FRANCE AND THE APRÈS GUERRE
1918–1924

Published with the assistance of the V. Ray Cardozier Fund,
an endowment created to support publication of scholarly books

FRANCE AND THE APRÈS GUERRE
1918–1924

Illusions and Disillusionment

Benjamin F. Martin

Louisiana State University Press   Baton Rouge

Copyright © 1999 by Louisiana State University Press
All rights reserved
Manufactured in the United States of America
First printing
00 02 04 06 08 07 05 03 01 99
2 4 5 3 1

Designer: Michele Myatt Quinn
Typeface: Granjon
Typesetter: Coghill Composition
Printer and binder: Edwards Brothers

Library of Congress Cataloging-in-Publication Data

Martin, Benjamin F., 1947–
    France and the Après Guerre, 1918–1924 : illusions and
disillusionment / Benjamin F. Martin.
        p.   cm.
    Includes bibliographical references and index.
    ISBN 0-8071-2399-4 (cloth : alk. paper) ISBN 0-8071-2509-1
    1. France—History—1914–1940.   2. World War, 1914–1918—France—
Influence.   3. Reconstruction (1914–1939)—France.   4. France—
Politics and government—1914–1940.   I. Title.
DC389.M27   1999
944.081'5—dc21   99-14903
                                                                          CIP

The paper in this book meets the guidelines for permanence and durability of
the Committee on Production Guidelines for Book Longevity of the Council on
Library Resources. ∞

For Jacqueline and Eugen Weber

CONTENTS

ILLUSTRATIONS

■ ■ ■

Preface and Acknowledgments

This book has been longer in the making than I intended. I began my writing of history with a biography of Albert de Mun, an interesting and substantial figure who had been largely overlooked, especially by Americans, and whose many-faceted career permitted me to examine political life in the Third Republic. De Mun died in October 1914, and I thought of continuing the story of Third Republic politics through the war he had warned of and into the victory he expected, again using biography, this time of the major figures from before 1914 who survived into the 1920s. If I had written this book then, it would have been wholly different from the pages that follow. Perhaps because I have lived through two additional decades, or perhaps because I set the project aside to study the ambiguities of French crime and French justice, I no longer entertain the sureties I once did. I am more convinced of contingency. I am less willing to credit good intentions. Yet my thinking remains profoundly influenced by a certain kind of education and by service as an army officer, revealed in my attitude toward loyalty, honor, courage, and betrayal. This book, more personal than my others, reflects the historian I have become. The reader will decide whether the change is for the better.

In Paris, at the Archives Nationales, the Bibliothèque Nationale, and the Archives de la Préfecture de Police, and in Baton Rouge at the Middleton Library of Louisiana State University, I received every possible assistance for my research. A Manship Fellowship from the College of Arts and Sciences at LSU supported my initial efforts. I acknowledge with appreciation permission to adapt and reprint some material from the introduction published as "Political Justice in France: The Dreyfus Affair and After," *The European Legacy: Toward New Paradigms* 2 (August 1997): 809–26, and the brief version of Chapter 2 that appeared as *"Briand à la barre:* Aristide Briand and the Politics of Betrayal" in *French Politics and Society* 15 (Summer 1997): 57–64. The illustrations are reproduced through license from the Corbis-Bettmann Archive. Leslie Beard compiled the index. Trudie Calvert copyedited the manuscript with consummate skill. At the Louisiana State University Press, my publisher for the third time, Leslie Phillabaum, Maureen Hewitt, John Easterly, and Catherine Kadair are without peers at the art of converting a manuscript into a book.

Ray Walser, Zofia Antrim, and Eugen Weber read my words—then challenged me to make them better. They were always right, and sometimes I did.

FRANCE AND THE APRÈS GUERRE,
1918–1924

Introduction: Small Change

Most history that is written and read is valued in the large notes of currency. The outbreak of the war in 1914, the Armistice in 1918, and the Paris Peace Conference in 1919 are ten-thousand-franc bills. Changes of cabinet, elections, and large-scale labor strife are at least the one thousand francs, with votes of confidence, legislative reports, perhaps an influential editorial the one hundreds. Concurrently, the small change of history, the ten-franc bills, the one-franc pieces, even the centimes of daily life, flows alongside the pricier events. In "The Crack-Up," F. Scott Fitzgerald rightly insisted that "at three o'clock in the morning, a forgotten package has the same tragic importance as a death sentence."[1] For during the Great War and the years immediately following—as always—seemingly minor incidents of scarcity, weather, the cost of individual vices, and now forgotten confrontations, worries, or slights could matter as much to many in France as the news that now dominates the historical reconstruction of the time.

In mid-January 1918, with the war more than 1,250 days old and bitter cold magnifying the discomfort and danger from the lack of coal for heating, rumors swirled about the German-Russian negotiations at Brest-Litovsk. Predictions were rife that a Russian capitulation would permit Germany to concentrate its army on the western front, and there was the

---

1. F. Scott Fitzgerald, "The Crack-Up: Pasting It Together," *Esquire,* 7 (March 1936): 35–39.

first open discussion about the Bolshevik government's repudiation of the tsarist debt. When the Chamber of Deputies considered these disastrous betrayals, the rightist Paul Pugliesi-Conti spoke from the tribune, lashing the Socialists with accusations of sympathy—or, why not, complicity— with the Bolsheviks. Before he could return to his seat, one of his principal targets, Barthélemy Mayéras, attacked him in the aisle and slugged him across the face. Pugliesi-Conti then staggered back to the tribune, drew a revolver from his jacket, and pointed it at the Socialist ranks. Amid great confusion, the session was suspended to restore order.[2]

Twelve days later, on the evening of 30 January, the German High Command introduced a new variety of chaos by sending Gotha bombers over Paris, leaving 36 dead, 190 injured—the first effective air raid on a civilian target. Bombs fell as the Chamber sat in session, and this time the deputies maintained their sangfroid. Most of Paris did not, and as the raids continued, the insurance giant Lloyd de France took advantage of the panic to sell policies against death from aerial attack, at the minimal cost of twenty francs for each ten thousand francs in coverage. A debate arose about the right of refuge: did householders have a responsibility to take in passersby during a bombardment? Le Figaro warned its bourgeois readers that such acts of mercy could lay them open to the dangers of theft and pillage. The union sacrée had split that far apart.[3]

The Gothas returned repeatedly, twenty-one times by mid-March alone. Sometimes the bombs fell ineffectively, at other times with devastating re-sults. The raid of 11 March left thirty-four dead, seventy-nine wounded, but from the desperation to find protection in the Métro stations, sixty-six more were crushed to death. Was it censorship or irony or false praise when Le Temps described the stoicism of the capital under attack? L'Intransigeant caught the emotion of the moment with a promise that Germany would pay dearly in the long run for this descent into barbarism.[4] But for now, the Germans added to the terror with long-range artillery, the so-called Big Berthas, which fired enormous shells from seventy-five miles away. Death from such a distance was unheard-of, and when the first attack began on

2. *Journal Officiel,* Chambre des Députés, Débats parlementaires (hereinafter cited as J.O.C., Débats), 18 January 1918.

3. *Le Figaro,* 1, 9, 14 February 1918.

4. *Le Figaro,* 9–13 March 1918; *Le Temps,* 12 March 1918; *L'Intransigeant,* 12 March 1918.

23 March, the skies were scanned for Gothas. On the ground, there were ten dead, fifteen wounded. The worst bombardment came on 29 March, when the church of St. Gervais was hit during Good Friday services, killing ninety-one and wounding one hundred.[5]

The Gothas and Berthas continued and even increased their attacks as the great German spring offensive of 1918 threatened to break through the Allied trench line. There were attempts at gallows humor, noting that on some days Paris was bombarded "only by rain." There was the grim satisfaction from Gothas shot down and from reports that some of the Berthas had exploded as they were fired. Yet the torrent of death prevailed until the Allied counterattacks in May, June, and July forced them out of range, just before the Germans perfected the incendiary bombs they had planned to set Paris ablaze. Even so, the Gothas caused 402 deaths and 809 wounded, the Berthas 196 deaths, 417 wounded. The accusation in *Le Figaro* sounds naïve to the late twentieth-century ear: "The *Kultur* of the Germans forgets no one! They have bombarded churches; they have bombarded hospitals and killed the sick in bed; they have thought of and killed little children."[6] But this burden was a new one for noncombatants to bear, to think of themselves and their civilian institutions as fair game, to be the victims of a malignantly total war, to reckon the tax of this anxiety.

The lack of food caused more constant anxiety. Throughout the war, Paris had been spared rationing, but on 22 January 1918, Victor Boret, the minister of supply, announced a 300-gram (10.5 ounce) per person limit on bread at bakeries. Restaurants would be able to serve no more than 100 grams to anyone at a meal. The Chamber of Deputies demanded to know the reasons for this change—especially because it affected them personally. Why had the rationing been imposed suddenly and without warning? Why, when some French cities where rationing had been in place for months were assigned a limit of 600 grams of bread per person each day, was Paris singled out for a "starvation" 300 grams? Why was the ration the same for all, when laborers, male and female, clearly expended more energy? And why was rationing unknown in rural areas? Boret's responses revealed a government pressed to the wall by the extremities of

5. *Le Figaro,* 24, 30–31 March 1918.

6. *Le Figaro,* April–July 1918, the accusation against German *Kultur* coming 7 June 1918; the totals of dead and wounded are from 18 December 1918.

war. Agreements with the Allies over delivery and division of food supplies had forced France's hand, he admitted, requiring the immediate imposition of rationing in the capital. The 300 grams per person was all that could be guaranteed at the moment, though an increase might come later. Equality of rationing had been decreed for fear that many citizens would cheat by falsely claiming the right to special supplements. The countryside was spared because peasant farmers threatened to hoard grain. A current of dissatisfaction ran through the Chamber at these admissions of weakness. Because a formal vote was likely to display too much disapproval, the deputies agreed that a show of hands could be used to pass a resolution accepting Boret's explanations.[7]

Within six weeks some exceptions were made: the bread ration was raised by 100 grams a day for laborers working at night, for women who were pregnant, and for anyone whose physician insisted must gain weight—but documentation was required in all cases. Yet with German submarines cutting deeply into supplies from the United States at the very moment when they were most needed for the increasing number of American troops, Boret urged restraint. Newspapers declared cutting back "un impérieux devoir." As a sop to public opinion and "pour encourager les autres," six bakers received brief jail terms for failing to observe the letter of the rationing rules, specifically for favoring their friends and relatives. Tribunals imposed harsher treatment on wholesalers speculating in potatoes, meat, sugar, and, spectacularly, gruyère cheese, for which there was a sentence of eight months in prison and a ten-thousand-franc fine. Amenities and small pleasures suffered. Hotels could not supply hot water except on Saturdays and Sundays. Arguing that preparation in bulk would save supplies, Boret established a central kitchen from which food was delivered to all but the deluxe Parisian restaurants. The Tour d'Argent, Le Grand Vefour, and the like, which escaped this signal indignity to French cuisine, were ordered to offer a repas à prix fixe set at twenty francs. The situation eased somewhat in the late fall as the Germans were beaten to their knees, but even then, the bread ration rose only to 500 grams per day for most adults and remained at 300 grams for anyone under the age of thirteen or over the age of sixty.[8]

7. J.O.C., Débats, 28 January 1918; Le Figaro, 23–24, 27 January 1918.

8. J.O.C., Débats, 14 May 1918; Le Figaro, 6 March, 8, 10, 15 April, 7, 11, 15, 23 May, 24 July, 24 September, 11 October 1918.

Were these privations partially responsible for the spread of the deadly Spanish influenza in the fall and winter of 1918? A session of the Académie de médecin on 16 October forced the first official acknowledgment of the epidemic. Soon, nearly 30 percent of railway workers had come down with *la grippe*, most likely because they were in contact with so many potentially contagious groups. At the end of the month, express trains had to be canceled for ten days, a fact that could not be concealed from the public. Nor could rising death rates: in Brittany, where the epidemic was especially severe, they were three times normal. When the number of infections soared in Paris itself, pharmacies made arrangements to provide medication throughout the night because the symptoms struck so swiftly. Predictably, the Chamber of Deputies fulminated against an "alien" disease. The government responded by releasing some physicians from the military to care for civilians and adopted nationwide a measure found effective in Lyon, closing cinemas and theaters, which were vectors for spreading the virus. By early November, the press was reporting that the epidemic had leveled off, in France at least. But on the day of the Armistice, there came the announcement that the avant-garde poet Guillaume Apollinaire, wounded severely at Verdun in 1916, had died two days earlier from influenza.[9]

Faits divers, the anecdotes that are the staple of popular journalism at all times, were a distraction from the Gothas, the Berthas, rationing, and *la grippe*. The fashions unveiled at the end of April for the "Salon of 1918" were proof, insisted *Le Figaro,* that culture and refinement continued in Paris despite artillery shells and bombs from barbarians. The survival of couturiers meant that France remained a rich nation even after all the war bond sales because there was a ready market for these creations. And buyers lined up at the gargantuan fur sale in early October sponsored by Funsten Frères et Cie. for the International Fur Exchange of St. Louis, Missouri—2,736,989 skins were auctioned, including those of 700 foxes, 80 mountain lions, 275 leopards, 1,275 black bears, 147 polar bears, and 8,500 badgers. Not all was gloomy if attention could be shifted from the human dead to the animal dead![10]

9. J.O.C., Débats, 25 October 1918; *Le Figaro,* 17–24, 26–27 October, 4, 11 November 1918. See Roger Shattuck, *The Banquet Years: The Origins of the Avant-Garde in France, 1885 to World War I* (Rev. ed.; New York, 1968), 288–97, for Apollinaire's last years.

10. *Le Figaro,* 1 May, 5 October 1918.

Crime also made good copy: a lawyer, Marcel Ferès, and his companion, Mireille Hennequin, given a six-month term for selling cocaine at the Palais de Justice, or a midwife, Laure Fournier, sentenced to eight years at hard labor for provoking an abortion, or the death in an asylum for the insane of Jeanne Weber, infamous as the Ogress de la Goutte d'Or for the child murders of 1906–7. The thrill of retribution, always keen among the suffering, combined with postures of moral rectitude to make such stories excellent for raising spirits. Best of all were the accounts of vengeance meted out to traitors, sentences of death imposed, for example, on Sidonie Ducret, for reporting to a German agent on artillery targets in the Paris region while working as a maid in a Geneva hotel, and Meyer Louis, for providing information about naval strength and morale at Bordeaux. Here was patriotism imbued with Jacobin severity.[11]

Faits divers with a connection to the tragedies of war were more dangerous to report because they set off ambiguous reactions. In March 1918, when a Russian officer, Captain Nicholas Wochnikov, despondent at his country's capitulation to Germany, played *la roulette russe* until he blew out his brains, the message could not have been inspirational to the many in France who feared that the German spring offensive might lead them to similar desperation. As a corollary to the prizes handed out in a prewar France troubled by the decline of natality to *familles nombreuses,* the war added "la plus grande famille," taking on the double meaning of *grande* as both *large* and *great.* The combination was meant to signal extraordinary sacrifice. In July 1918, a family from Nantes named Mariot was singled out for having sent ten sons, two sons-in-law, and ten grandsons into the army, with the result that of these twenty-two, five were dead, two were missing, and two were prisoners of war. Such an elevated blood tax— more than a third—might elicit grim determination that les Mariot had not fought in vain. They might also be seen to have endured, like France, enough.[12]

That kind of thinking led to war weariness, which had spread alarmingly in 1917. Although France was initially fighting a defensive battle for survival, by the end of 1914, anything short of "victory" over Germany

---

11. *Le Figaro,* 21 April, 14, 29 June, 11 July, 24, 28 August 1918.
12. *Le Figaro,* 21 March, 29 July 1918.

meant that the death and mutilation occurring at the front and the various degrees of privation at the rear were pointless. For what was their purpose if not to erase the shame of 1870–71, to regain Alsace and Lorraine, to end the threat of Prussian militarism? Yet after four years of fighting, how could the French not flinch at this theater of carnage, how not weep in the quite literally dark nights of national despair? Censorship, imposed immediately upon the outbreak of the war, was the stiff upper lip of public opinion, suppressing doubts and stoking patriotic fires. The political class had a special responsibility not to falter. Thus denunciations rained violently on Joseph Caillaux when he broke ranks. His meeting with Giovanni Giolitti in December 1916 was widely viewed as seeking to create a coalition for a negotiated peace—if Caillaux could become premier in France and Giolitti in Italy. The word *défaitisme* was created to describe his actions: hardly an exaggeration in the nationalist vocabulary, where between triumph and collapse fell only the shadow of sacrifice.

To stiffen spines, the government served notice of its determination to fight to the finish. During the last half of 1917, the arrest of Paul Bolo-Pasha, his confederate, Margaret Gertrud Zelle (alias Mata Hari), and the editors of *Le Bonnet rouge* as enemy agents suppressed German intriguing in public opinion. Charging Radical party leaders like Caillaux and Louis Malvy with treason for their défaitisme frightened politicians into closing ranks. The examples were all the more needed because even the die-hards despaired of France's cause. Maurice Barrès, the paragon of nationalism, told novelist François Mauriac in August 1917 that France could not hold out the two or three more years needed to win the war and predicted riot and collapse for the following spring. The right-wing portraitist Jacques-Emile Blanche wrote to Mauriac in April 1918 of finding Paris a cold, lifeless city surely to fall to the current German offensive. Mauriac replied, "And after ten years more, 'on les aura,' perhaps. But France will be dead from its victory."[13]

The certain knowledge that such opinions circulated privately absolutely proscribed their public expression. In March 1918, the government came down hard on Hélène Brion for "propos alarmistes," possessing and

---

13. Georges-Paul Collet, ed., *Correspondance (1916–1942): François Mauriac et Jacques-Emile Blanche* (Paris, 1976), 46, 64, 66.

distributing défaitiste pamphlets, in what was essentially a show trial before a court-martial in Paris. Prominent in the Syndicat des instituteurs, an association tolerated but technically illegal because the right to unionize did not extend to employees of the state, Brion was a perfect target: she could be held to the strictest standards of patriotism because of her status as a teacher at an *école maternelle*. With dozens of witnesses in her favor, she countered that she was only exercising her right of free speech and that, in campaigning for a negotiated peace, she was acting with the future of France's children foremost in her heart. The court-martial disagreed, imposed the harsh penalty of three years in prison, but then declared the sentence suspended. The message was clear that dissent on war was sedition, not to be excused by gender, ideology, or sentiment, and for which stern repression was possible.[14]

In April, Adelina Gaultier, convicted of handing out antiwar leaflets, also had her sentence of two years in prison suspended but had to pay a five-hundred-franc fine. A couple did find themselves in jail for a month because they shouted, among many other things while drunk, "The Germans will take Paris in two or three days!" The spring offensive raised the stakes to the maximum. That helps explain why a *civilian* court, the 15th Chambre correctionnelle of Paris, ruled in June that merely uttering the words "This damage is frightful!" before a building hit by a Gotha bomb was défaitiste. Courts-martial imposed exemplary punishment for singularly perilous times: to a Russian, Odokienko, from the nation of Bolsheviks and separate peace, five years in prison and a five-thousand-franc fine for daring to insist, "C'est la France qui a déclaré la guerre"; to an Austro-Hungarian, an enemy resident, two years in prison and a thousand-franc fine for claiming that "all French officers are thieves"; and to a M. Thuret, a municipal councillor and assistant to the mayor of the Parisian suburb Marly-le-Roi, who should have known better, a year in prison and a fine

14. *Le Figaro,* 26–30 March 1918; Judith Wishnia, *The Proletarianizing of the Fonction-naires: Civil Service Workers and the Labor Movement Under the Third Republic* (Baton Rouge, 1990), 183–85, 193–94. See also Persis Charles Hunt, "Revolutionary Syndicalism and Feminism Among Teachers in France, 1900–1921" (Ph.D. dissertation, Tufts University, 1975), 196. Brion files at the Bibliothèque Marguerite Durand include a rare printed résumé of the trial, *Le Défaitisme et les défaitistes: Le Procès Hélène Brion et Mouflard.*

of a thousand francs for saying in defense of an inebriated soldier, "What do you expect after four years—it's amazing that he hasn't mutinied!"[15]

As a bracing tonic, the government supplied the press with complete details about the prosecution of high-placed traitors. Their sentences were an overt warning, about which the public was encouraged to feel satisfaction. Bolo, Mata Hari, and the leader of the *Bonnet rouge* group were shot, its other editors escaping with terms at forced labor of five to ten years. The presentation of the défaitistes was equally brutal. When Henriette Caillaux was denied an audience at the Vatican, there was spiteful glee and a raking up of her scandalous past as proven adulteress and accused murderess. The formal charging of Joseph Caillaux with treason on 14 January brought headlines as large as for any battlefield advance. The tensions it engendered contributed to the acrimony four days later, when Pugliesi-Conti and Mayéras fought among the desks in the Chamber of Deputies. When Malvy's trial before the Senate began in July, *Le Figaro*'s editor, Alfred Capus, a close friend of Raymond Poincaré, president of the Republic, called it "symbolic of the nation's vitality and irrevocable decision for victory." The vote by the senators to convict Malvy of having "failed in, violated, and betrayed the duties of his office" while minister of the interior, for which he was banished from France for five years, led government-spokesman *Le Temps* to remind readers that conduct merely regrettable in peacetime was punishable when the nation was at war. In August and September, even as the fighting turned steadily in France's favor, there was the shocking news that yet another legislator, Senator Charles Humbert, was to be arrested for "intelligence with the enemy," synonymous with défaitisme. How Humbert's "treason" fit with that of Malvy or Caillaux the public would wait long to discover. In the meantime, the reminder that a government as implacable as Robespierre's imposed its will was sufficient.[16]

Victory, when it came in the second week of November, was unexpected. Although the approaching collapse of Austria-Hungary was re-

15. *Le Figaro,* 16, 19 April, 21–22 June, 31 August 1918.

16. *Le Figaro,* 9, 18, 29 April–16 May, 16 July 1918, for Bolo and the *Bonnet rouge* group; 3–31 January 1918, for Caillaux; 19 July–8 August 1918, for Malvy, the quotation from 19 July; 15 August, 18, 26–27 September 1918, for Humbert; *Le Temps,* 8 August 1918.

ported at the beginning of the month, Germany seemed strong enough to fight on alone until news arrived of revolution in Berlin. How hard to credit: Germany was finally beaten. On 11 November, as the glorious word *Armistice* was passed around, a huge crowd gathered at the Palais Bourbon to catch sight of Premier Georges Clemenceau, now "Père-la-Victoire," who before the Chamber of Deputies saluted Alsace and Lorraine and "nos grands morts" and, his seventy-seven-year-old eyes full of tears, "France, yesterday the soldier of God, today the soldier of Humanity, always the soldier of the Ideal." Across the Seine in the Place de la Concorde, the statues of Lille and Strasbourg sat in watch bedecked with flowers, while the streets were a single reveler with a million different names. It was everywhere the same in France: flags flew, church bells tolled, cannons fired salutes, the celebration contained for 1,561 days continued all this one day and all its night.[17]

In the moment of the Armistice, who among the French, holding this ten-thousand-franc bill of an event, counted the small change left over from the last year, ten-franc bills like the 300-gram rationing, the influenza, the lack of hot water or heat in the cold, the *faits divers* of petty meanness and despair? What were the dead and damaged from the Gothas and Berthas—certainly at least hundred-franc bills—what mattered Clemenceau's cabinet as Committee of Public Safety—perhaps a thousand-franc bill—beside the seeming historical justification of victory? But even as French men and women grasped their newly minted ten-thousand-franc bill, it began to slip through their fingers and was lost—or perhaps it was counterfeit. Victories are often illusory, as the 1920s and 1930s proved this one to be. The facts of daily life during the war have been ignored so thoroughly by historians that they escape even the footnotes of monographs. And that is ironic, for this small change ultimately was shown to be much harder currency than the Armistice.

17. J.O.C., Débats, 11 November 1918; *Le Figaro,* 1–12 November 1918.

1

▦ ▮ ▦

Of Noctambulists, Russian Bonds, and the Shooting of Tigers

Shortly before midnight on 24 May 1920, about nine miles north of Mont-argis, a small town in the department of the Loire, a track inspector for the Paris-Lyon-Méditerranée Railroad (P.-L.-M. R.R.) named André Ra-teau came upon a middle-aged man wandering along the right-of-way in his nightshirt. Challenged to identify himself, the man stared into the lan-tern light and answered guilelessly, "I am the president of the Republic." Incredulous at this response, the track inspector gently led Paul Deschanel, for that was his name and he was indeed president of the Third Republic, several hundred yards to the nearest signal house. As Deschanel waited, more befuddled than in shock, the subprefect at Montargis was alerted and, recognizing his head of state, took him to the safety of a French bu-reaucrat's office.[1]

Deschanel had boarded the presidential car of a special train in Paris at 9:30 that evening, heading for Montbrisson, where he was to unveil a bust

---

1. The traditional accounts of Deschanel's misadventure are Georges Bonnefous and Edouard Bonnefous, *Histoire politique de la IIIe République* (7 vols.; Paris, 1956–67), 3:158–61; Jacques Chastenet, *Histoire de la Troisième République* (7 vols.; Paris, 1952–63), 5:69; Leslie Derfler, *President and Parliament: A Short History of the French Presidency* (Boca Raton, Fla., 1983), 88–91; and Adrien Dansette, *Histoire des présidents de la République: De Louis Napoléon à Vincent Auriol* (Paris, 1953), 175–94. Dansette quotes Rateau's wife as knowing that Deschanel was a gentleman because his feet were so clean (189). See also Archives Nationales (hereinafter cited as A.N.), AP, 151, Papiers Deschanel.

of Emile Reymond, the senator from the Loire killed in October 1914 when German gunners shot down the observation plane he flew over their lines at Toul. The Senate had voted unanimously, on 22 November 1914, to commission a monument honoring one of their own, a man whose age, forty-nine, and status as a legislator would have kept him from the battle front but whose passion for flight had led him to be one of France's pioneer aviators and, when the war began, to volunteer for the dangerous assignment that brought his death. Reymond was a Third Republican Cincinnatus, and because he could never return to his plow, the ceremony was an occasion to commemorate civic virtue. And so the train also carried fifty-three other celebrants: Théodore Steeg, minister of the interior and the most powerful member of the cabinet assembled by Premier Alexandre Millerand, Pierre-Etienne Flandin, the undersecretary for aeronautics, who was not to leave much of a mark until the 1930s and whose presence was required to honor the vehicle in which Reymond died, and most of the legislators representing the Loire in the Senate and the Chamber of Deputies. Deschanel had left instructions to be awakened at 7:00 the following morning, just before the train was to pass through Roanne, about an hour's travel from Montbrisson, but when the valet entered the presidential car, he found the bed rumpled, the large window overlooking the tracks wide open, and no trace of Deschanel. Almost as soon as railway officials got this panicky and mystifying report, they had word from Montargis that the missing president had been rescued. This news was telegraphed to Premier Millerand in Paris, and he immediately decided to take personal charge of the situation. The P.-L.-M. R.R. cleared its tracks, and another special train, this one bearing Millerand, Deschanel's wife, and one of his sons, raced the two hundred miles to Montargis, where the president of the Republic had regained his senses and appeared relatively unaffected by his remarkable adventure. Having had his fill of trains for the moment, he insisted upon returning to Paris with his family in an automobile.

Millerand took the train back and used the time to prepare a cautious statement for the press, a best-foot-forward version of the truth, for too much was already well known to conceal anything but details. That evening, he met reporters at the Quai d'Orsay, the Ministry of Foreign Affairs, and told them that on the night before, President Deschanel had gone to bed in his railcar at 10:00 with the window closed because he always feared taking a chill, but woke up about an hour later feeling too warm. Not bothering to call his valet, he tried to lower the large trackside window. It was stuck, and when he pushed on it with all his strength, it opened wide, catapulting him headlong out of the car and onto the embankment of the right-of-way. Fortunately, because the train was going only thirty miles an hour at the time and the embankment where he landed was soft and grassy, he sustained just a few bruises and was temporarily stunned. It was in this state that he met the track inspector and the subprefect. Millerand assured a sympathetic press corps that Deschanel had been examined fully by several physicians and pronounced in good condition. Nevertheless, such a shock to the system of a man sixty-four years old led them to recommend a period of rest, which he could take at Rambouillet, the presidential retreat, and still be close enough to Paris to consult with the cabinet.

Because the president of the Republic was by tradition a nonpartisan and largely ceremonial head of state, the major newspapers, even in Paris, were willing to mute their reports, and more so their commentaries, about the incident. Almost all claimed to believe that a few weeks of relaxation would be a sufficient restorative. In the meantime, the vigorous Millerand and his cabinet ministers could stand in wherever necessary. Some humorists poked fun by recalling Deschanel's nocturnal ramble and inventing responses for the track inspector to "Je suis le président de la République," with "Et moi, je suis le pape!" quite the best in an officially anticlerical France. But overall, there was a careful effort neither to make Deschanel an object of ridicule nor to extend pity, for fear of damaging beyond repair his respect and authority. This attitude persisted until mid-July, when he was not yet well enough to preside over the Bastille Day military parade at Vincennes and had to send André Lefèvre, the minister of war, as his substitute. Discreet but open questions about his condition were then asked. Soon after his election as president on 17 January 1920, Deschanel had demonstrated a certain mental instability and on the advice of friends took a long holiday to the Côte d'Azur in April. Those closest to him had worried for some months earlier about a new tendency to exaltation and depression but marked it down to the stresses of the war. By the summer, the oscillating moods came more frequently, and with them occasional departures from reality. On 10 September the president of the Republic was discovered paddling happily naked in one of the fountains at Rambouillet. There could no longer be any hope for rapid recovery, and he submitted his resignation to the legislature a week later.[2]

The story of Paul Deschanel is all the more pathetic because he was able to hold for exactly eight months the office that it had become his life's ambition to attain. From birth he had a republican silver spoon in his mouth: born in Brussels because his father was a prominent exile from the Second Empire; reared among the new republican dynasties, his father first a deputy and then a life senator; his wife, Germaine Brice, herself the daughter of a deputy and granddaughter of the permanent secretary to the Académie française. Deschanel won his own election to the Chamber of Deputies in 1885, and he held the seat for the next thirty-five years. He was always polished, elegant, urbane, an inspiring if vacuous orator, and a moderate's moderate. Above all, he avoided making enemies except once, and then with almost fatal consequences. On 25 July 1894, he denounced the newspaper La Justice as a defender of anarchism, thereby incurring the wrath of its editor, Georges Clemenceau, who since his defeat in the 1893 elections was no longer a deputy. Clemenceau replied in an editorial on 27 July, calling Deschanel a scoundrel, a liar, and a coward. Despite Clemenceau's formidable reputation as a duelist, propriety required Deschanel to demand satisfaction, and at Boulogne-sur-Seine they faced off with foils. It was clear that Deschanel was terrified, backing away so fast that Clemenceau is supposed to have inquired, "Vous nous quittez, monsieur?" When Deschanel finally came within reach, Clemenceau was content to end the duel after slashing him across the right eyebrow, writing later, "If I had been spiteful, my little Paul would now be in very bad shape."[3]

The lesson of that July morning was not lost on Deschanel, who never again took a controversial stand. His reward was election to a vice-presidency of the Chamber for two years in 1896 and 1897, to its presidency for

2. For newspaper coverage, see, for example, Le Matin, Le Petit journal, Le Temps, and Le Figaro, 25–26 May, 14–15 July, 15–18 September 1920. Jean-Baptiste Duroselle, Clemenceau (Paris, 1988), 868, takes malicious glee in recounting the humor at Deschanel's expense.

3. J.O.C., Débats, 25 July 1894; Duroselle, Clemenceau, 425–26.

four years, from 1898 to 1902, and to the Académie française for life in May 1899—a set of memorably dull essays on foreign policy and colonialism, not his connections, cited as the rationale. He regained the presidency of the Chamber in May 1912 and was reelected every year through 1919. On 13 January 1920, he was all but unanimously returned to the presidential chair. This last proof of legislative popularity made him a serious candidate in the election later that same week for head of state and so confirmed his belief that presiding over the Chamber for twelve years was sufficient and proper preparation for presiding over the nation. Raymond Poincaré, whose seven-year term in the Elysée palace since February 1913 had paralleled Deschanel's in the Chamber of Deputies, was eager to relinquish the post. The obvious choice was Clemenceau, the Père-la-Victoire, whose *jusqu'auboutisme* as premier from November 1917 onward had held France together long enough to win the war. But during the year following the Armistice, Clemenceau's authoritarianism and willfulness had become far less tolerable to the senators and deputies, who were the presidential electors. Deschanel was to Clemenceau what accommodation is to recalcitrance. Deschanel refused, even during the war, to accept ministerial office for fear of offending some faction, any faction, and perhaps for fear of demonstrating that he was no more than a debonair master of ceremonies. Clemenceau also refused to join cabinets but for the opposite reason: his insistence on being premier or nothing, on running the government, and in November 1917 the war, his way. Deschanel would be a traditional president. Clemenceau, even more than the Poincaré of 1913 and 1914, would likely try to transform the office into a locus of power. Deschanel had hardly a single enemy. Clemenceau had a legion, and all of them in the legislature knew that revenge would come in denying him what he so clearly deserved.[4]

Too proud as always, Clemenceau refused to declare his candidacy, while letting it be known that he would serve if elected. Deschanel would never have challenged him directly—the scar over his right eye was a warning from twenty-five years before—yet that humiliating memory spurred him to exploit Clemenceau's tactical blunder of overestimating the

---

4. A.N., F7 12821, Elections des présidents Poincaré, Deschanel, Millerand et Doumergue (1912–24), reports of 4–18 January 1920.

gratitude he was due and underestimating the enmity he disdained. The formal vote was set for 17 January at Versailles, but custom called for a preliminary ballot the evening before by the "republican" legislators, any-one too far to the right of center unwelcome. After Deschanel's surprising victory here, 408 to 389 (with 30 votes scattered among others), deputies and senators crowded about Clemenceau to protest that they at least had been among his supporters. Clemenceau is said to have cupped his hand about his ear and asked, "Did I hear a cock crow?" Se non è vero, è ben trovato. In a white fury, he formally forbade the placing of his name in nomination the next day, even though eighty-nine legislators had not at-tended the preliminary meeting and might well have given him the presi-dency. Without formal opposition, Deschanel won as easily at Versailles as he had in the Chamber of Deputies four days earlier. After he returned to Paris, he thought to stop at the Ministry of War, on the rue St. Dominique, where Clemenceau kept his office. Clemenceau directed his orderly to in-form the new president of the Republic "que je n'y suis pas." On 18 Janu-ary, he wrote a curt letter of resignation as premier to Poincaré, whom he supposed to be in the cabal against him. Three days later, he left Paris and public life.[5]

As an episode in the Après Guerre (roughly the five years following the Armistice), the Deschanel presidency was distressing, a certain national embarrassment, but essentially minor. Its importance lies in the symbolism of a France exhausted from the war, recoiling from new responsibilities, yearning for a world lost between 1914 and 1918, disappointed when cal-culations based on these emotions produced wrong answers for present problems, and quite incapable of discerning that this aversion to reality was the prescription for national catastrophe.

Any discussion of the Après Guerre must begin with an analysis of French losses, statistics cited so often that they have all but lost their ca-pacity to elicit a proper reaction. During the Great War (to use the term before such conflicts were numbered), France mobilized 8,030,000 men,

5. Denis W. Brogan, *The Development of Modern France, 1870–1939* (London, 1940), 568, contains the anecdote of Clemenceau's remark to his supporters; Chastenet, *Histoire de la Troisième République,* 5:61–64; Duroselle, *Clemenceau,* 850–58, with the refusal to meet Deschanel, 857. All the newspapers published Clemenceau's rejection of nomination and his resignation.

20.2 percent of the total population in 1914 (39,800,000), 75 percent of the male population aged twenty to fifty-five. Of that number, 1,310,000 died or were never found, 3.3 percent of the total population, 12.2 percent of males aged twenty to fifty-five, 6.6 percent of all males. More than one-quarter of men aged twenty to twenty-seven were killed. Another 1,100,000 men were left with permanent disabilities, 56,000 of them amputees.[6] The recital of these figures is soul-numbing: Philippe Berthelot remarked cynically of them, "One man's death affects me; fifteen thousand deaths are only a statistic."[7] By comparison, the total of American dead in all the wars fought by the United States is slightly less than the French dead in the Great War alone. The American equivalent in 1995 to the French losses of 1914–18 would be 8,000,000 men killed. Civilian deaths were, in contrast, few—certainly no more than 200,000—for this was a war in which *soldiers* died. At a time of democratic armies, soldiers occupied a clearly defined segment of the demographic spectrum, the great bulk of men in their prime. The war took on, therefore, a horrifically anti-Darwinian character: the fittest were the ones to die. The remnants of their lives were left behind, 600,000 widows, 750,000 orphans.

The removal of so many young men to the front severely depressed the birth rate, which in France was already low (193 births per 10,000 inhabitants in 1913). Husbands and lovers who did not return from the trenches never fathered children, and because the military failed to arrange sufficient home leave for the troops until 1917, husbands and lovers who did survive fathered very few: the best estimate is a deficit of 1,400,000 births during the war. How curious that in *France* the imperatives of biology should be so ignored. Partly because of the long separations and surely from an unwillingness to act during the fighting, the number of divorces climbed steeply from 13,500 in 1913 to 41,300 in 1920, leveling at 21,500 over the next decade. There was also a pent-up demand for love, with 623,000 marriages in 1920, more than double the 299,000 of 1913, and a brief surge in the birth rate for that year and the next. But the drastic im-

6. The statistics for human losses are from Michel Huber, *La Population de la France pendant la guerre* (Paris, 1931), conveniently summarized in Alfred Sauvy, *Histoire économique de la France entre les deux guerres* (3 vols.; Paris, 1965–75), 1:19–23, 440–41, 443. Numbers have been rounded to the nearest hundred.

7. Chastenet, *Histoire de la Troisième République*, 5:78.

balance in the numbers of young men and young women forecast a decline soon enough in marriages and children. By 1931, the birth rate was down to 176 per 10,000. With so many soldiers dead and fewer children born, the old automatically bulked larger in proportion. Although life spans were the same in 1920 as in 1913, the proportion of men and women at least sixty years of age increased from 12.6 to 13.6 percent of the population. This *vieillissement* carried with it a threat that the weariness and passivity and resignation associated with aging could infect the society as a whole.[8]

Roughly four-fifths of the war on the western front was waged in France's ten northern departments, and the material damage justified their designation as the "devastated region." Although a mere 7 percent of the nation's land area and inhabited by only 10 percent of the population, these departments were an industrial giant, in 1913 accounting for 60 percent of French coal mining, 66 percent of textile production, and 55 percent of metallurgical production. After four and a half years of war, almost everything was in ruin: 564,300 private dwellings and 17,600 public buildings had been completely or largely destroyed; 860,400 acres of farmland and 172,700 of pasture had to be completely restored. German levies had taken 834,900 cattle, 376,400 horses and asses and mules, 890,800 sheep and goats, and 311,700 pigs. Of the 74,000 miles of road, 38,600 were impassable; 1,200 miles of canals and 3,500 of railroad were out of service. Agricultural production for 1919 was 34 percent of that for 1913 for wheat, 38 percent for oats, 60 percent for potatoes, 17 percent for sugar beets; industrial production was 43 percent of that in 1913 for iron ore, 28 percent for cast iron, 5 percent for steel, 4 percent for coal. In 1913, the eighteen coal companies of the Nord and the Pas-de-Calais dug 18,662,000 tons of coal, in 1920, even after a year of repairs, only 2,433,000 tons. For the purpose of imposing reparations on Germany, the monetary total for the damages in the devastated region was calculated to be 35 billion gold

8. Chastenet, *Histoire de la Troisième République,* 5:232–34, citing many statistical studies. For the purposes of comparison, 1913 is used because it was the last full year of peace, 1920 because it was the first year that demobilization was complete. In 1920, the proportion of men and women sixty years of age and older was 9.5 percent in England, 9 percent in Germany, 7.5 percent in the United States and the Soviet Union: see Sauvy, *Histoire économique,* 1:34.

francs (that is, the franc at its prewar level), an estimate that in spite of its tendentious origin is generally agreed to be reasonable. The equivalent in 1995 would be approximately $44 billion. This total does not include the loss to the nation and to private individuals of production between August 1914 and November 1918, when the region was under German control.[9]

The war had an extraordinary effect on the public treasury and private pocketbooks. Initially underestimating the length and the cost of the fighting and then unwilling to tax sufficiently a nation so drained of blood, French leaders financed it largely through loans. The budget for 1913 had a small surplus of 25 *million* francs, the budget for 1918 an enormous deficit of 34 *billion*. In between, the national debt rose from 33 billion francs at the end of 1913 to 175 billion at the end of 1918, with a concomitant increase in the amount of currency in circulation. Inevitably, this expansion of the money supply combined with wartime scarcities to drive up prices, slowly at first, then more rapidly, until at the Armistice they were about two and a half times what they had been in 1913. There were two exceptions: the government imposed controls on property rents by the decree of 14 August 1914 and on food by the law of 20 April 1916. The consequences, obvious to anyone familiar with the history of the French Revolution from the Year II to the Year X or living in the late twentieth century, were a surprise to a country accustomed by the experience of the nineteenth century to relative stability in prices and to the maintenance of value through the gold standard. Because fixed incomes—interest on most investments, pensions, and of course property rents—did not rise, rentiers were the first to suffer. For debt holders, repaid in money of decreased buying power, inflation was a cancer. Benefiting like private debtors, the government would pay off its war bonds during the 1920s in depreciated francs. Owners of productive assets such as farmland and factories were scarcely touched because the underlying worth tended to rise with inflation. The wages of workers sometimes lagged behind and, especially in

9. Sauvy, *Histoire économique,* 1:24–27, with the figures rounded to the nearest hundred and metric values converted to Anglo-Saxon equivalents. Sauvy notes that there is controversy over these statistics, but probably the best guide in detail is Edmond Michel, *Les Dommages de guerre de la France et leur réparation* (Paris, 1932). See also A.N., AJ 4 49–52, Mélanges: photographies, documents, coupures de presses, rapports sur la conduite des Allemands. I have calculated the 1995 buying power of the dollar to equal 1.25 gold francs.

the case of war industries, sometimes outpaced price increases. Failing to comprehend the economic factors behind these consequences, French leaders as well as the general population blamed inflation on *mercantis,* speculators, and generally believed that the end of the war and German reparations would permit an eventual return to 1913 indices. But in the meantime, fixed incomes had already by the Armistice lost two-thirds of their value.[10]

Besides the burden of 142 billion francs added to the national debt, France borrowed another 35 billion francs during the war from its ally, Great Britain (43 percent or 15.1 billion), and its associate, the United States (57 percent or 19.9 billion). The total, 177 billion francs, was equal to roughly two-thirds of the nation's gross national product in 1913. While inflation might make reimbursing government bondholders, mostly French citizens, less onerous, payments on foreign accounts had to be made in pounds and dollars. If the franc fell against these currencies, the amounts due were potentially open ended. French leaders hoped that these war debts could be combined with German reparations into a unified economic settlement, but the United States absolutely rejected any linkage between them.[11] France's financial position was especially difficult because so many of its own foreign loans had become worthless during the war, the greatest number through the Bolshevik renunciation of the imperial Russian debt. From a creditor nation in 1913—second only to Great Britain—holding 40 billion francs in foreign obligations, France in 1918 had become a debtor nation, owing 15 billion francs.[12]

"No one has written the history of the rentier," Eugen Weber claims, and he is correct, if a monograph is required. But Weber himself has elaborated the thesis and sketched several of the chapters for this work, and there are other important contributions that could be incorporated.[13] And,

10. Sauvy, *Histoire économique,* 1:26–27, 364–65, 513, 520, 524–25, though the statistics are in conflict on 364–65 and 520; Chastenet, *Histoire de la Troisième République,* 5:211–17.

11. Sauvy, *Histoire économique,* 1:169–72; Marc Trachtenberg, *Reparation in World Politics: France and European Economic Diplomacy, 1916–1923* (New York, 1980), 21–22, 54.

12. Sauvy, *Histoire économique,* 1:29–30.

13. Eugen Weber, *France: Fin de siècle* (Cambridge, Mass., 1986), 18, for the quotation. For Weber's contributions to a history of the rentier, see *France,* 9–104; "Inheritance, Dilettantism, and the Politics of Maurice Barrès," in *My France: Politics, Culture, Myth* (Cambridge, Mass., 1991), 226–43; and "The Secret World of Jean Barois: Notes on the Portrait

pace Weber, most accounts of the Third Republic during its first four and a half decades are a kind of history of the rentier. For the Republic's ethos was permeated by an economic conservatism solidly based on investments in state *rente* (government bonds) and *placements de père de famille* (blue-chip stocks) paying steady, certain, usually fixed returns. From 1873 until 1893, the twenty years of deflation sometimes called the "great nineteenth-century depression," wholesale prices in France declined so significantly, 40 to 50 percent, that the buying power of these fixed returns was doubled or occasionally tripled. After the economy began to grow again, inflation was all but unnoticeable. During the next twenty years, 1893 to 1913, wholesale prices increased only 30 percent, an average of 1.3 percent a year. From 1897 to 1913, the sixteen years of greatest expansion before the war, retail prices rose 15 percent, an annual average of a mere 0.9 percent. Even so, there were complaints of "la vie chère," but they are derisory in comparison to the inflation of the war and the Après Guerre.[14]

With no income tax to pare earnings, dividends, and interest, as little as five thousand francs a year meant that one could—just barely—*s'embourgeoiser*. And for rentiers, bourgeois values—above all public pro-prieties combined with financial prudence—were cherished in France, just as their counterpart, "Victorian" values, were cherished by the British middle class. Theirs was a world, hierarchical to be sure, of unquestioning faith in certain received verities: order, law, justice, science, and immuta-ble standards like the meter, the watt, and above all the franc, which had been defined since 1803 as 290 milligrams (4.35 grains) of pure gold and since then had remained the most stable monetary unit in the world.[15] Having a private income to pay for the necessities freed rentiers to do as they pleased with their time, to enjoy what Weber has frequently de-scribed as an antinecessitarian existence. Rentiers could be politicians who went unelected, lawyers and doctors who went unconsulted, writers who went unread, painters and sculptors who went without buyers— imagination alone limited choice. If by luck or talent there should be vot-

---

of an Age," in *The Origins of Modern Consciousness,* ed. John Weiss (Detroit, 1965), 79–109; among others. Shattuck, *Banquet Years,* is another contribution.

14. Weber, *France,* 22; Sauvy, *Histoire économique,* 1:314.

15. Chastenet, *Histoire de la Troisième République,* 4:152–56.

ers, clients, patients, readers, and buyers, *tant mieux;* but if not, *tant pis.* Practically every important political and cultural figure, a great many government officials, and most professionals were rentiers. The extraordinary freedom of the rentier is what gave the first forty-five years of the Third Republic its characteristic controlled pandemonium in politics and the arts: so many were free to try, to experiment, and if they failed, there was little rancor because the bills had already been paid.

The war thundered down upon the world of the rentiers and crushed it to powder. In *Les Thibault,* the roman-fleuve for which he would win the Nobel Prize in 1937, Roger Martin du Gard examined the emotions of his protagonist, Antoine Thibault, successful pediatric surgeon and rentier, on 31 July 1914: "His morale, till now intact, was badly shaken. The tempest breaking over Europe was rocking the very foundations on which he had built his life: science and human reason. He was suddenly discovering the impotence of intellect; and, confronted with this uprush from the world of instinct, the futility of the virtues which had been the mainstay of his industrious career: common sense, moderation, wisdom and experience, the cult of justice."[16] Although unnerved, Thibault did not glimpse the depth of the abyss—yet. Like most rentiers, he had eagerly bought Russian bonds. The interest rate was attractive, and the French government encouraged investment in its eastern ally. By 1917, even before the Bolshevik repudiation, they were quoted at barely two-thirds of par. There was every reason to fear that they would become worthless. Rentiers of military age, and especially professionals like Thibault, died in the war at a rate higher than average because so many were made officers and therefore expected to set an example of bravery. The death rate for French officers was 19 percent, for enlisted men, 16; for all adult males, 12.2 percent, but among professionals, 13.1. Martin du Gard closed his novel by having Thibault die a week after the Armistice from poison gas infection. In the days before, by now fully aware that his own death had been preceded by the death of the world he knew, Thibault embraced a nihilism unimaginable in 1914 among the men he personified: "The more one

16. Roger Martin du Gard, *Les Thibault* (8 vols.; Paris, 1922–40), translated by Stuart Gilbert as *The Thibaults* (Parts I-VI) and *Summer 1914* (Parts VII-VIII) (New York, 1939–41), this quotation from *Summer 1914,* 511–12.

thinks, the more one observes the outside world and one's own mind, the more apparent it becomes that life is pointless. . . . And nothing matters—except to get through . . . with the minimum of suffering."[17]

The portfolio of a real-life Thibault would likely have included Russian "1909 4.5 percents," the last tsarist obligation listed on the Paris Bourse before the war, a borrowing of 1.4 billion francs. As an incentive, the price at issue on 22 January 1909 was 89.25; thus, if held to maturity (the dates ranging from 1919 to 1959), the bonds, with a face value of 100, would yield a 12 percent capital gain as well as 4.5 percent interest paid semiannually. The offering was completely subscribed, and the bonds immediately began selling at a premium over the issue price, reaching 100 by January 1910, 104 by January 1911, and remaining above 100 throughout 1912 and 1913 before slipping into the high 90s during the first half of 1914. The threat of war drove the price down to 93, its declaration to 87. For the next two and a half years, there was relative confidence, the quotation fluctuating between 85 and 75, until Nicholas II's abdication in March 1917 dropped it quickly to the low 60s. By the end of the year and V. I. Lenin's renunciation of the tsarist debt, it fell to the high 40s. Hope that Allied intervention might somehow chase out the Bolsheviks propped up the price through 1918, 1919, and most of 1920, but after the rout of White forces and the withdrawal of the western contingents, it collapsed to 21. Speculators gambling on the uncertain future of the Soviet Union prevented a further decline. Bondholders who bought at issue and did not sell in the vain fantasy of recovery had by then lost 76 percent of their capital. Depending on the dates of purchase and sale, others fared better or worse.[18]

In August 1914, French investors held 13.897 billion francs of Russian government bonds and approximately 12 billion more of Russian commercial bonds. Because the war made direct payments from Russia impossible, the commercial bonds were forced into default, but for the government

17. Sauvy, *Histoire économique,* 1:441–42; Martin du Gard, *Summer 1914,* 112, 818–19, 986–87, the quotation from the last.

18. See the financial column and the Bourse quotations in *Le Figaro,* 1909–20. The 1909 4.5 percent Russian bonds paid interest each 15 January and 15 July. They were to be redeemed over a forty-year period, 1919–59, with the specific bonds for each redemption chosen by lot.

bonds, an arrangement was devised to remit the interest by tapping Russian gold reserves retained in France. When this resource was exhausted in February 1915, the French government assumed the payments for three years, until Russia signed a separate peace with Germany at Brest-Litovsk. This financial sacrifice to aid a beleaguered ally was a significant burden on the French treasury, costing about 630 million francs a year and therefore responsible for 1.9 billion francs of the deficit at the end of the war. This amount was paltry, nevertheless, compared to the ruin visited upon the bondholders, the effective confiscation of their entire 26 billion francs. Private capital in France has been estimated at 302 billion francs in 1913 but only 227 billion in 1919, a reduction of 75 billion, or 25 percent. Two-thirds of this decrease was owing to war damage, the other third to the loss of investments in Russia. The former could be made good, the latter, never.[19]

Because of inflation, even the private capital that remained was, by prewar standards, worth far less. Using 1913 as a base 100, the index of retail prices reached 238 at the end of 1918, making the real value of the 227 billion francs in capital only 95.3 billion. The erosion would continue as prices rose to 289 in December 1919 and 404 in December 1920. The effect is demonstrated dramatically by computing the real value, again using 1913 as a base 100, of investments listed on the Bourse. In January 1919, this figure for stocks paying a variable return, and therefore slightly able to adjust for inflation, was 49.2 and by December 1920, 30.6. Bonds and stocks paying a fixed return, of course, fared worse, standing at 34.8 in January 1919 and 18.3 in December 1920. Despite these cataclysmic losses in value, or perhaps because of them, investors often refused to sell, believing in the "espoir mythique d'un 'retour comme avant,'" the delusion that the losses could be made good, that everything would be all right, and that rentiers might live happily ever after. In fact, inflation created internal transfers to the detriment of rentiers, the dominant economic class of prewar France, and rather to the benefit of the subordinate, the working class. In December 1920, with capital at roughly one-sixth of its value in 1913,

19. *Le Figaro,* 27 March 1920; J.O.C., Débats, 26 March 1920, for the discussion of the government's attitude toward Russian bonds. See Sauvy, *Histoire économique,* 1:293–94, for the estimate of private capital.

industrial wages had kept up with price increases and would consistently surpass them during the next five years. The wealthy faced another threat as well, the income tax, which went into effect on 25 June 1920. The first six thousand francs of income was free of tax, but progressivity was steep thereafter, reaching 39.6 percent. To encourage births, there was a 10 percent surcharge on couples who had no children after two years of marriage and a 25 percent surcharge on bachelors thirty years of age and older. The new situation was expressed in the different attitude toward money. Before the war, the measure of wealth was how much a man *had*, his net worth; after, it was how much he *earned*, his income. And with this change came an end to the world the rentiers had made. As Maurice Barrès, a rentier par excellence, had written as long ago as 1889, "For without money, how to develop one's imagination? Without money, no more *homme libre.*"[20]

A governing elite has rarely been more poorly prepared by aptitude and training to confront such a radically altered economic reality. Given a classical education at their lycée or collège, French leaders could count to a thousand in Greek or Latin but had no conception of, for example, the effect of the money supply on prices. Clemenceau knew and cared little about these matters, unwisely entrusting them during 1918 and 1919 to Louis-Lucien Klotz, his minister of finance, whose limitations he knew well. Although no anti-Semite, Clemenceau called him "le seul Juif qui n'entende rien aux questions d'argent," and of Klotz's later personal financial irregularities and bankruptcy, shrugged, "He writes checks as others sign autographs." Aristide Briand, former premier and premier to be, was bored by any detail but by statistics most of all. Edouard Herriot, mayor of Lyon and postwar leader of the Radical party, cheerfully admitted his own ignorance of science and economics. He recounted how during the war a butcher protested that the government was permitting the slaughter of calves "with two teeth," instead of waiting for them to grow larger, when they would have "four teeth." This practice, he explained,

20. Sauvy, *Histoire économique,* 1:293, 317–18, 511, 532–34, and the quotation from 393. For the income tax provisions, see J.O.C., Débats, 22 April 1920, and *Le Figaro,* 23 April 1920. Barrès is quoted by Weber, who provides the translation, in "Inheritance, Dilettantism," 232.

provided tender veal for the wealthy who could afford it but limited the supply of meat during wartime. Herriot suggested a compromise, to slaughter calves when they had "three teeth," not realizing that the teeth appear two at a time. Raymond Poincaré was an exception to this general incomprehension of any subject outside the humanities, but he was known as such a pettifogger that his grasp of statistics and tables was hardly counted a virtue. The disdain descended throughout the bureaucracy. Alfred Sauvy has described what he terms "ce désordre de la rue de Rivoli," the Ministry of Finance, where almost no one could correctly add a column of figures, much less coherently present complex issues to the economically illiterate.[21]

These issues were all the more complex because they interlocked one with another and because the pattern of this radically altered economic reality was unknown, like pieces in a jigsaw puzzle for which there is no picture as a guide. French leaders had to demobilize a mass army, find work for these former soldiers, restore the devastated regions, solve problems of transportation, allocation, and rationing, slow the rapid rise of prices and the deficit, stay the fall of the franc against the pound and the dollar, and do so while challenged by a newly radical labor movement energized by the example of revolution in Germany and Russia. Confronted by such Herculean labors, it was tempting to succumb to the belief that German reparation payments would be the solution to everything.

After 1,561 days of war, French soldiers understandably wanted to leave behind the trenches in which they had fought as the *poilus* (the dirty, hairy ones) and return to their homes as soon as possible. Aside from the sheer administrative impossibility of immediately demobilizing an army of more than four million men, there were strategic and political reasons why they could not. Germany had asked for an armistice but had not surrendered. Until the German army withdrew completely from French and Belgian soil and was sufficiently disarmed, Allied troop strength had to be

---

21. For Clemenceau's cruel remark about Klotz, see Chastenet, *Histoire de la Troisième République*, 5:22, translated infamously by Brogan, *Development of Modern France*, 589, n. 1, as "the only Jew who couldn't count." For Clemenceau on Klotz and checks, see Duroselle, *Clemenceau*, 830–31; for Briand, see Edouard Herriot, *Jadis: D'une guerre à l'autre, 1914–1936* (2 vols.; Paris, 1952), 2:54; and for Herriot himself, his *Notes et maximes inédits* (Paris, 1961), 16–17. For Sauvy's assessment, *Histoire économique*, 1:364.

maintained at battle levels. And the peace negotiations were yet to begin. In France, at least, agreement was nearly universal that the provisions would be harsh and that force might be necessary to impose them. Nevertheless, by 28 June 1919, when Germany formally signed the Treaty of Versailles, 2.6 million men, mostly those aged thirty-five and older, had been demobilized. Another 1.4 million men were released during the remainder of the year, leaving only the "classes" of 1917–19 (men aged twenty-one to twenty-three) under arms.[22]

The demobilization was accompanied by three laws to restore what could be restored and to offer restitution for what could not be. The Loi Lugol of 31 March 1919, named after its sponsor, Deputy Jules Lugol, provided government pensions to soldiers and sailors left with wounds or continuing sickness from the war and to the widows, orphans, parents, and grandparents of men who were "mort pour la France." Civilian victims of war wounds or physical mistreatment under enemy occupation were granted similar payments by a second law, of 24 June 1919. At a cost of 3 billion francs a year in 1919 and 1920, approximately 1.2 million veterans and 25,000 noncombatants received pensions of varying amounts based on the degree of disability, while death benefits were paid to almost 1.5 million relatives. The restoration of material losses was based on the so-called Charte des sinistrés (Charter of Victims), which became law on 17 April 1919. Anyone suffering the loss of property in the devastated region as a result of the war could file a claim for restitution from the state according to rules written expressly to encourage restoration. If the owner did not *remployer* (reinvest or rebuild, according to the circumstances), simply pocketing the compensation, he received only the assessed value of the property as of 1914 minus depreciation, which for a building was usually set at 25 percent. Allowing for inflation, such an owner would thereby lose 75 percent of its value. If the owner did undertake to *remployer*, with the requirement that the reinvestment or rebuilding be in the same town or no further away than thirty miles and in no case outside the devastated region, he received the entire cost of replacement. *Remploi* was, in general, at least four times more expensive for the state, but the law had the intended effect. Fewer than 1 percent of the owners chose not to reinvest,

22. For the government's report on demobilization, see J.O.C., Débats, 4 July 1919.

and the devastated region was largely restored within a decade, much of it within five years. By the end of 1920, the Charte des sinistrés had provided for payments of 13.1 billion francs.[23]

At first, the French public regarded these heavy expenditures as certain to be reimbursed. After all, in May 1919, pending a final determination two years later of the total bill for reparations, Germany agreed to pay 25 billion gold francs in cash and in kind during the interim to cover the expense of restorations in France and Belgium. Before long, there was ample reason to doubt German good faith: by May 1921, this good faith had resulted in payments of 9.8 billion francs—slightly more than half, 5 billion, going to France—while Germany pretended that the cession of state buildings and utilities in Alsace and Lorraine made up the difference.[24] A suspicion grew that pensions and reconstruction were compensation to the French by the French. An offer by Germany in July 1919 of labor and materials for the restoration as payment in kind was met with an adamant rejection. German workers, likely to have been soldiers only months earlier, were unwelcome, especially in the devastated region, and French companies did not want to lose the work. The years needed to complete the rebuilding argue that there was more than enough to do, but the use of German labor would have negated an important collateral benefit of the Charte des sinistrés, the provision of additional jobs for war veterans. Another consequence, not so beneficial but hardly perceived during the Après Guerre, was how the rules of *remploi,* by guaranteeing the cost of "replacement," encouraged restoring houses, farms, shops, and factories just as they had been, often exactly where they had been, in 1914, without thought of modernization or relocation. A chance to build the future was wasted by rebuilding the past.

Although the Charte des sinistrés did mitigate the high unemployment usually accompanying the transition to a peacetime economy, the adjust-

23. See A.N., AJ 5 86–102, Dommages de guerre en France et évaluations; AJ 5 227–30, Evaluations des dommages: principes, études générales; AJ 5 231–41, Evaluation des dommages de la France: correspondances, rapports, observations des ministères; and Sauvy, *Histoire économique,* 1:183–87, 198–212, 453. The record keeping for the pensions, which were essentially life annuities, descended to a new category of the slipshod; by contrast, the records for reconstruction were superior.

24. Sauvy, *Histoire économique,* 1:138–40.

ments were painful, exacerbated by acute shortages of rail transportation and coal. As compensation for the seizure of French rolling stock in areas under occupation, the terms of the Armistice required Germany to hand over 5,000 locomotives and 150,000 freight cars, but they could not be used effectively because more than three thousand miles of track in the northern fifth of the country needed repair. Because German engineers deliberately destroyed French coal mines during the final months of the war, the Treaty of Versailles ordered Germany to deliver France 27 million tons of coal a year (2.25 million tons a month), the amount diminishing as French mines were repaired. From the beginning, Germany was in default—even though France agreed to a reduction, to 1.67 million tons a month in August 1919, raised to 2 million in July 1920—and never made a serious effort to fulfill the obligation. From January 1920 to May 1921, for example, the total of deliveries was not quite 20 million tons, less than 1.2 million a month. As Marc Trachtenberg tellingly observes, Paris, not Berlin, was dark by 10 P.M. for want of coal to generate electricity, and German leaders, by turning off the lights in hotels housing Allied commissions, hoped literally to keep them in the dark about this discrepancy. Without sufficient transportation and fuel, the French economy began its revival with crippling handicaps, itself a mutilé de guerre. Using 1913 as a base 100, industrial production in December 1920 was 67, the gross national product for the year, 80.7.[25]

The effects of these two critical shortages rippled through the economy of the Après Guerre, making everything less available and therefore more expensive. The privations of the war extended into the peace. Propaganda created the myth that the French endured hardships with little protest during the fighting, but in fact, grumbling was a constant undertone from mid-1916 until long after the war was over. When rationing replaced price controls, even press censorship could not conceal the discontent. In late January 1918, *Le Figaro* denounced the hoarding of bread before the system took effect as "panique imbécile" and "précaution égoïste." Three weeks later, Victor Boret, the minister of supply, publicly excoriated "a noisy minority incapable of voluntary sacrifice," the wealthy who com-

25. Sauvy, *Histoire économique,* 1:259–94, 464; Trachtenberg, *Reparation in World Politics,* 120–23; Chastenet, *Histoire de la Troisième République,* 4:333–34.

plained about the limits placed on the cuisine of restaurants. Worse was coming: the coal ration was cut by half for April and May, cut altogether for June and July; the sale of meat was limited to three days a week, the sale of *chocolat de luxe* and *fruit glacé* forbidden. When there was no fuel for heating, Parisians were told "on se chauffe au soleil," and when there was none for express trains, that they should enjoy a slower pace. The government's decision on 2 February 1919 to send price gougers and *mercantis* before courts-martial instead of the civilian criminal courts as before is a measure of how little these soothing words had comforted. A year after the Armistice, nearly everything remained difficult and expensive to obtain, and on 18 October, Louis Loucheur, the minister for reconstruction, admitted to the Chamber of Deputies that coal supplies would be insufficient through 1921.[26]

The shortages and inflation were sharp spurs for anyone receiving wages or a salary to seek a commensurate increase, even—perhaps especially—for the upper ranks of state service, traditionally filled by rentiers, and also traditionally poorly paid because an outside income was expected. With private fortunes laid waste, who could afford to be a magistrate or a diplomat or a secondary schoolmaster? *Professeurs* at lycées were trying to survive on salaries last adjusted in 1853 (testament to the stability of the nineteenth century): the starting level was 2,796 francs. Their lamentation was loud even before the Armistice and was heard with sympathy in the legislature, for after all, *every* deputy and senator was the product of a lycée or collège. In October 1919, the professoriat did receive a handsome raise, of 350 percent, well above the rate of inflation. But six months earlier, they were desperate enough to threaten a *chantage* of sorts against the government, a boycott of the June baccalaureate examinations.[27] What a

26. Jean-Jacques Becker, *Les Français dans la grande guerre* (Paris, 1983), translated by Arnold Pomerans as *The Great War and the French People* (New York, 1986), 132–40, 205–12, 217–35, 302–22; A.N., F7 12951, "Notes Jean," F 5, 126, 127, 210, 219, 260, 14 November–24 December 1918; F 5, 311, 338, 4–11 January 1919. J.O.C., Débats, 13 February and 18 October 1919, for Boret and Loucheur, respectively. *Le Figaro,* 4, 23, 24, 27 January, 10, 14, 24 February, 6, 20, 22 March, 8, 27 April, 6, 23 May, 24 September, 11, 23 October 1918, 8, 9, 13, 23 January, 3, 6, 12 February, 13 May, 19 July, 19, 29 October, 22, 27 December 1919, with the quotations from 27 January, 20 March, and 23 October 1918.

27. J.O.C., Débats, 8 October 1919; *Le Figaro,* 10 November, 25 December 1918, 7 January, 14 May, 16 June, 10, 12 September, 9 October 1919.

bourgeois professional corps could seriously consider doing, the working-class unions would not scruple to carry out.

For with the war of nations over, the war of classes resumed. Hypnotized by the barely imaginable victories of Bolshevism in Russia and socialism in Germany while retaining the old dream of a climacteric general strike, many French labor leaders let themselves be convinced that revolution was in the air. Their working-class followers had also come to believe that the sufferings of the war should be recompensed by more than a restoration of the capitalist hierarchical past. More than ever before, they joined unions—membership rose from 941,000 in 1913 to 1,473,000 by the end of 1919—and the unions, more than ever before, subscribed to the leadership of the increasingly radical Confédération Générale du Travail (C.G.T.). Clemenceau sought to disarm the threat by enacting on 23 April 1919 labor's longtime goal, the eight-hour day, with a provision that the reduction in hours would not mean a reduction in wages; men and women formerly working a sixty- or fifty-four-hour week would thus be paid the same for a forty-eight-hour week. But the demands of the C.G.T. now extended far beyond the social and economic: a "just" peace (for the benefit of the newly "socialist" Germany), no intervention against the Soviet Union, a general amnesty for political prisoners (for the benefit above all of the sailors who mutinied while on duty in the Black Sea as part of the French support for White forces in Russia), disarmament, an end to censorship (in force since 5 August 1914), and changes in taxation (shifting the burden onto the middle and upper classes). Flaunting its new strength, the C.G.T. organized a massive demonstration in Paris on May Day 1919, which Clemenceau countered with well-armed police and elite troops. Because both sides had something to prove to the treaty negotiators, bitter clashes were inevitable, leaving more than seven hundred injured and two young workers killed. When the C.G.T. leaders announced plans for a general strike on 21 July, in concert with trade unionists in Great Britain and Italy, to protest Allied intervention against Bolshevism, Clemenceau dodged a second confrontation by offering some slight concessions (more rapid demobilization and a partial amnesty) in return for a cancellation and brutal repression if not: any railroad or postal workers, employees of the state and forbidden to strike, taking part would be charged before courts-martial. This blandishment and threat made the C.G.T. back

down, and, to make the retreat less humiliating, Clemenceau sacrificed
Boret, the minister of supply, a particular bête noire of the working class,
through a contrived incident that forced his resignation. A general strike
was averted, but there were 2,026 work stoppages during the year.[28]

A second round of direct challenges to the state came the following
spring when Millerand was premier. Bitter disputes between the manage-
ment of the P.-M.-L. R.R. and its workers in February 1920 triggered an
explosion of animosity. Miners in the Pas-de-Calais and the Nord went on
strike in early March, cutting more than 780,000 tons of production from
already scarce coal supplies. The C.G.T. called a general railway strike for
May Day, aware that when the *état de siège* ("state of siege," martial law)
in effect since the outbreak of the war was lifted on 12 October 1919, the
government lost the power to send strikers before military courts. Not all
the railroad workers heeded the C.G.T., but other unions joined, first the
miners, dockers, and seamen, then those in the construction, metallurgical,
transportation, aviation, and automobile industries. More than three decades earlier, Millerand had begun his political career as a lawyer defending
strikes and, as an insider, had learned their points of greatest weakness.
With great dexterity and sangfroid, he outbid the C.G.T. and the unions
in public opinion by damning the harm done to reconstruction. He kept
the trains, buses, and subways going, for the most part, using army engineers and middle-class volunteers. And he went for the jugular by arresting union leaders, dismissing more than twenty thousand striking railroad
workers, and charging the C.G.T. with having violated the laws against
inciting a strike of government employees and therefore liable for dissolution. By the end of May, the strikes and labor's political challenge were
over. Workers abandoned unions faster than they had joined, total membership falling to six hundred thousand at the end of 1920. The most uncompromising of the extremists won control of the Socialist party—
renaming it Communist—and the C.G.T. in December 1920, genuflecting

28. J.O.C., Débats, 18 July 1919, for the Victor Boret incident. John M. Sherwood,
Georges Mandel and the Third Republic (Stanford, 1970), 31–32; Annie Kriegel, *Aux origines
du communisme français, 1914–1920* (2 vols.; Paris, 1964), 1:359–76; Charles S. Maier, *Recasting Bourgeois Europe: Stabilization in France, Germany, and Italy in the Decade After
World War I* (Princeton, 1975), 77–78; Duroselle, *Clemenceau,* 834–39; Chastenet, *Histoire
de la Troisième République,* 5:53–55.

before the god of Moscow, but theirs was the leadership of a rump. The great bulk of French workers gave up political aspirations, their abnegation made easier because industrial wages continued to outpace inflation. If the hierarchical capitalism they attacked in the strikes had then magnanimously granted social and economic concessions akin to the eight-hour day, could enduring labor peace have become a possibility? The chance, at least, was missed: it was easier—and cheaper—simply to blast "French Bolsheviks" and exult over their rout.[29]

What was decidedly not easy or cheap was solving France's fiscal crisis. The calendar testifies to the difficulty. Before the war, no year began without its budget approved and in place. By contrast, the budget prepared by Klotz for 1919 was passed four months late (9 April 1919), that of his successor as minister of finance, Frédéric François-Marsal, for 1920, seven months late (31 July 1920). Both based their figures more on wish fulfillment than on principles of accounting. Expenditures in traditional categories, labeled "ordinary," were balanced by receipts, supposing new taxes were passed; the cost of pensions and the enormous sums for reconstruction, labeled "extraordinary," were to be funded by loans, pending the payment of German reparations. Neither Klotz nor François-Marsal was foolish enough to believe that Germany would pay for everything lumped into the "extraordinary" column, but neither sufficiently disabused the legislature and the public of the notion that "le boche paiera."[30]

That simplistic idea had its unintended birth in a remark by Clemenceau before the Senate on 17 September 1918, almost two months before the Armistice but with German defeat possible to conceive: "Germany wanted a military decision and condemned us to pursue it. . . . Now, the awesome accounting of one people to another is being totaled, and it will be paid." Three months later, on 19 December, while the Chamber of

---

29. Marjorie Millbank Farrar, *Principled Pragmatist: The Political Career of Alexandre Millerand* (Oxford, 1991), 212–19; Adrian Jones, "The French Railway Strikes of January–May 1920: New Syndicalist Ideas and Emergent Communism," *French Historical Studies* 12 (Fall 1982): 508–40; Kriegel, *Aux origines du communisme,* 1:377–494; Maier, *Recasting Bourgeois Europe,* 154–58; Chastenet, *Histoire de la Troisième République,* 5:66–68; Sauvy, *Histoire économique,* 1:344–62. Censorship compromised press reports in 1919, but see *Le Figaro,* for example, 26 February–1 March, 30 March–1 April, 30 April–27 May 1920.

30. Sauvy, *Histoire économique,* 1:363–76.

Deputies discussed the damages of the war, Klotz emphasized that though Germany would be required to make reparation, whatever was left unpaid would become the responsibility of the French themselves. He repeated this warning on 13 March 1919, but ambiguously: "Nothing should be proposed as a financial charge against this nation until the debt of the enemy has been fixed." That fall, during the Chamber's debate over ratification of the Treaty of Versailles, André Tardieu, speaking for the government, was asked, "Mais qui paiera?" He replied simply, "l'Allemagne." Clemenceau, Klotz, and Tardieu all meant that Germany would pay *first*, but it was more comforting to assume that Germany might pay *all*.[31]

Klotz's budget for 1919 proposed total expenditures of 47.116 billion francs and receipts, to balance the "ordinary" outlays, of 8.7 billion. In 1913, the levies on tangible and intangible property—the so-called *quatre vieilles*, which dated from the 1789 Revolution—along with other income produced 5.092 billion francs. To make up the difference for the 1919 budget, the income tax was finally to be imposed, but that would not be enough. During the last year of the war, the government stiffened the assessment on inheritance (it ranged from 2 to 6 percent and a transfer fee of 15 to 25 percent) and added a luxury tax (of 10 percent on all *objets de luxe*, mostly jewelry, antiques, cameras, automobiles, and pleasure boats). In February 1919, Klotz bravely proposed a levy on capital, but a press campaign, led by the mass-circulation *Le Matin* and sponsored by the newspapers of the upper and middle classes such as *Le Figaro*, immediately began against it. The opposition of Raoul Péret, the powerful chairman of the Chamber's budget committee, was decisive: "German capital is intact; French capital is not," he declaimed to the deputies on 7 March. "We are unanimous in saying that Germany must make reparation." Klotz quickly abandoned taxing capital and offered his ambiguous version of "le boche paiera" first. Reassured, the legislators passed the budget, but at the Ministry of Finance, the need for additional revenue could not be ignored. Klotz delayed until 27 May but then asked for higher income tax

31. Sauvy, *Histoire économique*, 1:129–30; and Trachtenberg, *Reparation in World Politics*, 40–43. *Journal Officiel*, Sénat, Débats parlementaires (hereinafter cited as J.O.S., Débats), 17 September 1918, for Clemenceau; J.O.C., Débats, 19 December 1918, 13 March 1919, for Klotz; J.O.C., Débats, 2 September 1919, for Tardieu.

rates, various excise fees, and, for the first time in French history, a sales tax. Three days later, appalled at his colleagues' unreasoning resistance, Senator Alexandre Ribot, minister of finance during the first half of the war and at seventy-seven years old truly an elder statesman, urged them to recognize that German reparations would likely cover only a part, and not that large a part, of France's damage claims. Even assistance from Great Britain and the United States would not eliminate the need for sacrifices: "I cry out to all of France. . . . Work! Work! Work! That must be your order of the day!"[32]

Klotz was disturbingly ingenuous, telling the Chamber of Deputies on 9 July 1919, "My policy is simple . . . to tax, to borrow, and to wait for German payments." He had proposed the first, but the last depended on enforcing the treaty; in the meantime, all he could do was seek loans. During the war, the French government raised 55.395 billion francs through the sale of long-term bonds. Perhaps fearing that insufficient capital remained for another major borrowing, Klotz planned only a modest issue of 4 billion francs for 1919. He would cover the remainder of the deficit through short-term notes and currency advances from the Banque de France. Because of various delays, the bonds were not offered until February 1920, and by then François-Marsal was presiding at the Ministry of Finance. Unlike Klotz, he recognized that the vast expansion of the money supply—by 600 percent since 1913—was a primary cause of inflation. To reduce his dependency on further advances from the central bank, he eliminated the ceiling on the new loan, the gamble bringing in 15.730 billion francs, and convinced the Chamber and Senate to adopt a convention requiring the government to repay 2 billion francs a year to the Banque de France, beginning in 1921. To place the reconstruction of the devastated region on a sounder financial basis, he announced a loan in October 1920, paying the unusually high interest rate of 6 percent, specifically backed by the German reparation payments stipulated in the Treaty of Versailles. There followed the astounding subscription of 27 billion francs,

32. J.O.C., Débats, 18 February, 13 March, 27 May 1919; J.O.S., Débats, 30 May 1919, for Klotz; J.O.C., Débats, 7 March 1919, for Péret; J.O.S., Débats, 30 May 1919, for Ribot. For protests against the tax on capital, see *Le Matin,* 24–28 February 1919, and *Le Figaro,* 25, 28 February 1919, as well as the discussion in Pierre Miquel, *La Paix de Versailles et l'opinion publique française* (Paris, 1972), 13–19, 532–53.

testimony both to the attractive return and to the enduring belief that "le boche paiera."[33]

Despite their vastly different historical reputations, François-Marsal was in many ways merely a slightly wiser Klotz. His much vaunted efforts to control costs notwithstanding, the 1920 budget estimated total expenditures at 47.932 billion francs, a small excess of 1919. The more than doubled projection of income, 21.8 billion francs, was based on the hope of passing additional taxes, the same ones proposed the previous year. In May and again in December 1919, Klotz had called for a 1.1 percent *impôt sur le chiffre d'affaires,* a sales tax on business receipts, or "turnover." François-Marsal embraced the idea as his own and won its adoption on 20 July 1920. Unlike the income tax, it would be relatively simple to administer, calculate, and adjust upward or downward. As a concession to leftist complaints about its regressive quality, patrons of deluxe hotels and restaurants were condemned to pay a super sales tax of 10 percent on those bills. François-Marsal also resurrected Klotz's levy on capital, but in a new guise, as a tax on *enrichissement,* on the *increase* of capital between 1914 and 1920, couching it as an assessment against war profiteering. Although almost every rentier would have been exempt, the same forces that buried the capital tax of 1919 attacked and defeated what they termed "expropriation." Even so, the impact of new taxation was significant: in 1913, taxes equaled 8.5 percent of France's gross national product; by 1921, when all of the new ones were fully in effect, they would equal 13.6 percent. Writing in *Le Figaro,* the prominent conservative economist Louis H. Aubert calculated that the average inhabitant of France would be paying 453 francs a year in taxes, two-thirds more than his American counterpart at 272 francs. The French might validly question how this burden had become the victor's portion.[34]

33. J.O.C., Débats, 9 July 1919, for Klotz. The 1915 5 percent bonds raised 13.398 billion francs, the 1916 5 percents 10.082 billion, the 1917 4 percents 10.071 billion, and the 1918 4 percents 21.744 billion. On the expansion of the currency, see Sauvy, *Histoire économique,* 1:524–25, and François-Marsal's speech at Lyon, reported in *Le Figaro,* 7 March 1920. The 6 percent interest for the second 1920 loan was above the market rate: see Sauvy, *Histoire économique,* 1:531. François-Marsal, speaking at Strasbourg, claimed, "Et l'Allemagne paiera, parce qu'elle peut payer, et ceci quels que soient la situation budgétaire intérieure et le cours du monde"; quoted in *Le Figaro,* 21 October 1920.

34. For François-Marsal's policy, see J.O.C., Débats, 29 March, 14 April, 26 November 1920; J.O.S., Débats, 22 May 1920; and Sauvy, *Histoire économique,* 1:365–67; Chastenet,

And it was also the victor's portion to watch the proud franc, symbol of prosperity and stability, sink ever further on currency exchanges. Under the regime of the gold standard, the dollar was equal to 5.18 francs, the pound sterling to 25.22. Wartime controls negotiated with the United States and Great Britain kept these relationships all but constant until their termination in February 1919 (the quotations then were 5.45 and 25.97, respectively). Thereafter, the franc began to fall, slowly at first, then with greater speed: in June 1919, the dollar bought 6.38 francs, the pound 29.59; in December 1919, 10.87 and 41.81; by December 1920, 16.90 and 59.08. In twenty-two months, the franc fell 310 percent against the dollar, 227 percent against the pound. Put another way, in less than two years, the franc declined in value from eighteen cents to six cents. The public, politicians, and even most economists could not fathom the causes of this collapse and considered it a humiliation, placing them among those unciv- ilized peoples incapable of managing their affairs properly. Yet in the illu- mination of modern economic analysis, the explanation was cruelly sim- ple. The franc's enemies were a budget drastically out of balance, raging inflation, and a temporarily insolvable foreign trade deficit.[35]

The disarray in so much of the nation's agriculture and industry made imports vital to replace missing production while greatly decreasing the quantity of goods available for export. In 1913, imports amounted to 8.421 billion francs, exports to 6.880 billion, and the trade deficit was much more than offset by income from foreign investments. Six years later, in 1919, imports were 35.799 billion francs, exports only 11.879 billion, leaving a deficit of 23.920 billion francs—and France was now a debtor, not a credi- tor, nation. By 1920, the situation was improving: although imports were up further, to 49.905 billion francs, so were exports, and at a greater pace, to 26.895 billion, leaving the deficit almost the same as in 1919, 23.010 bil- lion francs, but the momentum was in the right direction. As production was restored, exports could rise (aided by the weak franc), imports would

---

Histoire de la Troisième République, 5:202–4. For the tax on the chiffre d'affaires, J.O.C., Débats, 27 May, 29 December 1919, 13, 23 April, 16 June 1920; J.O.S., Débats, 23 June 1920. For the tax on enrichissement, J.O.C., Débats, 14 April 1920; *Le Figaro,* 12, 22 April, 28 May 1920. For the tax burden, see Sauvy, *Histoire économique,* 1:387; and *Le Figaro,* 3 May 1920.

35. See the statistics in Sauvy, *Histoire économique,* 1:444–45, and the commentary, 1:58–59.

be less necessary, and the deficit would diminish. The formula was correct even if the proof was painfully protracted. Agriculture did not recover until the late 1920s. Industry was hardly more rapid: using 1913 as a base 100, its production hovered between 54 and 60 in 1919, between 56 and 67 in 1920. It would not reach 100 until January 1924, significantly, the year of the first postwar trade surplus.[36]

The year before, 1923, France lost all patience with Germany's obstinate refusal to meet its treaty obligations and occupied the Ruhr valley in an ultimately futile effort to compel compliance. If Germany had made the required reparation payments in cash and in kind, the enemies of the franc would have been largely disarmed: inflation considerably reduced, the trade and budget deficits much smaller. Instead, between November 1918 and December 1920, Germany paid France a mere 2.011 billion gold francs beyond the indemnities for reconstruction of the devastated region, which would reach 5 billion francs by April 1921. Over the following decade, until the Great Depression put an end to reparations in 1931, Germany made additional payments of 14.964 billion francs. The total, 21.975 billion francs, was a pittance compared to France's costs for reconstruction and pensions, which by the end of 1920 alone had reached 19 billion francs. The total was, in fact, only slightly greater than France's debt to the United States (19.9 billion francs) and far below France's combined debt to the United States and Great Britain (35 billion francs). Although the French did not know it before the end of the Après Guerre, any calculation based on the belief that "le boche paiera" was false, for le boche n'a pas payé.[37]

As Alfred Sauvy has sagely remarked, prewar France, which the Après Guerre increasingly called the "Belle Epoque" (the "good old days"), was "Malthusian" economically as well as demographically: a static society enjoying the luxury of freedom from the pains that accompany growth. Taxes and inflation were low, and with the population mostly of working age (before life spans so lengthened that care of the aged became a vexation), living standards for everyone were increasing. The war pressed this

---

36. Sauvy, *Histoire économique*: for balance of payments, 1:295–313, 477; for agriculture, 1:241–42, 257; for industry, 1:259–74, 464.

37. Sauvy, *Histoire économique*: on German reparations, 1:141–43, 165–67, 452.

society to the limit and was won at the cost of its destruction. To regain such a paradise lost—at least as it was seen from the far side of the Great War—engaged the fantasies of the political elite. Material prosperity could be restored and eventually was, just as the devastated region was reconstructed. But the character of the Belle Epoque, imbued with the liberating mentality of rentier wealth, was as beyond reclaiming as the Russian bonds in which so much of that wealth had been invested. The failure to recognize this reality, that longing cannot conjure a lost past, obscured clear thinking about the critical problems of economic policy.

These problems were staggeringly difficult, and all the more so because they appeared unique, certainly to the French. Each seemed bound up with all of the others, the solution of one dependent on the solution of all, and the economic problems further bound up with diplomatic and political issues. Thus reconstruction unbalanced the budget, contributing to a trade deficit, which, in turn, depressed confidence in the franc, which continued to slide because reparation payments were not forthcoming and because the legislature, spooked by "Bolshevism," refused to countenance any threat to bourgeois fortunes. Was there ever a chance to cut through this entanglement? Jean-Baptiste Duroselle points to what he considers a missed opportunity immediately after the Armistice, when "victory permitted a psychological shock." Clemenceau, he argues, should have committed his incomparable prestige as Père-la-Victoire behind a substantial tax on capital that would have reduced the enormous budget deficits of 1919 and 1920, thereby "saving" the franc. With its financial authority uncompromised, France could have acted more independently of Great Britain and the United States during the Paris Peace Conference and the diplomatic negotiations of the following eighteen months. Sauvy likewise censures "the great fault of not taking in hand the economic affairs of the nation." This unwillingness to assume bold risks and sacrifices passed the initiative to temporizers, who dreamed of restoring the Belle Epoque or who could call waiting for German reparations a policy. In the France of the Après Guerre, Sauvy writes, "self-deception was queen of the ball."[38]

38. Sauvy, *Histoire économique*: for the Belle Epoque, 1:430–37; for the quotations, 1:58–59; Duroselle, *Clemenceau,* 830. See also the extensive discussion, based on an immense literature, by Stephen A. Schuker, *The End of French Predominance in Europe: The Financial Crisis of 1924 and the Adoption of the Dawes Plan* (Chapel Hill, 1976), 3–88.

The determination to run risks, to make sacrifices, to adopt a resolute realism made French diplomacy over the quarter-century before the Great War so extraordinarily successful. By compromising political ideals to ally with Russia and colonial ambitions to ally with Great Britain, France constructed the Triple Entente, its sheer pragmatism as a bulwark against Germany overcoming the inherent mistrust of the partners. Italy was then weaned from the Triple Alliance and much of the Balkans turned toward the Entente. Even so, victory was hard-won and Pyrrhic. France expected an easier time at the negotiating table, but the diplomatic kaleidoscope had turned. The collapse of Romanov and Habsburg dominion left ethnic anarchy in eastern Europe. Russia had made a separate peace under the Bolsheviks. The United States, which had provided the final margin for victory, marked its rejection of traditional great-power relationships by Woodrow Wilson's insistence that his was an "associated," not an "allied," nation. To Great Britain, a defeated Germany appeared less menacing and thus affinity with France less necessary. In the immediate aftermath of the Armistice, France mistakenly thought that friendships solidified by common battlefield experience would last and forgot that pragmatism could cut in more than one direction.[39]

The first public blow to these illusions came when Wilson, so acclaimed when he arrived on French soil, refused to visit the devastated region for fear, he claimed, of prejudicing himself against the Germans. The second was the insistence by Wilson and David Lloyd George that English as well as French be an official language of the Paris Peace Conference—even the Prussians in 1871 had not demanded that French cede its place as the sole diplomatic language. Clemenceau and his cabinet were disabused of their misapprehension in private earlier by the refusal of British and American economic advisers to continue the wartime consortia and exchange agreements, although their termination would create difficult conditions for France. The attitude of Great Britain was disappointing but less than an utter surprise. Clemenceau told Lloyd George, "I have to tell you that from the very day after the Armistice I found you an enemy to France,"

---

39. The scholarship on these topics is vast. For a guide, see the bibliographic essay in Bernadotte E. Schmitt and Harold C. Vedeler, *The World in Crucible, 1914–1919* (New York, 1984), 489–517.

and Lloyd George replied, "Well, *was it not always our traditional policy?*" Paul Cambon, the longtime ambassador to the Court of St. James, remarked ironically that "the British unfortunately failed to realize that Napoleon had been dead for some time." The relative lack of sympathy from the United States, however, was regarded as betrayal. The arrival of American troops had stirred memories of Benjamin Franklin, the Marquis de Lafayette, and the birth of two republics conceived in great eighteenth-century revolutions. During the last year of the war, France celebrated all things American, from the Fourth of July and Thanksgiving to the heroic death in aerial combat of Quentin Roosevelt, youngest son of the former president, to baseball, "le sport national américain," which French troops were encouraged to learn for improving the accuracy of their grenade throws.[40]

Within the government, there was sharp division over strategy for the peace. Should France prepare to provide for its security alone, without depending on the uncertain support of allies and the untested idealism of the proposed League of Nations? Or should France recognize the impossibility of forever, alone, containing Germany and enlist at its side the wartime allies and the new League? Marshal Ferdinand Foch, lately commander in chief of the Allied armies, was the foremost proponent of a self-sufficient France and formulated the principal requirement in his memorandum of 28 November 1918 to Clemenceau demanding that the Rhine River be declared France's military frontier. Poincaré agreed but, in his address of welcome at the opening of the peace conference, veiled his desire for an independent Rhineland behind platitudes: "Justice . . . demands . . . sanctions against the guilty, and effective guarantees . . . to the nations which have been and which may still be exposed to aggressors or to threats." Clemenceau adopted the second proposition, that France should build a peace through a permanent alliance structure, but he did not reveal

---

40. Trachtenberg, *Reparation in World Politics,* 1–40. For the exchange between Clemenceau and Lloyd George, see Georges Clemenceau, *Grandeurs et misères d'une victoire* (Paris, 1930), translated by F. M. Atkinson as *Grandeur and Misery of Victory* (New York, 1930), 121. Paul Cambon is quoted in Piotr S. Wandycz, *France and Her Eastern Allies, 1919–1925: French-Czechoslovak-Polish Relations from the Paris Peace Conference to Locarno* (Minneapolis, 1962), 5. For the celebration of America, see *Le Figaro,* 23 April, 5, 15, 22 (Quentin Roosevelt) July, 21 August (baseball), 29 November 1918.

his position until after the conference was under way. At the end of December 1918, he secured for himself the leadership of the French delegation and a blank check for the negotiations from the Chamber of Deputies and the Senate by promising to submit the finished treaty for legislative approval. He dared would-be Talleyrands like Aristide Briand to seek the overthrow of his cabinet if they found his refusal to accept their counsel objectionable, and the continuation of censorship kept all but the highest officials from gauging the progress of diplomacy except through rumor.[41]

Clemenceau knew early on—perhaps even before the conference opened—that neither Wilson nor Lloyd George would agree to dismembering Germany in any fashion. He advanced the proposal to gain counteroffers, eventually winning the permanent demilitarization and temporary occupation of the Rhineland and the promise of defensive alliances with Great Britain and the United States. Clemenceau had the structure he sought, but Foch was appalled and lectured the conference, to no avail, on the military imperative of a Rhenish buffer state. Poincaré then asked the French delegation to demand that the occupation terminate only when the last franc due in reparation had been paid. This interference provoked Clemenceau's comment in English to Wilson, "You must give me help from those two fools." Although believing that a peace without the participation of the United States would fail, Clemenceau more clearly than most measured Wilson's merits. On 29 December 1918, he described him to the Chamber of Deputies as a man who inspired respect "par la noble candeur de son esprit," knowing well from his years in the United States as a young man and his unfortunate marriage to an American that "candor" in English means "sincere," while in French, "candeur" means "naïveté." Whatever the shortcomings of the treaty they negotiated, he was deeply grateful for Wilson's attempt to forge a lasting peace. Once the details

41. For Poincaré's speech, *Le Figaro,* 19 January 1919; for Clemenceau, J.O.C., Débats, 29–30 December 1918; Duroselle, *Clemenceau,* 724–25, 737–38, 746–68. During the negotiations, Clemenceau would rely almost entirely on his own judgment and that of André Tardieu (deputy, France's high commissioner for Franco-American relations during the war, and a member of the French treaty delegation). This isolation occasioned misgivings: see Ribot in his *Journal d'Alexandre Ribot et correspondances inédits, 1914–1922* (Paris, 1936), 273, noting Poincaré's anxiety and commenting: "Clemenceau has become irritable. He has no one beside him but Tardieu, who is not a sure guide."

were public, most of the French did not share this gratitude. On 28 June 1919, following the formal signing in the Hall of Mirrors at Versailles, cries of "Vive Wilson" were few as the American president boarded his train at the Gare des Invalides to leave for Brest, the *George Washington,* and a country that was also turning against him. But Clemenceau put his arms around Wilson and with tears in his eyes said without reserve, "I feel as if I am losing one of the best friends I have ever had."[42]

Because the Treaty of Versailles was based on Clemenceau's, not Foch's, conception of security for France, making vital the continued participation of the United States in European affairs, the extent of Wilson's political difficulties overshadowed all other issues when the Chamber of Deputies opened its debate. On 24 September, Louis Barthou, deputy since 1889, former premier, and eight times a cabinet minister, asked André Tardieu, Clemenceau's closest foreign policy adviser, what would be the fate of the promised defensive pact between the United States and France if the American Senate failed to ratify the treaty. Tardieu's guarded reply that he expected approval did not satisfy Barthou, who continued, "I have the firm hope that the United States will ratify the treaty, but between hope and assurance there is a period of anguish." He then called for an adjournment of the Chamber's debate until after the American outcome was known. With an uncertain number of deputies apparently ready to follow his lead, Clemenceau intervened personally for the first time to insist on immediate consideration. As he had done nine months before, he challenged those opposing him to seek his overthrow and the following day took the tribune to defend his work. The treaty was, he conceded, "imperfect, written hastily and under conditions you do not understand"—a cryptic reference to the economic pressures Wilson and Lloyd George could mobilize against France to compel compromises. Yet, "I say that it is a good treaty, and I will have little difficulty in demonstrating so and winning your support." The American role was the critical question, and Clemenceau spoke forthrightly: "We are counting on America. And do you want to know what I truly believe? If there were no written treaty, I would count on America all the same!" During the war, "Nothing obliged

42. J.O.C., Débats, 29 December 1918; Duroselle, *Clemenceau,* 738 (for "candeur"), 753 (for "two fools"), 768 (for "best friends").

the Americans to come to our aid. They came." When one of the conservative deputies, Louis Marin, complained that the complexities and ambiguities of the treaty "reduce us to the politics of vigilance," Clemenceau rejoined, "I, myself, see life as a perpetual struggle, in peace as in war. . . . All existence is but a struggle."[43]

Reassured, and perhaps shamed by Clemenceau's fate-defying courage, the deputies approved the treaty on 2 October by a vote of 372 to 53; one of the votes against was from Marin. Ironically, on the same day, Woodrow Wilson suffered a debilitating stroke after breaking off the campaign of speeches by which he hoped to rouse popular support for the treaty. At first, French leaders wore a brave face about Wilson's health and publicly asserted that the American Senate would eventually recognize its responsibilities. The French Senate approved the treaty unanimously on 11 October. But by the end of 1919, the mask of confidence turned to openly bitter resentment in reaction to the spectacular influence in Great Britain and the United States of John Maynard Keynes's diatribe against Wilson, Clemenceau, and the treaty, *The Economic Consequences of the Peace,* and to Lloyd George's remark to the House of Commons on 18 December that an American refusal to conclude the defensive pact with France meant that Britain need not do so either. This mood intensified during the first months of 1920, as American senators invoked the Monroe Doctrine against the League of Nations, clamored for the rapid repayment of war debts, and, on 19 March, definitively rejected the Treaty of Versailles. A week before the vote, Alfred Capus, a close friend of Poincaré's and editor in chief of *Le Figaro,* wrote in his newspaper, "The services rendered by President Wilson to France are unforgettable, but the errors he has committed at the expense of our country are not less so." A week after the vote, Gabriel Hanotaux, a former minister of foreign affairs, advised bluntly in print: "We must take up for ourselves, and as soon as possible. Neither America nor anyone else will come to our aid." The two comments represented the response to Clemenceau that had been lacking the previous September. When the victory by Warren G. Harding in the November 1920 presidential election signified the final American turning away from

43. J.O.C., Débats, 24–25 September 1919.

Wilson and his ideas, an editorial expressed the wish that Europe could *déwilsoner* itself as the United States had just done.[44]

The other overriding issue of the treaty for France was reparations, which complexly linked economic and foreign policy. In 1871, Bismarck had imposed on the nascent Third Republic an indemnity amounting to 5.69 billion francs. An arithmetically minded columnist for *Le Figaro* calculated that this sum at 5 percent compound interest per year (the return of some Russian bonds if reinvested) would be worth about 60 billion francs by the end of 1918, a total, he suggested, that would make an appropriate German restitution for their crimes of both wars. In fact, Clemenceau and his principal economic advisers, Louis Loucheur and Etienne Clémentel, initially did not plan to ask for reparations beyond the amount needed to restore the devastated region, approximately 35 billion gold francs. To them, continuation of the wartime economic consortia with Great Britain and the United States, by which the three could control the price and distribution of raw materials worldwide, combined with tariff and currency accords was much more important. Such agreements would have greatly assisted the French recovery and checked German aggression. But Wilson and Lloyd George, convinced that the arrangements would work most to the benefit of France and that their nations would gain more from free trade and financial independence, adamantly refused to maintain what they regarded as emergency provisions. The fallback position for the French was to insist on heavy reparations from Germany as France's only means of recovering from the war damage, hoping that the British and Americans would prefer consortia to reparations. The plan backfired when Lloyd George enthusiastically embraced German payments as an unexpected windfall to cover British war expenses such as pensions. What the French had conceived as a negotiating ploy became harnessed to British demands and, for want of an alternative, pulled Wilson along in tow. The treaty did not specify a total sum for reparations because Clemenceau and Lloyd George asked more than Wilson considered acceptable, but it did include the famous German "war-guilt" clause

44. J.O.C., Débats, 2 October 1919; J.O.S., Débats, 11 October 1919. *Le Figaro*, 11 March (Capus), 25 March (Hanotaux), 5 November (*déwilsoner*) 1920.

as the justification for the bill to be presented. The Reparations Commission was charged to set the figure by May 1921.[45]

During the interim—and beyond—French political and economic leaders pursued two complementary strategies. The first was to seek an alternative consortium with Germany by pledging to reduce reparation payments in return for the provision of Ruhr valley coke to be used in the regained iron mills of Lorraine. Although occasionally seeming to hold promise, these negotiations failed because the German industrialists believed that they could outclass their French rivals whatever the circumstances and because they were fundamentally opposed to assisting their "enemy" in any fashion, especially if doing so involved the emotionally charged issue of Alsace and Lorraine. The second strategy was to settle on a fixed and "final" figure for reparations with the German government even as the commission undertook its deliberations. Armed with this proof of German *willing* compliance, the French could "mobilize" their share of the total (set at 52 percent by the Spa conference in July 1920) by selling bonds, most likely in the United States, backed by the guarantee of reparations. A lump sum would thus be available immediately, and the bondholders, not France, would assume the onus of ensuring German payments. This approach also led to nothing because German leaders always rejected proposed totals or attached unacceptable political conditions to agreement, while demonstrating a determination to pay as little as possible. Combined with the almost complete withdrawal of the United States government from European affairs, Germany's attitude rendered ludicrous the idea of finding a market among American investors for bonds backed by reparations.[46]

The only course left for France was to insist on strict enforcement of the treaty and payment in full of the total set by the Reparations Commission, 132 billion gold marks, of which the French share was 85.8 billion gold francs. But doing so was handicapped by the reluctance, sometimes the refusal, of the British to cooperate. Eager for German customers and unaccountably fearful of a new French dominion on the Continent, Great

45. Charles Vallée in *Le Figaro,* 8 September 1918. For the strategy of the peace conference, see Trachtenberg, *Reparation in World Politics,* 1–54.
46. Trachtenberg, *Reparation in World Politics,* 54–96, 110–14, 130–91.

Britain left France to discipline Germany alone. And so was born the reputation of France as a strong-arm bully, a militaristic nation greedy for the last franc of reparation, a myth encouraged by André Tardieu's widely read *La Paix* of 1921, in which he portrayed Clemenceau calling for stern treatment of Germany but overwhelmed by objections from Wilson and Lloyd George. Tardieu was writing to defend himself, not just Clemenceau, now that the shortcomings of the treaty he recommended had been so starkly revealed.[47]

Further troubles for France lay in the chaos of eastern Europe, though less from the outcome of the peace conference than from a nostalgia for the Russia of the Triple Entente. Ambiguity and contradiction in policy were the result. What the Clemenceau and Millerand cabinets wished for most fervently and vainly was a restored Russia, whether tsarist or reformist, that would honor past debts and take up again its French-appointed role as eastern counterweight to Germany. With the United States and Great Britain adamantly against intervention, France's best hope for the destruction of Bolshevism was to mount an invasion supporting the fissiparous White forces by arming and leading men from the bordering ethnic groups, from among the Poles, Lithuanians, Ukrainians, Byelorussians, and Romanians. But if that worked—and Lenin, for one, was convinced that it might—Russia "one and indivisible" would be lost. The new ethnic nations could not be denied large territorial claims, and that, White leaders insisted, was unacceptable. By betting on the Whites to win by themselves, France lost one of the crucial wagers of the twentieth century.[48]

And having lost, France needed a new eastern counterweight, a bloc of the ethnic successor states, which for strategic reasons would have to include both Poland and Czechoslovakia. Concerned only to create a defensive structure, French leaders begged the question of mutual antagonism between the two, even while increasing it through obtuse diplomacy. The Czechoslovak foreign minister, Eduard Benes, so thoroughly ingratiated himself in Paris—Clemenceau, who dispensed few compliments, called

---

47. Trachtenberg, *Reparation in World Politics,* 101–2, 192–289. André Tardieu, *La Paix* (Paris, 1921), translated as *The Truth About the Treaty* (Indianapolis, 1921).

48. Wandycz, *France and Her Eastern Allies,* 103–19.

him "one of the best of them all"—that France adopted his egregiously inequitable position on the partition of Teschen, to the great economic injury and permanent indignation of the Poles. In August 1920, when the Soviet Red Army struck to within a few miles of Warsaw, Millerand did send Poland a military mission under General Maxime Weygand, when no other nation, notably including Czechoslovakia, would come to the rescue. Yet this aid went largely unappreciated because the Polish leader, Marshal Josef Pilsudski, whose strategy threw back the Bolsheviks, resented the implication that France had won Poland's war. Once the Russians were in retreat, Millerand urged the Poles to settle for moderate border gains in order that some future non-Bolshevik government might not take exception to them. Here was the absurdity of a foreign policy offending an important existing government to placate one that might never come to power. The perceptive royalist historian Jacques Bainville wrote in *L'Action française* that France should act "as if Russia were lost to us. . . . [We] shall never organize anything in Europe if we cannot detach ourselves from the first love of the Third Republic." Shrewd as he was, Bainville forgot that no one, not even a regime, forgets a first love, especially when bereft.[49]

The first and abiding love of most French politicians was a species of narcissism, legislative dominance. This beloved had been a casualty of the war, first to the army General Staff and, from November 1917 on, to Clemenceau, who required a blind confidence from everyone who wished to avoid the charge of défaitisme. Ironically, Clemenceau had always been the champion of executive weakness, winning the name "Tiger" for savagely overthrowing cabinets and proclaiming his contempt for the presidency of the Republic by his injunction, "I vote for the stupidest." After the examples made of Louis Malvy and Joseph Caillaux for their too limited faith in the religion of total victory, deputies and senators offered not even token resistance as long as the war continued, an exception made for the approximately fifty Socialists in the Chamber, whose noisy but ineffectual protests were useful to Clemenceau and his chef de cabinet, éminence grise, Georges Mandel, in discrediting the extreme Left by linking it to

49. Wandycz, *France and Her Eastern Allies*, 21–185, quoting Bainville in *L'Action française*, 9 September 1920, 177. For Clemenceau, see his *Grandeur and Misery of Victory*, 149.

Bolshevism. But once the Armistice was signed, rebellion could not be long in rising.[50]

The first sign came during the debate on foreign policy, 29–30 December 1918, when Clemenceau sought sole authority at the peace conference. There were nearly fifty more votes against the cabinet this time, coming from a faction around Briand, who put his partisan Henry Franklin-Bouillon up to proposing that the delegation include "the political elite . . . whom public opinion recognizes as having a real competence for the task," an allusion to Briand as well as an implicit attack on Clemenceau, who had no previous negotiating experience. The second came during the ratification of the treaty in September 1919, but neither was a serious threat. Clemenceau taunted his opponents with the challenge to overthrow him if they could. They could not and they dared not. Because of the war, the Chamber had sat long past the expiration of its mandate in June 1918, and Clemenceau set new elections for mid-November 1919. What would the voters think of their humiliating the Père-la-Victoire?[51]

While awaiting their turn to debate the treaty, the deputies changed the procedure for the forthcoming ballot, adopting proportional representation (*répartition proportionnelle*, or RP), the goal of parties on the Right and Left, as well as a few Centrists led by Briand, since the last decade before the war because the system of single-member districts (*scrutin d'arrondissement*) underrepresented groups with a scattered following. The new RP required voting department-wide, with each party or parties acting together to sponsor a list of candidates. If a single list won an absolute majority of the department's votes, it received all the seats for the department; if not, the seats were apportioned according to the percentage of votes for each list. The possibility of combining lists put a premium on making electoral alliances, and in 1919, the parties of the Right (excluding only the obvious monarchists) and the Center were the ones at least superficially in agreement. The Radicals of the moderate Left found themselves without a partner, for the Socialists, with whom they were accustomed to join at

50. Duroselle, *Clemenceau,* 637; Sherwood, *Georges Mandel,* 18–28; Herriot, *Jadis,* 2:72–73; Joseph Paul-Boncour, *Entre deux guerres: Souvenirs sur la Troisième République* (3 vols.; Paris, 1945–46), 1:281.

51. J.O.C., *Débats,* 29–30 December 1918, 27–29 August, 2–5, 9–12, 16, 18, 23–26, 30 September, 1–2 October 1919; Duroselle, *Clemenceau,* 737–40, 768–73.

the polls, were bent on ideological purity and were besides already tarred with the brush of Bolshevism. The result of the voting was the first victory for a coalition including the Right since 1871. The other distinguishing characteristic of the elections was the choice of so many new men, through the defeat of 360 incumbents. The swing to the Right produced some of the change, and the rest was owing to a sense among the voters that the deputies were *embusqués,* shirkers, who sat out the war in relative comfort, and that *poilus* might better understand the needs of the nation. So many of the new deputies wore their sky-blue military dress uniforms when the Chamber convened on 8 December 1919 that it was dubbed the Chambre bleu horizon—the Chamber of the Blue Horizon.[52]

The coalition of Center and Right parties, the so-called Bloc national, was presented to the voters as the means of constituting a majority for continuing the clemenciste program. The premier himself encouraged this portrayal during his major speech of the campaign, on 4 November at Strasbourg, the emotional center of Alsace and Lorraine and symbol of his victorious policies. Clemenceau called for a new *union sacrée* of the true France, excommunicating those renegade French "bolsheviks . . . who do not hide their intention to install upon the ruins of our republican regime their bloody dictatorship of anarchy. To them, truly, we have nothing to say. Between them and us, c'est une question de force." The notorious "priest-eater," who had refused to permit any official attendance, above all Poincaré's, at the *Te Deum* celebrated by the cardinal-archbishop of Paris six days after the Armistice, now extended his hand to the Catholic conservatives, vowing that the laicity of the state would not compromise the "rights and liberties of citizens whatever their faith as long as religious peace is maintained." But this pledge was, perhaps intentionally, vague, just as he was on the other critical issues. To the complaint that his treaty condemned France to a perpetual alert, he rejoined, "As if it had ever been any different!" Of the budget, "we must ask whatever is necessary in taxes." On economic recovery, "Enough investments abroad; let French savings invest in France." The speech was a triumph of rhetoric, a magnificent façade for a political symbol now seventy-eight years old.[53]

52. Sherwood, *Georges Mandel,* 89, unnumbered content note; Chastenet, *Histoire de la Troisième République,* 5:55–60.

53. The full text of the speech was published in *Le Figaro,* 5 November 1919; Duroselle, *Clemenceau,* 839–50.

Behind the façade and the symbol, the success of the Bloc national belonged to a clever strategist, Adolphe Carnot, and two immeasurably ambitious deputies, Briand and Millerand. Carnot, who since 1901 had assembled many of the Centrist deputies in the Alliance républicaine démocratique and was an oddity in not holding elective office himself, pulled together the most important figures from two-thirds of the Chamber's hemicycle. By promising to bar the route to Bolshevism, he tapped the political slush funds of the major business groups in France, the Comité républicain du commerce et de l'industrie and the Union des intérêts économiques, to cover the much greater costs of department-wide campaigning. His address in the Salle Wagram of Paris on 20 October, proclaiming the coalition's goals, was the first mention of the name "Bloc national." Briand, though a premier before and during the war, recognized that he might have to wait to regain power because he was known as a conciliator and conciliation was hardly the mood of the day. But he also believed that his return would come all the sooner through a majority elected by RP, which he had sponsored from the first. With his usual facility for choosing the winning side, he bet on the Bloc national instead of the Radicals, with whom he remained on good terms. He made the decision clear in a speech at Nantes on 29 October, emphasizing the need for the elections to produce a "homogeneous majority" providing "sustained support of republican policies," sentiments more enigmatic than Clemenceau's but, in the idiom of 1919, unmistakable. Briand's participation reassured the left wing of the Center that the Bloc national was not too heavily weighted toward the conservatives and was also proof that it was not securely clemenciste.[54]

The most powerful figure in the coalition was Millerand, since March the high commissioner for Alsace and Lorraine and regarded as the heir apparent to Clemenceau, who would likely seek the presidency of the Republic in January 1920 or tire from old age. Millerand began his career as a Socialist—the first, in 1899, to hold a cabinet post—and then moved steadily across the political spectrum, winning his highest marks as a stri-

54. See the account of Carnot's speech in *Le Figaro,* 21 October 1919; a long article and interview followed two weeks later, 7 November 1919. For Briand, see Georges Suarez, *Briand: Sa vie, son oeuvre, avec son journal et de nombreux documents inédits* (6 vols.; Paris, 1938–52), 5:41–54; and Bernard Oudin, *Aristide Briand, biographie* (Paris, 1987), 388–89.

dently nationalistic minister of war from January 1912 to January 1913 and from August 1914 to October 1915. Recognizing that his constituency lay among the voters for the Right and the Center, he described a program appealing to them at the Paris Ba-Ta-Clan hall on 7 November in what was immediately recognized as the most important speech of the campaign. Where Clemenceau and Briand were obscure, Millerand was explicit. For Catholics, he promised an end to criticism of the church in state schools, permission for some of the religious congregations, banned since the early 1900s, to return, and the strong possibility of restoring diplomatic relations with the Vatican broken in 1904. For businessmen, he pledged the defeat of Bolshevism, opposition to any further government monopolies or nationalization, and determination to change conflict between classes into solidarity among them. To loosen the stranglehold of Parisian centralization, he proposed regional assemblies charged with encouraging local initiative. And most controversially, like Clemenceau, Millerand had changed his mind about the balance point between the legislature and the executive. Confronting the crises of the postwar world, he claimed, required augmenting the powers of the presidency by reviving prerogatives that had fallen into desuetude and by expanding the presidential electors beyond the deputies and senators. In every line of the speech, Millerand posed as the new emblem of order and authority.[55]

To what extent the French electorate embraced the proposals of the Bloc national, specific or not, is difficult to conclude. In the voting on 16 November, the coalition won 380 of the 616 seats, three-fifths of the Chamber. Another 57 right-wing deputies, mostly monarchists, would likely be occasional supporters. By placing Captain Jacques Sadoul, a deserter to the Soviet Red Army under sentence of death after court-martial in absentia, at the head of their list for the Paris region, the Socialists provided the rationale for believing even the most extreme accusations of their Bolshevist intention. Yet the Socialists received more popular votes than in 1914, the Radicals about the same, even as they lost a third and a half, respectively, of their seats. Soon afterward, in the December municipal elections and in the balloting for the Senate on 11 January 1920, for which RP did not apply, the Radicals and Socialists held their own. The

55. Farrar, *Principled Pragmatist,* 205–9.

tactical failure of the Left to comprehend that RP compelled organizing a competing alliance to the Bloc national was almost certainly more important than any rightward shift of public opinion in creating the Chambre bleu horizon.[56]

So many and so diverse, the Bloc national fell into feuding almost immediately. Although unwilling openly to declare his candidacy for president, Clemenceau spoke carelessly of his plans after taking possession of the Elysée palace. He had recently acquired a dossier of letters that appeared to prove the rumors about Briand's irregular contacts with German agents during the war. In September 1917, he was ordered to break off negotiations with Baron Oskar von der Lancken-Wackenitz about a compromise peace but, according to the evidence, secretly continued them until mid-January 1918 and counted on the fall of the Lloyd George and Clemenceau cabinets to clear the way for his proposals. Malvy had been banished to exile for five years, and Caillaux was in prison waiting trial before the Senate on charges of treason, for less. On 18 November, only two days after the Bloc national's sweeping victory, Clemenceau suggested to several colleagues that Briand be tried with Caillaux. Perhaps he was not serious because he also said, "On 17 January, I will take charge at the Elysée for seven years, and for those seven years Briand will stamp his feet in vain seeking to become premier." To save his political skin and maybe his life, Briand retaliated.[57]

Clemenceau had always gloried in his enemies. Even as Père-la-Victoire he was respected and feared but not loved. Now he underestimated their danger. Although he was the obvious choice for president, he refused to eliminate potential rivals by soliciting election. His arrogance as premier offended many legislators, and there was the threat that he would be authoritarian at the Elysée. The Socialists were certain to oppose him, and many Radicals, resenting his treatment of Malvy and Caillaux, would join them. Briand was a relatively new enemy, Poincaré an old one. Profoundly angered by Clemenceau's open disdain since becoming premier, Poincaré

---

56. Sherwood, *Georges Mandel,* 39–43; Duroselle, *Clemenceau,* 844–50; Chastenet, *Histoire de la Troisième République,* 5:59–60. A strike by printers shut down Parisian newspapers from 11 November through 1 December 1919.

57. Duroselle, *Clemenceau,* 850–53.

described him as "heedless, excessive, vain, bickering, jesting, shockingly reckless, deaf intellectually as well as physically, incapable of reasoning, of reflecting, of following a discussion. . . . This is the madman the nation has made a god." He had never forgiven a letter from Clemenceau on 17 January 1913, the day of his own election as president of the Republic, that closed, "I have the pleasure to announce that I no longer know you." But because the victory of the Bloc national had brought a majority of practicing Catholics to the Chamber of Deputies for the first time under the Third Republic, the greatest jeopardy for Clemenceau lay in his bitter antagonism toward the church. Even as an adolescent, having broken a statuette of the Virgin in anger, he mounted the head atop an inkwell, which he kept on his desk for the rest of his life. How easy it was for Briand to exploit the animosity toward Clemenceau when the secret ballot of the presidential vote ensured that he could never know exactly whom to blame. Making his cause more certain, Briand whispered ironically to Catholics that when Clemenceau died in office—he was, after all, seventy-eight years old—France would be treated to a spectacular *civil* funeral. The cardinal-archbishop of Paris, recalling the slight after the Armistice, advised pious legislators to vote for someone else. All that remained was to choose an alternative, and Deschanel, with his record of consecutive elections to the presidency of the Chamber and his willingness to be a figurehead, seemed the perfect reversion to prewar type. Mandel and Tardieu sensed the looming disaster for Clemenceau but could not persuade him of the peril. Millerand, called by his recent biographer a "principled pragmatist," remained neutral, displaying more pragmatism than principle in his recognition that Clemenceau's defeat would clear his own path to power. And so Paul Deschanel became president of the Third Republic.[58]

On 19 February 1919, at 8:40 in the morning, an anarchist named Eu-

58. Duroselle, *Clemenceau,* recounts the story of the inkwell, 34; quotes Poincaré's description, 750; and analyzes the presidential election, 853–58. The letter is quoted in Fernand Payen, *Raymond Poincaré: L'Homme, le parlementaire, l'avocat* (Paris, 1936), 396, n. 1. See also Pierre Miquel, *Poincaré* (Paris, 1961), 276–309, 407–8; John F. V. Keiger, *Raymond Poincaré* (Cambridge, Eng., 1997), 267–68; Gordon Wright, *Raymond Poincaré and the French Presidency* (Stanford, 1942), 239–40; Sherwood, *Georges Mandel,* 44–51; Farrar, *Principled Pragmatist,* 210, n. 4; Suarez, *Briand,* 5:56–70; and Oudin, *Briand,* 389–93.

gène Cottin fired ten bullets at Clemenceau, hitting him three times but injuring him only slightly. Within eight days he resumed his responsibilities. On 16 January 1920, the deputies and senators at the preliminary presidential ballot took better aim, this time shooting the Tiger in his vitals. Like a desperately wounded animal, he dragged himself into the brush away from his tormentors, to live nearly ten more angry years. With the concurrence of Deschanel, who would not take office until mid-February, Poincaré selected Millerand to be the new premier. He promptly offended Catholics and courted the moderate Left by choosing Théodore Steeg, a Radical well known for his anticlerical rigor, as minister of the interior. Following the best tradition of Third Republican premiers, Millerand was wary of depending on the Right. The Radicals would be grateful simply to reenter the majority and showed it by joining with the Bloc national for a vote of 510 to 70 on the motion of confidence installing the cabinet. The conservatives would expect him to fulfill campaign promises, especially restoring diplomatic relations with the Vatican. Where the church was concerned, nothing was ever enough to please them. In May, Millerand sent Gabriel Hanotaux to represent France at the canonization of Jeanne d'Arc in St. Peter's Basilica—a gesture unimaginable at any point during the preceding forty years—but General Edouard de Curières de Castelnau, a war hero elected in 1919, insisted on leading eighty other deputies as an unofficial delegation. During eight months in power, the cabinet could boast of barring the way to Bolshevism, facing down French labor militants in May, and helping Poland turn back the Red Army from the gates of Warsaw in August. Yet François-Marsal was no more capable than Klotz of grappling effectively with the frightening fiscal and economic difficulties, and despite Millerand's vigorous efforts, German intransigence grew with the realization that the American withdrawal from European affairs and the persistent British reluctance to support strong action enforcing the treaty left France increasingly isolated.

After Deschanel's resignation, Millerand was elected president of the Republic on 23 September. Any fear of his determination, expressed less than a year earlier, to strengthen the office was overlooked because of the need to elevate a prominent figure in the wake of the embarrassment over Deschanel and because Millerand enjoyed support across the political spectrum from Left-Center to Right. Millerand had not forgotten, however, and in naming Georges Leygues, a moderate, as premier, he chose an excellent administrator who had served with distinction as Clemenceau's naval minister but was wholly without experience in diplomacy. Millerand intended to, and did, run France's foreign policy from the Elysée, a vital step in molding the kind of presidency he wanted. Although the deputies should not have been surprised, they were resentful, and in that Briand found an opportunity. At his encouragement, Leygues was pressed to hold a debate on foreign relations, and when he kept postponing it, the Chamber overturned the cabinet on 12 January 1921. Briand was the obvious successor, forming his own cabinet four days later, exactly a year after organizing the conspiracy that defeated Clemenceau. The future was ominous: the franc still falling, industrial and agricultural production in a shambles, rebuilding far from complete, and whether in the west or the east of Europe, French interests in jeopardy. But the music of corridor intrigue was being played again, and dance cards were filled with possible partners. The deputies seemed relieved.[59]

Beforehand, there was one last moment of national union evoking the sacrifices of the war, the burial of the *soldat inconnu* beneath the Arc de Triomphe on 11 November. Millerand led the solemn cortege, followed by Leygues, Poincaré, Marshals Foch, Joseph Joffre, and Philippe Pétain, the deputies and senators, all manner of government officials national and local, generals, lesser officers and their troops, widows, and *mutilés de la guerre*. The ceremony was superbly affecting. Of France's heroes, only Clemenceau was missing. In the months after his abrupt and dramatic withdrawal from public life, he planned a trip as far away from France as possible, to India, leaving in mid-September and not returning until nine months later. On 14 January 1921, two days from the anniversary of the vote that ended his career, he went on a hunting expedition in Gwalior province and shot two tigers. Surely, he appreciated the macabre irony.[60]

59. Rudolph Binion, *Defeated Leaders: The Political Fate of Caillaux, Jouvenel, and Tardieu* (New York, 1960), 284–85; Sherwood, *Georges Mandel*, 52–72; Farrar, *Principled Pragmatist*, 209–317; Chastenet, *Histoire de la Troisième République*, 5:65–71. See J.O.C., Débats, 20 January 1920, for the vote of confidence.

60. Duroselle, *Clemenceau*, 868–74. For the ceremony of the *soldat inconnu*, see *Le Figaro*, 12 November 1920.

2

Briand à la barre

Georges Clemenceau and Aristide Briand were almost of different generations, born twenty-one years apart, 1841 and 1862, in the west of France, Clemenceau to a family from the interior of the Vendée described sometimes as bourgeois, sometimes as minor nobility, Briand to a fishergirl on the coast at Nantes who claimed a liaison with a nobleman of her own. They died not so long apart—Clemenceau in 1929, Briand in 1932— among the last of the leaders from the Belle Epoque who had somehow won the war and, yet again somehow, lost the peace. Far from the adulation of political crowds, both met death nearly alone. In the isolation of his angry self-exile, Clemenceau railed at his enemies and often his friends even as they went to the grave before him. At the funeral for Marshal Ferdinand Foch, only a few months before his own, he complained, "They are all going away and leaving me." Even death he confronted on his own terms, finally agreeing to lie down but keeping on his clothes. He asked to be buried upright, without benefit of clergy. Once a bon-vivant connoisseur of friends, food, and women, Briand became a surly and untidy cynic, drinking by himself, scowling at the latest editorials. His mourners were scarcely a dozen. Georges Suarez, the biographer of both, insisted on their essential contrast: "Clemenceau despised the fool, Briand allowed for him"; Clemenceau sought the definitive, Briand the indeterminate. He claimed that the secret to Briand's political success lay in his being "stranger to no human weakness." But Clemenceau's conviction was a close neighbor: "The greatest sin of the soul is to lack warmth." And at the end, if only out of necessity, Briand must have embraced another of Clemenceau's aphorisms, "There is strength in expecting nothing except from oneself."[1]

It had not been this way for most of Briand's life. Since his youth he had surrounded himself with companions male and female. From the men, Fernand Pelloutier, Alexandre Millerand, René Viviani, he took his politics, an independent socialism trusting in the general strike to transform society. But the unions early noted his lukewarm commitment, how his eloquent speeches lacked "véritable haine" against the established order. No wonder: like the best bourgeois, Briand carefully entered his expenditures in notebooks, husbanded his resources, and by 1897 took satisfaction in a modest fortune of fifty thousand francs. For through his friends he had prospered as a journalist of the Left and, soon enough, won election to the Chamber of Deputies from Saint Etienne in 1902. Already he was moving toward the Center, defending Millerand's decision to join the Waldeck-Rousseau cabinet three years earlier. Soon, the seductive blend of his entrancing words and his ambiguous allegiances made him the rapporteur for legislation in 1904 ending the 1801 Concordat and two years later minister of religion to implement it, almost the only honest broker in the separation of ultramontane church from laic state. To Camille Pelletan's sardonic question, "Is the road to Canossa beautiful?" Clemenceau replied, "I don't know; Briand takes us there in a closed carriage."

From a woman he had learned the cost of constancy. As an upstart socialist lawyer in Saint-Nazaire, he began an affair with Jeanne Giraudau, whose outraged husband had the police catch them en flagrant délit. Briand was suspended from the bar, and following conviction for public indecency, both were sentenced to brief jail terms. Although the case was reversed on appeal, the humiliation drove Briand to Paris, where Jeanne followed after her divorce. "Have confidence, my angel, have confidence in me," he wrote her on leaving, "I love you, I adore you." It was early

---

1. Suarez, *Briand,* 1:vii, 74; Clemenceau, *Grandeurs et misères d'une victoire,* iii; Janet Flanner [Genêt], *Paris Was Yesterday, 1925–1939,* ed. Irving Drutman, from *The New Yorker Magazine,* 1925–29; originally published in book form in 1972 (New York, 1979), 52, 59–60, 82.

1893, and his career was yet to be made. During the next eleven years as he created himself, he lived sporadically with Jeanne, the devotion broken often by her infidelities until finally he could not bear the betrayal. Now he wrote what he could not say: "Truly, my dear Jeanne, this time it is serious. . . . I have seen. . . . another breech of my self-respect added to so many others. But when one loves, there is no longer any self-respect or pride or anything. . . . I will be the one to go, and now you are alone, Jeanne, completely and for good." He would not find such passion again for anyone—or any cause. To the cynicism politics and experience had already bred, he added a crust of wary guile.[2]

At the right time: because he was leaving the relatively safe obscurity of the background for a quarter-century of risks at the front of the stage. Salons celebrating republican luminaries introduced Briand to realms of society higher than he could imagine—and, his liaison with Jeanne ended—to "aventures féminines . . . nombreuses et variées" among those wishing to "enter the antechamber of history through love." The government of Premier Emile Combes, which had hammered France on the anvil of anticlericalism for two and a half years, fell in January 1905. Its support had been shaky for months, since Clemenceau discovered that the suspicious Combes had set agents of the Sûreté générale to follow him. "A big laundry wagon parked in front of my door," Clemenceau explained to his friends, and "my inspector, noticing me, slipped behind it. I cried out, 'peek-a-boo!' . . . That afternoon at the Senate, Combes came toward me with his hand held out. I put both of mine in my pockets." The weak successor coalition under Maurice Rouvier collapsed in March 1906 before demonstrations by fervent Catholics against the Separation Law. With elections looming in two months, Jean Sarrien sought to form a ministry of strength and talent, recruiting Clemenceau, Raymond Poincaré, and Briand. Although the story is likely apocryphal—and Poincaré formally insisted it was—Sarrien gathered his cabinet for drinks at his house before assigning them portfolios. When he asked Clemenceau, "Que prenez-vous?" the reply came back, "l'Intérieur." Poincaré took finance, Briand, religion.

The combination was compelling: Clemenceau insolent, ardent, indom-

2. Suarez, *Briand,* 1:1–439, quotations from 121, 126, 438–39.

itable; Poincaré brilliant, brittle, distant; Briand supple, shrewd, sympathetic. They won the elections, restored order, calmed passions, and quickly eclipsed Sarrien. By October, he was gone, Clemenceau becoming premier for the first time, at age sixty-five. Louis Barthou, minister of public works, had taken a photograph of the cabinet leaving a train at Rambouillet and commemorated the occasion for Briand in verse:

> Do you recall? It was your first ministry
> And your finest top hat?
> Life has its mystery.
> Do you recall how Sarrien was so quickly
> The Tiger's meal—just like that?

Uncomfortable with the change, Poincaré left the Ministry of Finance to Joseph Caillaux. Barthou stayed on and so did Briand, his sense of compromise—it was never the "accommodation" always associated with Paul Deschanel—meshing well with Clemenceau's intemperance.

Perhaps that was what gave the new cabinet its unlikely equipoise, permitting it to last for thirty-three months, a record for the Third Republic. In January 1907, Briand almost resigned when Clemenceau criticized his willingness to treat with the Catholic church: the famous remark to Pelletan about Canossa and the closed carriage—"impossible d'admirer le paysage"—came a few days later. Uncharacteristically, Clemenceau made up to Briand, who returned the favor later by short-circuiting a proposed mutiny in the cabinet by Caillaux, Millerand, and Viviani. And Briand tried to restrain Clemenceau from the outburst against Théophile Delcassé in July 1909 that provoked the Chamber of Deputies finally to overturn him, long tired of what Albert de Mun called "the extraordinary wantonness that had always prevented his being a statesman." Afterward, an unrepentant Clemenceau raged: "Yes, they told me to shut up, but je m'en foutais! . . . Nothing in the world could have stopped me!"[3]

Almost to his surprise, it was now Briand's turn. The deputies who had

3. Suarez, *Briand,* 1:439–40, 2:1–224, quotations from 2:63, 1:440, 2:87, 98–99 (in the original, Barthou's verse went: "Te souviens-tu? Ce fut ton premier ministère / Et ton plus beau chapeau. / La vie a son mystère. / Te souviens-tu comment de Sarrien débonnaire / Le Tigre eut si vite la peau?"), 156, 220. See Benjamin F. Martin, *Count Albert de Mun: Paladin of the Third Republic* (Chapel Hill, 1978), 219.

supported Clemenceau for nearly three years expected him to continue the same policies without the arrogance. But Briand was moving—had been moving—steadily away from the Left, toward the Center and even the moderate Right. Millerand, another veteran of labor lawyering on the same political track, and Barthou, who was already where they were headed, accepted his offer of ministries. Caillaux, going in the opposite direction, declined. In October 1909, Briand began the long campaign for *répartition proportionnelle* (proportional representation), offending the long-dominant Radicals, who depended on *scrutin d'arrondissement* (single-member districts), while winning the praise of conservatives, who expected to gain. Against attacks by Jean Jaurès and the Socialists bitter at Millerand's defection, Briand replied by calling him "one of my best colleagues, one of my friends," and staked a vote of confidence on that. When railroad workers went on strike in October 1910, he had them recalled to military service and kept the trains running by threat of court-martial. The Right applauded again, but too fervently for Briand's political sensibilities. Reliance on a clearly conservative majority might make him unacceptable in the future to the moderate Left—and anyway would restrict his field of maneuver. The risk dictated a tactical withdrawal, which Briand managed by voluntarily stepping down as premier in February 1911.

The next year made stark the political battle lines for the future. Under Ernest Monis until the end of June and then Caillaux, a leftist coalition of Radicals and Socialists tripped precariously through the financial scandal of Henri Rochette and the diplomatic crisis of Agadir. By January 1912, hints of peculation along with the accusation of failing to uphold national honor in the face of German threats forced Caillaux's resignation. The successor was obvious: Poincaré, pillar of rectitude, epitome of nationalism; and so his chief allies: Briand and Millerand. Twelve months of this leadership, followed by Poincaré's successful candidacy in January 1913 to become the Third Republic's first forceful president in two decades, made the pot of political antagonisms boil over. For Jean Jaurès and the openly antimilitarist Socialists, for Caillaux, whose migration leftward brought him the leadership of the Radicals, stiffer attitudes toward Germany, cultivation of a "nationalist revival," and abandoning previous efforts to pass an income tax were variously warmongering or fiscal class oppression— bad enough but merely issues of principle. Issues of personality had the makings of a blood feud. Although riled by the Poincaré cabinet's forays right of center, Clemenceau was a Radical of the original stamp, his Jacobin nationalism scorning Caillaux and Jaurès as weaklings at best. But he had always opposed a strong man at the Elysée, and he regarded the vote that made the premier into the president as a personal affront. Clemenceau ended even correct relations with Poincaré—and Poincaré's allies as well could expect a raking from the Tiger's claws. Briand did not consider Clemenceau exactly an enemy, but he had every reason to rank Caillaux as one, for as minister of justice under Poincaré, he had come to hold proof of Caillaux's improper intervention into the judicial proceedings of the Rochette financial scandal, a memorandum of confession by the magistrate involved, Victor Fabre.

Taking over as premier, Briand introduced the centerpiece of the new nationalism, an increase in required military service from two years to three, and the linchpin of his political strategy, répartition proportionnelle. In March, Clemenceau led the Senate to reject the new voting procedure and overturn the cabinet. The claws had flashed first. Caillaux's machinations took longer. As Briand's successor, Barthou won passage of three-year service by late summer but fell before attacks from the Left over how to pay for it. An angry Briand reacted to the threat that Poincaré's entire program was now in jeopardy by warning, "The service law has become an organic instrument in the national defense; it was not voted with the intention of modifying it every six months." But could that be prevented when Radical and Socialist candidates were already campaigning for the following spring's legislative elections by emphasizing the human and financial costs of the nationalist agenda? As a counter, Briand and Barthou organized an alliance of the centrist groups, for which they gained the tacit support of the moderate Right—a precursor of the Bloc national in 1919. And with Poincaré, they attacked Caillaux directly. Briand ridiculed the leftist pose of this wealthy bourgeois, this "ploutocrate démagogue." Gaston Calmette, the editor of Le Figaro, was promised documents compromising Caillaux, and so began the famously vicious editorials. Calmette hinted at treason in the Agadir negotiations, at malfeasance in the Rochette scandal, at rakish philandering in his marriages. The last provoked Caillaux's wife to shoot Calmette dead in March 1914 and force the withdrawal of her husband from political life that had been the objective. For good measure, Barthou read aloud the Fabre memorandum before the Chamber of Deputies. Even so, the elections were a dead heat, until the outbreak of the war in August made everyone a nationalist at least temporarily, a condition best denoted by the sense of *union sacrée*.[4]

René Viviani was premier during the first fifteen months of the fighting, but this ineffectual and ambiguous man quickly ceded control of the cabinet to Briand, serving as minister of justice. For the first time, the ground was completely clear for him: Caillaux in disgrace, Jaurès murdered as mobilization was announced, Poincaré at the Elysée and feuding with Clemenceau, who refused to serve in any cabinet but his own. From late October 1915 until mid-March 1917, Briand was premier in fact, thus effectively leading France through more than half of the war. He had to his credit restoring the parliamentary direction of the generals that had been lost in 1914 and early 1915, maintaining the national nerve during the hell of fighting at Verdun and along the Somme, and establishing the diplomatic framework that would eventually permit a unified allied military command on the western front. But victory was still desperately far away—all the more so with Russia in revolution—and defeatism was growing. Briand was accused of failing to recognize the danger: the proof was in his having kept on as minister of the interior Louis Malvy, friend of the *Bonnet rouge* group, whom Clemenceau would denounce in July as the consort of traitors. Most of all, Briand was blamed for the failure of his principal strategic initiative, the dispatch of French troops to Salonika in October 1915, ostensibly to save the remnants of the Serbian army laid waste by the Austrians. There were rumors from the beginning—coming even from the commander of the expedition, General Maurice Sarrail, a Caillaux ally—about another objective, dislodging the pro-German king of Greece, Constantine, in favor of his brother, Prince George, whose young wife, Marie Bonaparte, had for the past two years pursued an *affaire de coeur* with Briand. During a secret session of the Chamber's foreign affairs committee in June 1916, Georges Leygues implied that French policy

4. J.O.C., Débats, 11 December 1913, for Briand's warning; Suarez, *Briand,* 2:394–508; Benjamin F. Martin, *The Hypocrisy of Justice in the Belle Epoque* (Baton Rouge, 1984), 151–206; Edward Berenson, *The Trial of Madame Caillaux* (Berkeley, 1992); Robert J. Young, *Power and Pleasure: Louis Barthou and the Third Republic* (Montreal, 1991), 92–131.

in Greece had been confused with the premier's personal attachments. Briand replied imperiously: "I know that there are those who pretend that my relations with Prince George and with his family have blinded me and that they add to these insinuations odious calumnies. Because there are such who seek to gain ministerial portfolios in this mud, I invite them to trample around in it with me right now."[5]

That deputies who had maintained, and would continue to maintain, Briand in office as wartime premier could suspect he might distort strategic policy to seek a throne for his mistress provides one measure of paranoia in France after Verdun. It also reveals the degree to which they had come to expect—even to accept—the cynical and the devious from him. And that is why many readily believed the much more serious allegation later that he engaged in unauthorized compromise peace negotiations during 1917 and 1918. In this instance, however, all the evidence was on Briand's side. In January 1917, a German representative, Baron Oskar von der Lancken-Wackenitz, sought to open unofficial talks with three Belgian aristocrats acting as intermediaries. Keeping Poincaré fully informed, Briand met secretly with the intermediaries in Paris once without result. Eight months later, in September, weighing the entrance of the United States into the war against the likely collapse of Russia, the Germans renewed their approach, seeking an agreement in the West that would permit them a free hand in the East. Lancken now proposed to negotiate directly with Briand at Lausanne, in neutral Switzerland. Poincaré had been suspicious of German intrigues from the outset, and Alexandre Ribot, now minister of foreign affairs, feared *un piège,* a trap that would separate France from her allies. Briand could not proceed without the absolute sanction of his government, and lacking it, he refused to meet Lancken. But this new approach, when he had been out of office since March, cast him in a questionable light, especially as the campaign against *défaitisme* gained momentum. In mid-October before the Chamber of Deputies, Ribot portrayed him as almost the dupe of the Germans, and although

---

5. Oudin, *Briand,* 322–51, the quotation from 344; and see 333: for some years Briand had maintained a liaison with Berthe Cerny, who applied considerable polish to his provincial ways. After discovering his affair with Princess Marie, she exclaimed to friends, "Men! You teach them to dress, to hold their forks, and then they betray you with royal highnesses!"; Suarez, *Briand,* 3:1–490, 4:1–223.

Briand replied effectively, some doubt remained. From this moment, Clemenceau never fully trusted him again. Asked in March 1918, at the height of the final German offensive, to add Briand to his cabinet, Clemenceau reacted with contempt, "You don't harness a thoroughbred with a frog!" And once the war was won, he set the Sûreté générale scrounging for whatever could be found against Briand. The agents eventually returned with the dossier of which Clemenceau boasted in late 1919, entirely forged by a refugee German Spartacist named Alfred Leopol.[6]

Until a fraud it was proved to be, Briand had to defend himself with all his reputed cynicism, cunning, and duplicity. For at least these months of crisis, he justified Léon Daudet's caricature as "a special beast, with a head for deceit and guile, a body for haranguing, paws for prowling the lobbies, a pouch full of rancor and malice, and a remarkable facility for twisting, retwisting, and countertwisting." Sensing that the répartition proportionnelle he had so long championed would lead to a landslide victory for the Bloc national, Briand made certain that he was counted among them, even if he had to move from his district at Saint Etienne to Nantes to find the appropriate list, even if he was on the new majority's left edge. Yet he patched up his quarrel with the Radicals by testifying for Malvy and by refusing to testify against Caillaux—a remarkable abnegation. He led the intrigues against Clemenceau's ambition to be elected president of the Republic and sponsored Deschanel's improbably successful candidacy. When he brought down the Leygues cabinet in January 1921, he won revenge indeed for the malign aspersion about Princess Marie. Four days later, Briand was premier again. He had twisted, retwisted, and countertwisted. For now, after tramping around with his enemies in the mud, he alone was left standing. It was a bravura performance.[7]

Was this the real Briand, nothing left of the man who laid bare his heart in a letter of farewell to the faithless beloved Jeanne? Entries in his personal journal during the last year of the war present a keen-eyed but de-

6. Oudin, *Briand,* 355–80; Suarez, *Briand,* 4:224–320; Raymond Poincaré, *Au service de la France* (11 vols.; Paris, 1926–74), 9:284–86, 333, 338, 370; Guy Pedroncini, *Les Négotiations secrètes pendant la Grande Guerre* (Paris, 1969), 71.

7. Léon Daudet, *Souvenirs des milieux littéraires, politiques, artistiques et médicaux* (2 vols.; Paris, 1926), 2:238; Suarez, *Briand,* 5:1–89; Oudin, *Briand,* 381–95.

tached observer. Several times he walked out into the open spaces of the Bois de Boulogne for a better view of the Gotha attacks on Paris, but the sight elicited only bloodless lines: "Numerous bombs scattered throughout" (31 January); "The bombardment of open cities is the most stupid, the most odious, and the most useless thing conceivable" (1 February); "The victims are numerous. A panic in a Métro station has killed more than the German planes" (12 March). When the Big Berthas launched their shells, what struck him was not the damage but the distance, "Cent vingt kilomètres!" (23 March). After visiting the Citroen armaments factory, he meditated: "It's a city. Fifteen thousand men and women working; forty thousand artillery shells a day. In one immense workroom, six thousand women labor competently at great steel machines while losing nothing of their parisienne grace. What will become of all this after the peace? What will these machines make? What will be the life of these women? There is the problem of tomorrow—not easy to resolve. Yet there are those who complacently believe that once the war is over everyone can take up the peaceful course and humdrum of the days before" (28 February). On 8 November, the Senate voted that Clemenceau and Foch "ont bien mérité de la patrie," of which Briand wrote, "And the others?" including himself in those omitted. Three days later, when the Armistice was announced, Briand's emotion seeped into the entry as he described "the firing of cannons, no longer the cannons that kill but the cannons of joy for victory," the scene at the Chamber of Deputies, where in "a stirring session . . . I was asked to speak. . . . A few words. . . . Acclamations. . . . The Armistice read by Clemenceau. . . . It is the collapse of Germany," and the crowds on the boulevards, "singing the Marseillaise in delirium." But on the following day the aloof tone returned when he recounted how political colleagues insisted to him that Clemenceau was being given too large a part in the triumph: "They speak of an injustice to repair. I calm them. The crowd is simplistic, not wanting to disperse its favors; and besides, it is poor, never having enough gold for two idols at a time."[8]

When the Leygues ministry fell exactly twenty-six months later, the crowd did not seem to have enough gold for any idol. All of the economic

8. Suarez, *Briand,* 4:321–90, quotations from 337, 338, 348, 350, 347, 388, 389, 390, respectively.

problems from the war remained to be solved—and solution seemed dependent on German reparations. But with the United States refusing to be
a party to the treaty Wilson had negotiated and with France and Great
Britain at loggerheads over what and how much to enforce, Germany's
recalcitrance was ever more flagrant. In preparation for another confrontation with the Germans, scheduled for London at the beginning of
March, French and British leaders were to seek a common strategy by
meeting in late January at Paris. Because he was permitting Millerand to
set foreign policy from the Elysée, Leygues resisted answering questions
about his plans. And at that time, resentment about the assertion of un-
precedented presidential prerogatives and frustration from a year of in-
conclusive results at the San Remo, Hythe, and Spa conferences boiled
over. On 12 January, the Bloc national majority massively deserted the
cabinet, by a vote of 463 to 125 refusing to grant "confidence without explanations, confidence in the dark."[9] Briand was an obvious successor. His
experience ensured an end to Millerand's interference, while the ruthless
and unsavory methods by which he had rebuilt his political position might
be exactly the tactics French diplomacy needed in dealing with both Great
Britain and Germany.

The accusations from the war years, the spiking of Clemenceau, and
now this indirect slap through Leygues had significantly weakened the ties
between Briand and Millerand, who had come to regard his old friend as
inconstant and unscrupulous, if still charming. But because other possible
choices for premier were reluctant, Millerand completed Briand's restoration. This news reached him as he celebrated his nephew's wedding at
Larue's, the famous restaurant on the place de la Madeleine. Between
champagne toasts, Briand laid out a cabinet of apparent strength for the
critical portfolios, foreign affairs to himself, war to his old colleague Barthou, finance to the austere Paul Doumer, reconstruction to Clemenceau's
economic adviser at the peace conference, Louis Loucheur. And with
them, he won a vote of confidence from the Chamber of Deputies on 20
January by a margin, 475 to 68, even more decisive than Leygues's defeat,

9. The principal conferences of 1920 were at San Remo (19–26 April), Hythe (19–22
June), and Spa (5–16 July). See J.O.C., Débats, 12 January 1921, the quotation from
Laurent Bonnevay.

after striking exactly the right tone: "We have a peace treaty with Germany; we do not yet have peace. . . . We have the strength; we will be able, we will know how, to use it if necessary to impose respect for formal commitments." But not alone: "For me, before striking, I want to reason . . . and in any event, to coordinate with our allies." By this caveat, Briand made clear that he would follow the line adopted by Clemenceau during the 1919 peace negotiations, that France could control Germany only through an alliance structure containing Great Britain—and if possible, the United States. Throughout 1920, first as premier and then as president, Millerand pursued a version of this policy, but the price of British support for a unified front toward the Germans had been a steady retreat from French positions. As ambiguous as Millerand was forthright, Briand might do better with the same strategy. For the moment, the Chamber was permitting him the chance to prove it.[10]

Or to fail, for some of the deputies voting with the cabinet were convinced that Briand was proceeding from wrong assumptions. Chief among them, ironically, were the clemencistes, the triumvirate from the Père-la-Victoire's inner circle, who loathed Briand for humiliating Clemenceau and who could defend his peace treaty only by interpreting how he would have applied it. André Tardieu was their leader, brilliant, eloquent, haughty, uncompromising—under the ancien régime he would have fit the mold of a court noble, but in the Third Republic, he had to settle for having been the diplomatic analyst for Le Temps, France's principal liaison with the Americans during the war, and at Clemenceau's side throughout the peace negotiations. By writing La Paix to defend his work, he betrayed his anxiety about it. Yet more dangerous was Georges Mandel, who had been with Clemenceau since 1903, almost his only longtime companion, so much his collaborator that Clemenceau once jested, "When Mandel farts, I am accused of eating beans." If Clemenceau was Robespierre, Mandel was Saint-Just; if Clemenceau was Napoleon, Mandel was Joseph Fouché: the real minister of the interior during the last year of the war, imposing censorship, headhunter of the défaitistes. From his mentor he learned icy

10. Farrar, Principled Pragmatist, 318; Stephen D. Carls, Louis Loucheur and the Shaping of Modern France, 1916–1931 (Baton Rouge, 1993), 210–12; Suarez, Briand, 5:76–114; Oudin, Briand, 396–99; J.O.C., Débats, 20 January 1921.

authority, audacity, courage, vindictiveness, a spirit of opposition. His best friend was the third member, Edouard Ignace, head of military justice for Clemenceau, a grand inquisitor who implacably prosecuted the suspects Mandel turned up. Like Fouquier-Tinville during the Terror, he was dominated by simple ideas and simpler truths. Though lacking a following in the Chamber, they were prophets among politicians but all the more a threat for presenting themselves, rightfully or not, as a moral absolute to which Briand could not pretend, against which clever duplicity could ultimately appear shabby.[11]

And then there was Poincaré. He had departed the Elysée gloriously, the legislators voting that like Clemenceau and Foch he had "bien mérité de la patrie." Without campaigning, he was immediately elected to the Senate, where he was given charge of the committee on foreign affairs. From January to May 1920, he presided over the Reparations Commission, created by the Treaty of Versailles to establish the total owed by the Germans. In 1921, he was sixty-one, only two years older than Briand. More than any other political figure, he represented the sentiment widely abroad in France and famously crystallized by Jacques Bainville in *L'Action française* that the treaty was "too gentle for its severity." Writing bimonthly articles in the *Revue des deux mondes*, where he was read above all by the rentiers ruined through the war, he came to embody the desperate hopes of all who believed that if only the treaty were strictly enforced their lives and their fortunes could be restored. With him, they were skeptical about the League of Nations, hostile to disarmament, doubting of international arbitration, opposed to any new taxes or new expenditures, for a politics of rigor and austerity. Poincaré had warned from the beginning against Clemenceau's diplomacy at the peace conference and since then had deplored a foreign policy that sacrificed French interests to curry favor with Great Britain while acting with reluctance against clear German violations of the treaty. Would Briand be firmer? Writing of him in *Le Temps* on 23 January, Poincaré shaded his words: "But, thank God, he has the cunning to know how to be resolute."[12]

11. Binion, *Defeated Leaders*; Sherwood, *Georges Mandel*; Suarez, *Briand*, 5:142–48; the quotation about Clemenceau and Mandel is from Oudin, *Briand*, 391.

12. Miquel, *Poincaré*, 404–35; Bainville's comment, "trop douce pour ce qu'elle a de dur," appeared in *L'Action française*, 8 May 1919; *Le Temps*, 23 January 1921.

Against these critics lying in wait, Briand armed himself with the counsel of Philippe Berthelot, since 1920 secretary-general for the Foreign Ministry, the highest-ranking permanent official. They were a likely pair,
holding similar assumptions about human nature and diplomacy. Berthelot had about him a haughty brilliance that was reflected in his extraordinary ability as a linguist—he was fluent in most western European lan-
guages and had a working knowledge of several Oriental ones—and
attracted the friendship of intellectuals as disparate as Maurice Barrès,
Paul Claudel, and Jean Cocteau. Profoundly cynical, he claimed that civil
wars were preferable to foreign because those to be killed were familiar.
His remark during the hecatombs of trench fighting about deaths and statistics gained a grim notoriety. The number of his mistresses had been
counted remarkable, even for the Belle Epoque, and a rumor persisted
that he gave one of them the German declaration of war against France as
a trophy. Early in his career as a junior secretary at Lisbon, he was accused
of embezzlement, but the charge was dropped when his father, Marcellin
Berthelot, distinguished chemist and republican worthy, briefly served as
foreign minister in 1895. Given a second chance, he made the most of a
rare—in the Quai d'Orsay—financial expertise to advance French economic interests through diplomacy, especially in China. He was rewarded
with a series of rapid promotions that brought him near the top by 1914.
Clemenceau omitted him from the delegation to the peace conference, and
this snub represented an honor in Briand's eyes. But more important was
an appreciation for how the two men might be complementary. A glutton
for hard work, first in, last out, reading each memorandum and retaining
every detail in his encyclopedic memory, Berthelot could be indispensable
at the side of the increasingly indolent Briand—even if, as he would say
famously of him: "It's astonishing. He doesn't listen, but he understands
all the same." And like Briand, Berthelot believed that individuals were
more important than issues—"Tout est question de personnes," he insisted—and therefore that anything could be negotiated.[13]

13. M. B. Hayne, *The French Foreign Office and the Origins of the First World War, 1898–
1914* (Oxford, 1993), 124–78, the quotation about people and issues from 146; Jean-Luc
Barré, *Le Seigneur-chat: Philippe Berthelot, 1866–1934* (Paris, 1988); Auguste Bréal, *Philippe
Berthelot* (Paris, 1937); Richard D. Challener, "The French Foreign Office: The Era of

Anything included the vital question of early 1921, reparations. During the year and a half since the signing of the Versailles Treaty, French and British officials had met at a seemingly continuous series of conferences to discuss its implementation, their attitudes and proposals conditioned by completely different experiences since the Armistice. The end of war spending combined with the demobilization of soldiers seeking employment to throw Great Britain into a deep economic slump. Like most British leaders, David Lloyd George, the prime minister, and George Nathaniel, Lord Curzon, the foreign secretary, were convinced that recovery depended on the revival of trade, above all with Germany, traditionally Britain's greatest European market. To reduce Germany to penury through large reparations payments, they believed, would continue the economic havoc throughout Europe, undermine the Weimar Republic's creation of moderate constitutional government, and threaten British prosperity both short- and long-term. In France, if the necessity of rebuilding the devastated regions absorbed returning poilus and kept industries busy, lack of coal because the Germans failed to make promised deliveries, inflation because of budget deficits to pay for reconstruction, and the fall of the franc because imports far exceeded exports meant economic dislocation different from but as severe as that in Great Britain. All French political leaders right of the Socialists agreed that German reparations were the solution to these present problems and would secure the future by keeping Germany relatively weak whether or not the Weimar Republic survived. Yet even those of Poincaré's persuasion recognized that imposing the treaty would be difficult without British participation, and they suspected that Lloyd George was not above threatening to sever the entente to pressure France into adopting the British view.

Here was the origin of French attempts at accommodation during 1920, as Millerand succumbed to the bluff. In an effort to arrive at a fixed total for reparations—their share eventually set at 52 percent—to which the Germans would agree, French leaders first had to win British support. Although the Reparations Commission was considering a figure as high as

---

Philippe Berthelot," in *The Diplomats, 1919–1939,* ed. Gordon A. Craig and Felix Gilbert (Princeton, 1953), 65–69; Suarez, *Briand,* 5:125–29, the quotation about Briand from 128.

150 billion gold marks, Millerand was by May openly willing to settle for 120 billion. Despite attacks from Poincaré and Tardieu, the Chamber of Deputies backed him. A month later, because of British pressure, he provisionally accepted what came to be called the "Boulogne scheme," a series of payments running from 1921 to 1963 that amounted to an initial German obligation of 100 billion on which interest would be paid—much like a mortgage. But if with British help the French could "mobilize" the money, obtaining a lump sum through selling bonds backed by the guarantee of these payments, he would take 35 billion gold marks as payment in full of France's share: even so low a figure available immediately was preferable to dunning the Germans for four decades. Nothing was said about war debts, which if paid from the mobilized sum—and so avoiding interest charges—to Great Britain and the United States would leave France with only approximately 10 billion gold marks from Germany, considerably less than had already been spent on reconstruction. And even then, Lloyd George sought to force the French down to an initial German obligation of 85 billion. Correctly recognizing reparations as the great flash point between their wartime antagonists, the Germans had every incentive to reject any proposal involving impositions on them or to attach unacceptable political conditions, such as a claim to all of Upper Silesia.[14]

By the beginning of 1921, with Germany remaining defiant and Britain ever exigent, Millerand was regretting this diplomacy of concession. In the Chamber of Deputies, the Bloc national was increasingly restive: the overthrow of Leygues was fire across the presidential bow. Lloyd George also paid heed to the shot. British policy had perhaps pushed France too hard. If he did not come to terms with the new French premier, the next cabinet change might face him with Poincaré, whose attitudes were as well known in Britain as they were unwelcome. It was time to make up with Briand. They did, after all, have in common a celebration of Celtic origin—Lloyd George Welsh, Briand Breton—a notorious string of love affairs, and the reputation among their enemies for a certain plasticity in principle and looseness with fact. Briand had to be given something to flaunt before the deputies, evidence of British solidarity with France. And so he was. When

14. Trachtenberg, *Reparation in World Politics*, 119–81; J.O.C., Débats, 28 May 1920, for Millerand's defense of the 120 billion gold mark total.

Lloyd George and Curzon met with Briand and Berthelot in Paris from 24 to 29 January, they agreed to present Germany with basically the Boulogne scheme as a means of fulfilling reparations and to impose sanctions, occupation of additional German territory, for further recalcitrance.[15]

Afterward, at a press conference, Briand was exultant, and even some of the newspapers most suspicious of his cabinet managed praise: "They have fulfilled their mandate better than we dared hope." At the Palais Bourbon, the agreement partially disarmed his most dangerous critics. When Mandel, Ignace, Louis-Lucien Klotz, and most of all Tardieu complained that accepting the Boulogne scheme was another retreat, reducing further the reparations dearly bought with French blood, requiring in their stead more taxes and more borrowing, Briand brought the clemencistes up short by quoting Clemenceau that "the treaty, born of allied accord, can be executed only through allied accord." France, he reminded the deputies, had only one seat—and one vote—out of the four on the Reparations Commission (Great Britain, Italy, and Belgium were the other members): would it be better to break off all talks until the British capitulated to the French position—if ever? "Tardieu," Briand continued in that disingenuous tone he used so effectively to taunt, "as one of the principal architects of the Versailles Treaty, knows the difficulties of its negotiation. He should consequently be indulgent toward a man who, having to apply the treaty in arduous times, has done his best by the nation's interests. I would not dream that M. Tardieu has already dispensed in the interest of his work all the indulgence of which he disposes and that he has none left for me." Undeterred, Pierre Forgeot, one of the most intransigent of the younger deputies in the Bloc national although an *embusqué* during the war, demanded to know whether Briand would impose sanctions alone if the rest of the allies refused and all but accused him of lacking the fortitude to do so. Redolent of the rumor that he sought a compromise peace during the war, this charge attacked Briand's character as well as his policy. The mood changed abruptly: dignity clearly asserted had to replace

15. Trachtenberg, *Reparation in World Politics,* 181–91; Suarez, *Briand,* 5:119–21; Oudin, *Briand,* 404–6. The Paris press claimed the British government had indicated to Millerand that a cabinet headed by Poincaré would be displeasing to it, an account formally denied by the British embassy: see *Le Figaro,* 19 January 1921.

banter. Briand ended the debate with an unequivocal declaration, the basis on which the Chamber could either vote its confidence in his cabinet or not: "Six times premier, I will find in my patriotism the energy to make the rights of France respected. If tomorrow I encounter resistance, you will see whether I lead a weak government. But if I must act by myself in such an operation, I shall not do so. I shall act only with our allies." The count went 387 to 125 in his favor—for the moment, he was in control.[16]

Briand first met Lloyd George in February 1915, forming then an impression of him that he maintained six years later: "too unstable to be sincere, too inconstant to be engaging . . . passing from cordiality to attack with an imaginative eloquence full of historical references but disdainful of technical arguments . . . an exceptional gift for comprehending broad horizons and conceiving of vast enterprises . . . but an inability to grasp the power of psychological factors and a failure to perceive the tragic misery of individuals or the immensity of ruin done to France." Binding this mercurial man to France and to himself was Briand's task if a policy of "allied accord" in executing the treaty was to succeed. Germany immediately provided assistance, its press and politicians exploding in anger at the unexpected agreement and generating a highly negative reaction among British and French leaders. Delighted with this opportunity, Briand brought his team of experts headed by Berthelot across the Channel on 20 February, a full week before the conference with the Germans. He used the time to offer soothing words about disputed oil reserves in the Middle East, considering some compromise of French interests there well worth British support in Europe. More important, the talks in freezing weather before roaring fires and over strong drink made for "a warm Celtic reveling that engendered a genuine bond."[17]

How much so became apparent when the conference opened on 1 March. The German foreign minister, Walther Simons, replied to the Boulogne scheme by offering an initial obligation of only 30 billion gold marks, and that contingent on Germany's not having to cede any of Upper

16. *Le Figaro*, 30 January–10 February 1921, the quotation from 30 January; *L'Echo de Paris* and *L'Action française*, 8 February 1921; J.O.C., Débats, 4, 8–9 February 1921.

17. Suarez, *Briand*, 3:94–95, for the impressions of Lloyd George; 5:164, for "ces agapes celtiques."

Silesia to Poland. These proposals were so patently unacceptable that an astonished Lloyd George turned to Briand and said, "It's time to end this session, because in five minutes more it will be we who owe money to the Germans." As Simons argued his brief, Briand took out his pocket watch, waited while five minutes passed, and then slid it along the table to Lloyd George with a note reading, "Here is my watch. All that is left to do is for you to hand over your shirt." The humor concealed real anger, and this time German recalcitrance was met with sanctions as promised at Paris. A united Franco-British front increased tariffs on German goods, established a customs line along the Rhine under the control of allied troops, and most decisively, on 13 March, occupied three additional German cities, Duisburg, Ruhrort, and Düsseldorf. Briand's report to the Chamber of Deputies three days later was a speech of triumph, interrupted frequently by acclamation, as he praised the support of his cabinet and called Lloyd George a true friend of France. Despite some minor quibbling, there was among the deputies an overwhelming sense of satisfaction—and relief— that Briand had been willing to act, to take *un gage,* a security deposit against the payment of reparations, as a creditor demands collateral. This time, they voted 491 to 66 for him.[18]

Converting mere acclamation into roaring admiration required only a few strident phrases. On 5 April before the Senate, Briand replied to questions about how he would deal with further German defiance, especially over the 12 billion gold mark payment due on 1 May to satisfy the interim reparations imposed by the treaty in June 1919 for initial restoration: "We will say to our allies, the creditor has the right to exercise coercion . . . and I proclaim to you proudly today that if Germany tries again to evade her obligations, her engagements, a firm hand will fall upon her collar!" A week later, on 12 April, he addressed the Chamber with less flourish but the same determination: "Once the bailiff has been sent, if the debtor remains recalcitrant, the constable must accompany him. It is not a question of war or of troubling the peace or of recommencing military operations

---

18. The exchange, recounted in Suarez, *Briand,* 5:164, and Oudin, *Briand,* 408, was in French: "Il est temps de lever la séance, car, dans cinq minutes, nous finirons par devoir de l'argent à l'Allemagne." "Voici ma montre. Il ne rest plus qu'à donner votre chemise." J.O.C., Débats, 15–16 March 1921.

that Germany imposes on us. It is a question, I say, of going to find the debtor, and if he does not want to pay, of constraining him by all the measures of coercion at our disposal. It is a question of pure justice. The first of May, in accord with our allies, we will present ourselves at the rendez-vous."[19]

Did Briand understand how fragmentary the solidarity with Lloyd George might be or how fugitive the roaring admiration? Despite his experience and cynicism, he seems to have underestimated the inconstancy of both. On 27 April, the Reparations Commission issued its report, declaring that Germany owed an initial sum of 132 billion gold marks, significantly more than the 100 billion figure of the Boulogne scheme. German leaders furiously pleaded that they could not pay, vowed that they would not pay such tribute to oppressors—and that included the 12 billion due on 1 May. Anticipating this response, Briand with Berthelot and Loucheur returned to London on 30 April and expected Lloyd George to join them in "sending the constable": imposing the ultimate sanction short of war, occupation of the Ruhr Valley, Germany's industrial heartland. Lloyd George refused point-blank. British public opinion, he claimed, could not support further coercion, especially when it would roil markets. Briand retorted that *French* public opinion could not accept further concessions, and on 2 May he authorized Barthou, the minister of war, to recall the recently demobilized class of 1919 as a reserve for occupation troops. To this challenge, Lloyd George threatened that for the French to act alone "would be the end of our alliance, and it is you who will take the responsibility." But the harsh exchange did not require an immediate break because Barthou reported that the soldiers would not be fully prepared until 12 May. In that space, there was time for allied reconciliation and then to stare down the Germans. Over the next two days, the four nations of the Reparations Commission agreed on a structure for the payments, the so-called London schedule. Germany was to issue three sets of bonds: "A" class, retroactively dated 1 May 1921, for 12 billion gold marks, "B" class, dated 1 November 1921, for 38 billion, and "C" class, on a date to be determined, for 82 billion. Until the staggering details of the plan

19. J.O.S., Débats, 5 April 1921; J.O.C., Débats, 12 April 1921; *Le Figaro,* 8 April 1921, praised what came to be called "la main au collet" speech.

were devised, Germany would pay 2 billion gold marks each year and 26 percent of export revenue, estimated to be an additional 1 billion marks. The German government was then given the deadline of 12 May to accept the plan or face occupation of the Ruhr. After nearly a week of hesitation, German leaders capitulated.[20]

Could these German bonds be "mobilized"? Germany had hardly given a *willing* acquiescence, and lacking that, what investors were going to place their capital in peril? Without "mobilization," France, due 52 percent of the reparations, assumed the major risk of German default. Could France count on Great Britain to assist in compelling compliance? Would Lloyd George have dispatched his troops to join a French occupation of the Ruhr in May 1921? Would Briand have sent in his forces without them? Would any French cabinet do so? This fundamental question about allied enforcement of the treaty did not yet have to be answered because this time German nerve failed. But Briand's confidence in Lloyd George's support was shaken, and all the more so as the question of Upper Silesia immediately led to further tension between them. The bonhomie of Celtic charm and the passing of notes was over. Over as well was the brief suspension of suspicion by the moderate and conservative press. During March and April, editorialists such as Marcel Hutin in *L'Echo de Paris,* Jacques Bainville in *L'Action française,* and Maurice Geneste in *L'Avenir* were giving Briand the benefit of the doubt, Bainville writing on 7 March, "Force alone will not suffice if the success is not accompanied by diplomacy; an intelligent foreign policy is as necessary as the appeal to arms." Even Clemenceau had been optimistic and gracious, saying at Toulon as he disembarked after his long trip to the Far East: "I believe that all is going well. Everything will be all right. I am not worried." By May, anxious for a demonstration of French backbone, *Le Figaro* asked how it could take ten days to mobilize eighty thousand men—in 1914, at that rate, the Battle of the Marne would have been fought on the Garonne. Its editor, Louis Latzarus, spoke for the nationalist position: either Germany had to give material guarantees for payment of reparation or France had

---

20. Suarez, *Briand,* 5:176–87, Lloyd George quoted on 182; Trachtenberg, *Reparation in World Politics,* 206–11; 385, n. 85, for a discussion of the value represented by these bonds and the 132 billion gold mark initial sum.

to take them herself: "Tout le reste est chicane et illusion." *Le Temps* was as blunt in asking, "What is the German capitulation worth?"[21]

The Upper Silesia question exacerbated all the existing tensions. Germany regarded the recreation of Poland from the debris of the Romanov, Habsburg, and Hohenzollern empires as the most grievous of the wrongs imposed on the map by the Versailles Treaty. The "corridor" to the sea placed historically German lands under Polish rule and separated East Prussia from the rest of Germany—a problem Foch proposed solving by the gift of that province to the Poles. The final boundary line for Poland in the west was to be established by a plebiscite in Upper Silesia, ore-rich, an industrial powerhouse, and ethnically mixed. When the voting took place on 20 March 1921, Germans outnumbered Poles 707,605 to 479,359, and in townships, 844 to 678. Germany demanded the entire territory, while Poland held out for division as provided under the treaty.

The French position was both inevitable and long prepared. In the summer and fall of 1920, only France had come to Poland's aid against the Red Army. Despite a decided nostalgia for the prewar alliance with tsarist Russia, French leaders had to recognize that with Bolshevism there triumphant, Poland alone could be the eastern counterweight to Germany. In the following months, both governments moved closer together by encouraging French investment in the oil fields of eastern Galicia, an economic stake that made concluding a military arrangement on 19 February 1921—France guaranteeing Poland against German or Soviet aggression—a natural step. A loan of 400 million francs for the arming of Polish forces, with the requirement that all the matériel be purchased in France, interlaced them further. Berthelot, whose bias toward Czechoslovakia showed in his lack of rapport with Polish leaders, was wary, but Briand sided with Millerand, who had sent the military mission under Weygand and had handled the negotiations almost until the end, and with Barthou, who had lost his only son in the war and hungered for every means of

---

21. *L'Echo de Paris,* 2 March 1921; *L'Avenir,* 6 March 1921; *L'Action française,* 6–7 March 1921, *Le Figaro,* 2, 4 May 1921, Latzarus in the latter; *Le Temps,* 11 May 1921; Clemenceau was quoted in *Le Figaro,* 22 March 1921, and described as "astonishingly fresh and alert," not a compliment; two days later, on 24 March, it reported that a woman remarked of Clemenceau, "He is well preserved!" to which a man replied, "He has just come back from the land of the mummies."

revenge against Germany. In declaring for division of Upper Silesia after the plebiscite, France was supporting an ally but also holding to the letter of the treaty.[22]

This loyal and juridical stance, seemingly straightforward and without risk, attracted fire almost immediately. Neither the Poles nor the Germans were willing to concede anything in Upper Silesia. Both prepared for killing and dying by recruiting militias in the thousands, which they equipped with everything up to field artillery. By early May, the region was aflame in fighting. The ever-acute Bainville had written on 21 March, "Germany will erase the results of the war first in the East—that has begun; the turn of the West will come next." And he added, "More so than yesterday, we are forced to watch over fragile Poland." For Lloyd George would watch over the interests of Germany. From conversations with him, Briand knew of his deep antipathy—verging on hatred—toward the Poles, Catholics and victors over Bolshevik Russia with which he proposed to extend diplomatic and commercial ties. "To ruin Poland and make it disappear from the map," Briand once judged, Lloyd George "would ally himself with the devil." But Briand was as shocked as the rest of the French political world at his vehemence before the House of Commons on 13 May, when he called for Germany to receive all of Upper Silesia and disdainfully claimed that the allies should permit the Germans to impose their will on the Poles because the territory had been Prussian for two hundred years and certainly not Polish for six centuries. Were these the words of entente cordiale? From the Right, *Le Figaro* denounced Lloyd George for "taking joy in aggravating our anxieties and destroying our hopes." From the Left, *La Lanterne* suggested that if Germany seized Upper Silesia, France should seize the Ruhr.[23]

The pressure on Briand to respond directly was overwhelming. This open affront to an important French position so soon after the barely avoided split over reparations raised the gravest doubts about his foreign policy and with it the survival of his cabinet. On 14 May, his tone cold but correct, he gave Lloyd George a public lesson in history and international

22. Wandycz, *France and Her Eastern Allies*, 186–223; Young, *Power and Pleasure*, 138.
23. Bainville in *L'Action française*, 21 March 1921; Briand's assessment is from Suarez, *Briand*, 5:194; *Le Figaro*, 17 May 1921; *La Lanterne*, 24 May 1921.

law: although taken as a prize during the War of the Austrian Succession by Prussia in 1740—*not quite* two hundred years before—Upper Silesia had then and continued to have a substantial Polish population; for that reason, it was allocated to Poland—the boundary with Germany to be drawn on the basis of townships after a plebiscite—by the Versailles Treaty, to which all the parties were signatories. The following day, he warned the German government that it faced "prompt coercive action" if regular army troops were sent into Upper Silesia. And on 16 May, in a formal note to London, he assured Lloyd George that "in the case of a German-Polish war, France would not adopt a passive attitude."[24] Briand now had two days left before the legislature reconvened after a month-long recess. His enemies had been waiting for a reversal in fortune before attacking. They had their chance.

Tardieu was ready to make the most of it. His denunciations fell like hammer blows: accepting too little in reparations, failing to press sanctions, yielding to British pressure, and failing to derive any benefit after having done so. He threw Briand's rhetoric back at him, his "firm hand on the collar," his "constable with the bailiff." "That is what you have said. Is that what you have done? No!" Led by the firebrand Forgeot, prominent figures from the Bloc national joined the assault. Léon Daudet, coeditor of *L'Action française* and a deputy himself, writing that "each day the sky grows darker," demanded that Millerand dismiss Briand, "whose account with the nation will be reckoned later by the High Court," and appoint a cabinet headed by Clemenceau as minister of war and with Poincaré as minister of foreign affairs. In *L'Echo de Paris,* the well-connected Pertinax predicted, "The hour has come to change approaches."[25]

But Briand still held one great advantage: however much the deputies longed to flout Great Britain and humiliate Germany—and cheered doing so in speeches and in print—most of them still feared the ultimate consequences of such an independent course. Briand pressed this point in his defense. "We came out of the war with a treaty involving enormous diffi-

24. *Le Figaro,* 15 May 1921, for Briand's statement; Suarez, *Briand,* 5:195–96, for the notes to Berlin and London.

25. J.O.C., Débats, 19–20 May 1921; *L'Action française,* 19, 24 May 1921; *L'Echo de Paris,* 19 May 1921: Pertinax was the pseudonym of Charles Joseph André Géraud.

culties in application and execution." Three weeks ago he could, he declared, have won short-term praise by insisting on occupying the Ruhr, but his policy of restraint forced Germany to submit all the same: "Ah yes, force! I prefer to obtain a result by threatening it rather than use it without result. I prefer that to a gesture which, in isolating France, would have placed in our hands only a useless forfeit. I believe I have well interpreted the interest of the country in doing so." To cinch his argument, he revealed that Germany had made a payment of 150 million gold marks on 17 May, with assurances of a much larger one by the end of the month. Acrimony there might be with Lloyd George, but the gains were incontestable, and Briand asked a vote of confidence on that basis. Whether or not they approved of his methods, the deputies gave him the right to continue, 419 to 171, his majority considerably less than in mid-April but not significantly different from what he had been glad to have at the beginning of February. *Le Figaro* was undoubtedly correct in concluding that the Chamber was more resigned than content, for to overthrow Briand would condemn his successor to a policy of force. That left the Senate, and not for the trial proposed by Daudet. Tardieu and Mandel tried to stir up trouble there, but when the Germans handed over one billion gold marks on 28 May, no senator, and especially not Poincaré, wanted to argue against that success.[26]

So reparations proved trumps again: churlish Lloyd George, put-upon Poland—these and much more could be tolerated or ignored by the legislators and public opinion as long as Germany made payments. In this interim, gold marks bought Briand time to put out the fire in Upper Silesia. During June and early July, the flames flared as German militias attacked French observers, wounding five and killing a ranking officer. When Briand threatened to restore order by sending in two divisions of troops, Curzon protested bitterly—at least in part because he had read a severely unfriendly critique of himself in papers mislaid by the French ambassador, Count Auguste de Saint Aulaire. Yet with much ill grace, the British acknowledged that a decision had to be imposed from without. At the end of July, Lloyd George agreed to abide by the judgment from a panel of

26. J.O.C., Débats, 24–25 May 1921; *Le Figaro,* 27 May 1921; J.O.S., Débats, 30 May 1921.

experts, but a week later, when it awarded a significant portion of the region's industrial zone to the Poles, he reneged. In Paris to press his case, he attacked the integrity of the panel and accused Briand of instigating a campaign of abuse against him in "ses" newspapers—to which Briand replied that *L'Action française* was not yet an official publication. A dinner held in his honor by Millerand at the presidential retreat in Rambouillet turned out badly when the car carrying Lloyd George, Curzon, Briand, and Loucheur broke down returning to Paris. Lloyd George launched into curses in English of such astounding profanity that Loucheur had trouble translating them for Briand. On the following day, 12 August, they agreed to submit the issue to the League of Nations, where Lloyd George hoped to win because of the large Commonwealth representation, Briand because of the treaty language. And Briand was right: on 20 October the League's committee granted about two-thirds of Upper Silesia to the Germans but the greater share of the mineral wealth and industry to Poland because Poles were in the majority there. The partition pleased no one entirely— perhaps its best endorsement—but the Germans and the British were the most disappointed.[27]

On the same day as Millerand's dinner party, 11 August, the American president, Warren G. Harding, issued invitations to the world's naval powers for a disarmament conference to be held at Washington in November. For Briand, the proposed agenda meant little compared to the possible return of the United States to involvement in Europe. Here was his opportunity to retrieve for France the support of America, to reconstitute the alliance of the three Western democracies that had defeated Germany and, under the Versailles Treaty, were supposed to guarantee the peace. In Paris, nearly half a world away from the isolationist "normalcy" of Washington and strident complaints of French "imperialism" from the Hearst newspapers, Briand's reverie could seem almost within reach. Hugh Campbell Wallace, ambassador since December 1914 and a Wilsonian, formally disavowed the Hearst charges and continually stressed the goodwill of the American people for France. In his last official act, ad-

---

27. Wandycz, *France and Her Eastern Allies,* 223–37; Oudin, *Briand,* 411–13; Suarez, *Briand,* 5:199–208. See Briand's brief comments, J.O.C., Débats, 11 July 1921; Poincaré in *Le Matin,* 9 June, 7 August 1921; *Le Figaro,* 8–13 August 1921.

dressing a celebration on the fourth of July, he insisted that "Germany *must pay,* and must pay all." And he concluded, "Friends for a hundred and fifty years, French and Americans ought to be brothers in everything but blood." His successor, Myron T. Herrick, had also been his predecessor for nearly three years and was as openly Francophile. No French politician had forgotten his refusal to leave Paris in September 1914 as the Germans approached. Herrick timed his return for Bastille Day, to hug his old friend Briand, to lay flowers on the tomb of the *soldat inconnu* beneath the Arc de Triomphe, to declare, in presenting his credentials to Millerand at the Elysée, that he was returning to friends. That was Paris.[28]

About three months earlier, at the end of March, Briand had chosen René Viviani as his personal representative to sound out the new Harding administration because Viviani was remembered in Washington from a similar assignment almost exactly four years earlier, in 1917. Then, with Woodrow Wilson leading the United States into war beside France, Columbia University contributed to international diplomacy by awarding Viviani an honorary doctorate. Now, with the rejection of all that Wilson stood for, Washington seemed to regard France with suspicion and even hostility. During one meeting, Senator Henry Cabot Lodge, more responsible than anyone else for defeating the treaty and spurning the League of Nations, demanded a promise that war debts would be paid and pilloried Viviani for comments in the French press about the failure of the United States to recompense France for monies spent in defeating the British during the struggle of the colonies for independence. On his return, Viviani admitted encountering "an atmosphere sometimes troubled by intrigue" but insisted, lamely, that "a reorganization of Franco-American politics is near at hand." That was Washington. And this Washington perspective was more clearly enunciated by Nicholas Murray Butler, another ardent Francophile, president of Columbia University, who had awarded Viviani his honorary degree and who during his visit to Paris in July 1921 received the supreme honor for an intellectual of being received by the Académie française. Americans, Butler said, had a high regard for the French people, for their courage, for their civilization, but Americans in the aftermath of the war would not sign a treaty of alliance with even their closest friends

28. *Le Figaro,* 12 January, 7 April, 5–6, 15–16 July 1921.

and especially would not countenance submitting to a super government like the League of Nations.[29]

Was Briand listening? Or was he confident that his charm and words could win over les Américains as they had—at times—Lloyd George? Was he counting on men like Wallace and Herrick? That was a judgment not without basis: in April and May, the United States had reacted to German appeals about reparations and possible occupation with stern indifference. And so Briand announced that he would personally lead the French delegation to Washington in November, rejecting advice that he was radically raising the stakes—as Wilson had in coming to Paris for the peace conference. The most ominous warning, because of its author, came from Poincaré. Correctly assuming that Briand was crossing the Atlantic not to discuss naval disarmament but to attempt the restoration of the wartime alliance, he cautioned, "But I greatly fear that in trying to recapture, in its original form, the tripartite pact, we are grasping at a will-o'-the-wisp."[30] Yet who better than Briand to try?

Certainly, Briand thought that, and he said so. On 9 October, he went to Saint Nazaire, at the mouth of the Loire River and a few miles from his constituents at Nantes, for a parade of France's Atlantic fleet, toured the new cruiser *Strasbourg,* and then addressed a banquet of his supporters. With the Chamber of Deputies and the Senate soon to reconvene after a long late summer recess, Briand reviewed his nearly nine months in power. He claimed for his policies the authority of Clemenceau, the fundamental proposition that the Versailles Treaty was dead without allied harmony. When he took office in January, there was no fixed figure for reparations payments, and Germany disdained threats of sanction. That was before the occupation of Ruhrort, Duisburg, and Düsseldorf, before the London schedule, both possible because of close cooperation with Great Britain. "The strength of the alliance is indisputable": from this reality, France should draw the lesson that the control of Germany required avoiding isolation. For that reason, he was going to Washington, not just

29. *Le Figaro,* 29 March, 1–2, 20–21, 28 April 1921, for Viviani, the quotation from the last; 17, 22 July 1921, for Butler, the interview from the former.

30. See *La Liberté,* 22 September 1921, for a friendly warning to Briand; for Poincaré, *Le Temps,* 19 September 1921.

to defend French interests but to seek a revival of France's long friendship with the United States. To those—and he left them unnamed—who might flaunt a policy of force instead, to "men who play easily at being soldiers, I say frankly, there are too many mourning veils in this country, too many young men who have suffered amputations, for our hearts not to shudder at the thought." But if they were determined to have their way, Briand challenged them to overthrow him, as Clemenceau had done his opponents in December 1918: "I am not attached to power: if someone possesses the secret of doing better than me, I will immediately cede him my place."[31]

Eleven days later, on 20 October, the League of Nations announced its partition of Upper Silesia. This apparent victory for French diplomacy and the Polish nation, for international arbitration and the sanctity of treaties, for ethnic self-determination and repressed minorities was utterly Pyrrhic. The consequences were evidence that no good deed goes unpunished, that for France in the Après Guerre, one step forward was always followed by one step—sometimes more—backward. On 7 October, following quiet negotiations during the summer, Louis Loucheur, the minister for reconstruction, had signed the Wiesbaden accords with his German counterpart, Walther Rathenau, by which up to seven billion marks of reparations due France could be paid in kind. After fulminating about the League's ruling, the German government declared the agreement void. British leaders, already making common complaint with the Germans over the partition, were delighted because the deliveries in kind would have eliminated lucrative sales to the French. And so Germany and Great Britain drew closer together—and further from France. Vague talk of a new formal alliance between France and Great Britain, heard since Winston Churchill proposed it in June, faded. Lloyd George was furious at having been maneuvered by Briand into submitting the Upper Silesia question to the League. Curzon was angry at the latest French diplomacy in the Near East, where France favored the Turks, Britain the Greeks. They determined to exact revenge at Washington. So much for allied harmony. But the true calamity for Briand came in rumors that the fall of the mark on currency markets would give Germany an excuse to avoid mak-

31. *Le Figaro*, 10 October 1921; Suarez, *Briand*, 5:211–14.

ing its reparation payment of 500 million gold marks in January 1922. Briand knew that reparations were trumps in French politics. Without them, he had a losing hand.[32]

To Briand's political opponents, his entire policy appeared at risk, this fragility the proof of its weakness. But Briand had seemed vulnerable in May, and whatever the potential for disaster now, it remained intangible. The state of play was revealed by three speeches on 16 October, a week after his at Saint Nazaire. Presiding over the unveiling of a statue at Metz of Paul Déroulède, the secular saint of *revanchisme* who died on the eve of the war that restored Alsace and Lorraine to France, Barthou called this founder of the bullying Ligue des patriotes "the Knight of the Fatherland," the animator of "l'alliance franco-française," the union of all the French for the strength of France. Any reference to the anti-Dreyfusard violence that led to his conviction and exile for plots against the state was absent. Yet even this glossing away of unfortunate details was insufficient for Maurice Barrès, who had perhaps forgotten his doubts of victory during the war. "The vow of Déroulède has been fulfilled, but the destinies of France remain to be achieved," he declaimed, his eyes on the Rhineland across the border. At Avignon, Paul Painlevé, a wartime premier and important figure in the Radical party, described that portion as leading "France and Europe together to a future of massacre, blood, and ruin."[33]

Briand stood between Barthou and Painlevé: the great question for the Bloc national that had sustained him thus far was exactly where. With the Chamber of Deputies back in session, Barrès blamed the cabinet for "une politique d'abandons," and Daudet complained, "What you said you would do, you have not done"—more of the same from May. The danger to Briand came from Mandel, who charged him with sliding away from the Bloc national toward the Radicals, of cultivating the Left with a foreign policy of compromise and a refusal to crack down on French Bolsheviks while expecting to retain the votes of the Right and Center with empty promises. The accusation of betrayal with its implicit reference to the défaitisme of Caillaux and Malvy was all the more sensational because

32. Carls, *Louis Loucheur*, 228–34; for reaction to Churchill's proposal, see *Le Figaro*, 10 June 1921.
33. *Le Figaro*, 17 October 1921.

on 19 October, leftist radicals reacted to the death sentences of Nicola Sacco and Bartolomeo Vanzetti in the United States by sending a mail bomb to the American embassy. More bombs in protest exploded over the following two days.[34]

When Briand replied, he must have had those bombs on his mind: "By walking around a barrel of gunpowder cigarette in hand, one creates all manner of risks, without having either the desire or the intention of provoking an explosion. In Europe—I might say almost the entire world—there are not a few barrels of gunpowder, and to want peace means to avoid doing anything that could set a spark off. For France, which has suffered so much from war and since the Armistice has endured a series of provocations that justify impatience, to want peace means to forbear. If the nation has the right to be nervous and excitable, the duty of remaining calm and of abstaining from any impulsive act which might lead to irreparable consequences is all the more important for its government." Having suggested that his critics lacked sangfroid, he defended his foreign policies with the same arguments, even the same words, he had used since January: "The whole question comes down to whether the cabinet has done all that it could do or whether someone else could do better. . . . The treaty—that's the agreement of the allies." Just because *France* wanted to do something did not mean that it would be done. "That is a fact. Every act under the treaty must be carried out in concert, in combination, in common." Yes, he had talked in the spring of placing a firm hand on Germany's collar, but he had done so in accord with the allies, not without them. For to stand alone against Germany was to invite the isolation of 1870 again. "Germany is a nation of seventy million with enormous industrial capabilities. The cannons we destroy today can be replaced tomorrow." Facing the potential of such a foe, France had to grasp at the chances offered by going to the naval disarmament talks in Washington. How could France fail to play the role her presence in the world demanded, how not attend the first great international conference ever held in the United States, how snub the sister republic that had come to France's aid? And there he would proclaim the rationale for France's armed might: "It is because the French soldier was there, armed, courageous, heroic, in 1914, that liberty was saved!"

34. J.O.C., Débats, 18–20 October 1921; *Le Figaro,* 20 October 1921.

Liberty saved was also the gist of Briand's answer, oblique but obvious, to Mandel. "The 'Republic' is not merely a word . . . it is authority resigning itself to having adversaries, a regime under which representatives elected to oversee the government can do so in complete freedom. When they have attacked the cabinet from the tribune, when they have voted against it, they can be certain in returning to their homes that no attempt will be made to punish them. . . . There are men who have taken, under the pretext of union sacrée, such an attitude toward the regime that they cannot be counted in a 'republican majority.' " He did not want their votes any longer, and he did not expect them. But who exactly was he reading out and exactly for what? The Far Right of Daudet and his ilk were certainly condemned, but what of less extreme nationalists like Forgeot? And what about the clemencistes, all of whom—especially Mandel—had a pronounced authoritarian streak? Briand named no one but demanded a majority to his liking or he would not continue. As at Saint Nazaire, he was daring his opponents to overthrow the cabinet, but he had shifted the odds against himself by refusing to count the votes of some who might support him grudgingly and alienating others who approved of his policies but resented his attack on their colleagues.[35]

The moment had come for Tardieu. In May he had been the vanguard of the assault; now he was cast as the coup de grace. To the usual clemenciste complaint of coddling Germany, he added a prediction that at the Washington he knew so well France would find pressure to make concessions, not offers of alliance. These words and arguments were as hackneyed as Briand's—the deputies had heard them from both for months, and their repetition would change few minds. The crux of the attack was an elaboration on the charge laid by Mandel at the beginning of the debate days earlier. Briand, Tardieu exclaimed, was no true member of the Bloc national but instead a crypto-Radical. Briand had betrayed Clemenceau, testified for Malvy, was carrying out a foreign policy worthy of Caillaux. Briand's definition of "republican" was an invitation for the Radicals to join the majority even as he excommunicated loyal patriots. But victory for the Bloc national had been the response of French voters to years of Radical domination after 1902 that nearly brought the nation to ruin and

35. J.O.C., Débats, 21 October 1921; Suarez, *Briand,* 5:214–30.

defeat. Unable to escape his past, devoid of any vision for the future, allowing Britain, the United States, and even Germany to define the parameters of French action, Briand had become, in Tardieu's pungent and deadly line, "un chien crevé qui suit le fil de l'eau"—a dead-tired dog going with the stream. As if to prove Tardieu's point, Edouard Herriot, the leader of the Radicals, demanded to speak, to decry this depiction of men he claimed had rescued the Republic during the Dreyfus Affair, saved it from clericalism and militarism, and had the duty of defending its values against the likes of Mandel and Tardieu. In staking out a "republican majority," Herriot was as specific as Briand had been vague. When Briand answered Tardieu, he tried to undo the damage by setting a single condition, clearly accepting the Republic, for inclusion in his majority: an attempt to restore the ambiguity by begging the question of defining either "accepting" or "Republic." But by now, the deputies had a clear idea of where the lines were being drawn, and as Briand finished, from the Far Right Armand Baudry d'Asson cried out, "A policy of vassalage!" with Daudet adding, "And of treason!" Although Briand did win the vote of confidence 338 to 172, he had 80 votes fewer in his favor than in May, and for the first time since the Chambre bleu horizon took their seats in January 1920, the Bloc national split down the middle, half continuing to support Briand, the other half, not yet ready to abandon him, abstaining.[36] The voyage to the United States beginning three days later on 29 October was already under dark clouds.

From Le Havre, the appropriately chosen *Lafayette* steamed into the late fall Atlantic laden with two thousand bottles of champagne and brandy to circumvent American Prohibition. The French delegation of diplomatic, legal, and military experts was formally headed by Albert Sarraut, the minister for colonies, because Briand could not be away for much more than a month and, allowing for crossings, would have only about two weeks in the United States. As always, Briand was assisted by Berthelot, who brought along—ever so discreetly—his current mistress. Viviani begged to return to Washington, and Briand acceded but gave him no official function. For Viviani was exhibiting signs of decreasing mental

36. J.O.C., Débats, 25–26 October 1921, Tardieu on the former, Briand and Herriot on the latter; Suarez, *Briand,* 5:230–37.

stability—which could make for malicious fun, as when Briand concocted a false cable warning of icebergs ahead to make him shiver in terror, and for acute embarrassment, because Viviani propositioned so many women aboard ship so grossly that Briand had to intervene personally. During the voyage, Sarraut was confined to his cabin with an attack of malaria exacerbated by his fear that Briand had only the slightest grasp of the issues facing France in Washington, especially complications involving Japan and China and how naval disarmament might affect the French Empire.

Briand's mind was instead set on reviving the lost defensive pact with the United States. His hopes were buoyed by enthusiastic crowds in New York, where the *Lafayette* landed, and a triumphal train trip down to Washington on 8 November, where the secretary of state, Charles Evans Hughes, and the former commander of United States forces in France, General John Joseph Pershing, waited to greet the delegation. Briand then met briefly with President Harding and joined him to commemorate the Armistice on 11 November as the body of an American infantryman recently brought back from France was interred in the Tomb of the Unknown Soldier. After such a promising prologue, Briand was brought up short on the following day at the first plenary meeting of the conference when he discovered that he had not been placed at the head table but among the representatives of the British Dominions. Although the mistake was quickly rectified, he was unable to conceal completely an ill humor that intensified over the next week as Hughes and the head of the British delegation, Arthur James Balfour, pressured the French not only to accept humiliating limitations on battleships but to reduce land forces as well. How could former wartime partners fail so utterly to comprehend France's obligations? Instinctively choosing persuasion over confrontation, Briand tried again to explain when his turn to speak arrived on 21 November. "To have peace, there must be two partners. . . . Disarmament must be moral as well as material. I have to say that in Europe today there are grave elements of instability, conditions that France must confront as threats to national security." All of Germany's enemies in the war had undergone sacrifices, but France, he reminded the conference, had sacrificed the most. To weaken France was to encourage certain men—referring to militant German nationalists such as General Erich Ludendorff—in their plans for revenge. "Germany in a few weeks can raise an army of six to seven million men. . . . We French must protect our nation. We cannot disarm in the face of such menaces. We cannot bargain away our security. We must be permitted to establish it in terms compatible with present needs. The danger is there. It is on the prowl. It is just above our heads. . . . The true condition for disarmament is for Germany to know well that France is not alone."[37]

The argument was compelling only from the vantage point of Paris. The other delegates acknowledged the quality of Briand's rhetoric but appeared unmoved. In the following day's *New York World*, a long article by H. G. Wells accused the French of preparing the next war. One day more brought Curzon's outrageous comment from London that France constituted a perpetual menace to world peace. Persuasion had failed, his time in the United States was used up, and a disappointed Briand permitted himself a Parthian shot of indignation. On 24 November, he declared to the conference that he had come with a clear mandate: "France can accept reductions in armaments if French security is guaranteed. If France stands alone, France can accept nothing. No nation facing a question of life or death would answer differently. No statesman conscious of his responsibilities would act otherwise." And at a final press conference, when a hostile Hearst reporter asked sarcastically whether French tanks were doves of peace, he replied with his own question, whether the new American battleships were launched to fish for sardines. He had recovered his equipoise by the evening and a farewell dinner. In his toast, he thanked the government of the United States for the invitation that permitted him, as the first French premier to visit while in office, to convey personally the profound gratitude of France for America's aid in the war. And he concluded with an invocation for the cause of peace in the name of the dead from both nations: "If their supreme hope were to be disappointed, if their heroic sacrifice were to be in vain, it would be a defiance to their memory and an insult to their tomb."[38]

After Briand and Berthelot boarded the *Paris* on 26 November for a gloomy return home, the conference abandoned any attempt to restrict

37. Suarez, *Briand,* 5:239–79; Oudin, *Briand,* 418–21; *Le Figaro,* 22 November 1921.

38. Suarez, *Briand,* 5:280–92, the Hearst reporter from 287, the toast from 292; Oudin, *Briand,* 422; *Le Figaro,* 25 November 1921.

ground troops but quickly adopted the originally proposed limitations on capital ships, in the formula of 5 to 5 to 3 to 1.67 to 1.67: Great Britain and the United States were each permitted a battleship fleet totaling 525,000 tons, Japan 315,000, France and Italy 175,000 each. Although the French delegation complained that "Anglo-Saxon" naval domination was now codified and bitterly resented accepting parity with Italy, their only argument was wounded pride. For France had allowed its navy—in 1914 the world's third greatest—to deteriorate badly during the war while Britain carried out most of the operations at sea: of the five, only France would not have to *disarm*, would not have to decommission ships to satisfy the tonnage requirement. Almost as a token, to assuage the abasement, the French were made a member of the Four Power Treaty, by which the United States, Great Britain, France, and Japan agreed to guarantee each other's island possessions in the Pacific, and the Nine Power Treaty, promising to preserve the territorial integrity and administrative independence of China and the "Open Door" trading rights. Sarraut devised a different form of reciprocation: to make up for France's inferior position in battleships, he prevented any limitation on submarines, provoking a howl of protest from the British, who could not imagine against whom, other than themselves, these submarines might be used. By the end of the conference in early February 1922, French and British military leaders had adopted a thoroughly mutual mistrust, while United States officials regarded France as dangerously obstructionist.[39]

Briand was surely the wrong man to come courting the Americans. Judging national perceptions is always risky, but he ought to have noticed how two celebrated visitors from France had been received in the United States earlier during the year, the boxer Georges Carpentier and the tennis player Suzanne Lenglen. An authentic war hero as an aviator, decorated with the Croix de Guerre and the Médaille militaire, intelligent, modest, friendly, photogenic, Carpentier was the emblem of French manhood. He met Jack Dempsey in New York on 2 July 1921 to fight for the heavyweight championship and was knocked out in the fourth round. Coura-

39. Henry Blumenthal, *Illusion and Reality in Franco-American Diplomacy, 1914–1945* (Baton Rouge, 1986), 103–11; *Le Figaro,* 27, 30 December 1921, for the pleasure at British unhappiness over the submarine issue.

geous and gritty, he kept going until he could not stand and afterward made no excuses. Lenglen was temperamental, excessive in manner, outrageous in dress. In 1921, she was already the singles winner at Wimbledon and of the French championship, where she beat the top-ranked American, Molla Bjursted Mallory, in the finals. At Forest Hills for the United States championship, she met Mallory again on 16 August. After losing the initial set 6–2—the first set she had lost since winning Wimbledon in 1919—Lenglen defaulted before completing a single game in the next, complaining that she suffered from bronchitis and that Prohibition denied her "restorative" brandy. Everyone present believed she preferred to quit rather than be defeated. The vice-president of the French Tennis Federation, Albert de Joannis, refused to defend her and resigned. Carpentier never won a title, but Americans adopted him as one of their own. Lenglen was the greatest woman tennis player of her time, victorious in singles at Wimbledon for six years, three times winning women's doubles and mixed doubles as well. Americans cheered for her opponents the rest of her brilliant career.[40] Briand was too little like Carpentier—a foxy cynic— too much like Lenglen—a complaining trimmer—and Americans never took to him. When Clemenceau, aged but unbowed and unrepentant for anything, came over in 1922, he was venerated.

Like wolves sensing the weakening of their prey, Briand's political enemies awaited his arrival at Le Havre on 2 December. They knew that he had lost the confidence of half the deputies in the Bloc national. They had the condemnation of his diplomacy at Washington: *Le Figaro*'s Jacques Roujon led the Paris press in their assessment, "We must not mistake the gravity of the current Franco-British rift." They had further reports of German plans to withhold reparations. At that, Poincaré, until now noticeably silent, spoke before the Cercle national (National Club) in Bordeaux on 27 November to establish himself as the alternative to Briand and briandiste policies: "For two years, the allies have shown a singular forbearance toward the Germans which they have insolently abused and which they endeavor even today to exploit for new advantages. . . . The hour has come

40. Larry Engelmann, *The Goddess and the American Girl: The Story of Suzanne Lenglen and Helen Wills* (New York, 1988), 27–38; see the accounts in *Le Figaro*, 3, 24 July for Carpentier; 26, 27 August, 9, 11, 13, 15, 18, 19 September 1921 for Lenglen.

to repeat to them as at Verdun, 'That is it! You go no further!' . . . If the German government is bankrupt, the German nation is then liable, and its wealth present and future is the collateral of its creditors."[41] To draw blood immediately, they had a scandal involving Berthelot.

In 1913, when Philippe Berthelot was under secretary for Asia at the Foreign Ministry, his brothers, André and Daniel, founded the Banque industrielle de Chine (B.I.C.), which with ministry support quickly became the principal instrument of French credit in the Far East. The postwar slump brought severe financial difficulties, and on 13 January 1921, immediately after the fall of the Leygues cabinet, Berthelot, on his own initiative but with the authority of his office as secretary-general, sent a telegram to France's embassies in Peking, Tokyo, Shanghai, Hong Kong, and London officially denying that the B.I.C. was facing imminent collapse. And it did not because Berthelot's intervention prevented a run by depositors and because he convinced the Banque de Paris et des Pays-Bas to provide a temporary infusion of funds. The effort was to no avail: within months, there was more trouble, and on 30 June the B.I.C. closed insolvent. At the beginning of July, Briand faced questions from the Chamber of Deputies about the bank's collapse and Berthelot's role. He answered by reading aloud the telegram of 13 January and declaring that he would have approved it had he been in office, thereby "covering" the action by his retroactive warrant. Briand was then surprised by how many deputies from across the political spectrum were appalled at Berthelot's having acted in the name of the government to protect the investments of his family. Afterward, he promised General Edouard de Castelnau, moral paragon of the Bloc national, that he would investigate the issues fully and, if necessary, "reassign" Berthelot.

Briand did no such thing. He accepted an exculpatory accounting from Berthelot and assumed that the "indelicacy" would be forgotten. He did not count on how he himself might be attacked through the disgrace of his principal diplomatic aide or on the Calvinist rigor of Edouard Soulier. Pastor Soulier chose the same day Tardieu applied the riverine canine metaphor to Briand to demolish Berthelot's excuse that his telegram was sent to refute false rumors about the B.I.C. spread by the Reuters news

41. For Roujon, *Le Figaro,* 24, 26 November 1921, quotation from the latter; for Poincaré, *Le Figaro,* 28 November 1921, and Miquel, *Poincaré,* 436.

agency: Reuters had not carried any items about the B.I.C. Hard-pressed already, Briand replied irritably, "At the moment when the delegation to Washington is about to depart, I cannot understand how an elected representative of France can try to diminish its moral authority." The case festered while they were away. On 24 December, Pierre Taittinger, one of those read out of the "republican majority" in October, offered a poisoned Christmas stocking, revealing that Berthelot had sent a second unsanctioned telegram about the B.I.C., on 22 January, two days after Briand took office as premier and minister of foreign affairs. In this one, which he had concealed from Briand all along, Berthelot claimed, falsely, that the French government would make good any losses from the bank. Stunned by such duplicity, Briand could only respond mechanically that "it would be unfair not to recognize the formidable labors and intelligence of this high official." Clearly, Berthelot had to go, but not even then did he acknowledge his disloyalty: "I have against me appearances . . . continual attacks, abominable calumnies, absurd reproaches." When Briand announced Berthelot's resignation before the Chamber on 27 December, the wound opened by this betrayal was too apparent: "He has gone, and you must pardon me, for this has been one of the saddest and most painful moments of my life." After Poincaré became premier, he convoked Berthelot before a disciplinary hearing on 13 March 1922 and suspended him from government service for ten years. Berthelot did not deserve the pardon Briand granted him four years later.[42]

On the day that Briand announced Berthelot's resignation, *Le Figaro* seriously asked whether the premier's would be next. The B.I.C. scandal took so long to play out after their return from Washington because the reports about Germany and reparations were accurate. At the end of November, Rathenau had sought British support for relief from the 500 million gold mark payment due 15 January 1922 (as the quarterly installment toward the 2 billion gold marks a year under the London schedule). Encouraged by Lloyd George, the German government then formally applied to the Reparations Commission for a moratorium, which refused,

---

42. J.O.C., Débats, 5, 8 July, 25 October, 24, 27 December 1921; *L'Echo de Paris,* 8 July 1921; *Le Figaro,* 25, 27, 28 December 1921; Suarez, *Briand,* 5:319–33, the resignation letter from 329; Oudin, *Briand,* 425–28.

over British objections. Once again, Great Britain and France were colliding over enforcement of the treaty and this time when relations were already strained severely by Upper Silesia, the Near East, and the naval conference. As he had nearly a year before in January, Lloyd George now feared that if he did not grant Briand a *tangible* prize, he would soon be negotiating with Poincaré. Briand likewise sensed that the point of crisis for his cabinet was close. At London from 18 to 22 December, they tried to establish the outline of a deal: in return for French concessions on reparations, Britain would sign a treaty of mutual defense with France.

The details remained unsorted. Lloyd George proposed a renunciation of war debts among Britain, France, and the United States and of Britain's share of reparations if the total required of Germany were reduced. Opposed to relaxing the reins on the Germans, Briand thought to offer the United States the "C" class reparation bonds in satisfaction of the war debts. Both plans were condemned without reprieve when American officials declared that debts owed the United States from the war would henceforth accrue 5 percent interest and were due in full by 1947. This response left Lloyd George merely pursuing a general French "accommodation" toward German payments, and that meant granting the moratorium. To risk touching reparations, Briand needed a firm pledge of British military support. He initially suggested a worldwide compact but quickly fell back on his real aim, a commitment by Britain and France that Germany's boundaries remain unalterable. Lloyd George replied that Britain could never accept responsibilities involving eastern Europe but could guarantee the western boundary with France and Belgium. Nothing was absolutely agreed, but the outline could be filled in during the conference of the four reparation powers scheduled to begin at Cannes on 4 January.[43]

At least that is what Briand said on returning to Paris. In winning a postponement of new debate over his policies until after Cannes, he told the Chamber, "France will cede none of the reparations due." Senate patriarch Alexandre Ribot, not usually a friend, this time endorsed him unequivocally: "The premier has foreseen all the dangers which can result from this conference. He will take the necessary precautions. He will insist on a solid

43. *Le Figaro,* 27 December 1921; Carls, *Louis Loucheur,* 234–37; Suarez, *Briand,* 5:336–51.

public accord between France and Great Britain. That is the true and proper policy for France." Even after the depressing voyage home from America, Briand had not forsaken his belief in diplomacy, negotiation, reason, talk, charm. Of Lloyd George he said: "We get along. We compromise. We settle important matters as best we can. We remain united. That's how allies act." Briand might think so. Others who had backed him to this point now changed their minds. Among them were Millerand at the Elysée and, from the cabinet itself, Barthou and Doumer.[44]

At first, Cannes was a relief for Briand from the welter of criticism in Paris. Seeming anxious to patch up relations, Lloyd George had ready a memorandum proposing a guarantee of full military assistance to France upon any German attack. As its price, he asked French support for limits on submarines, for an appearance at Cannes by German representatives to plead for a moratorium, and for a general European conference on economic matters at which Germany and Russia would be full participants. The last had become Lloyd George's scheme to restore prosperity: opening post-tsarist Russia to trade might tame and civilize the Bolsheviks while making money for the Germans with which to pay reparations. Although Briand preferred a wider conception of a French military convention with Britain and was leery of rewarding Russia and Germany in trade arrangements, the lure of a firm alliance was irresistible. After further discussions with Lloyd George, he sent a long and optimistic cable to Millerand. From Paris came back an almost hostile reply: Lloyd George's language for the defensive pact required both partners to abstain from "all aggression against their neighbors," implying that France would be forbidden to enforce the Versailles Treaty by occupation; the inclusion of Russia would force France to accept the Bolshevik government without having granted it diplomatic recognition or having received compensation for repudiated tsarist debts; permitting the Germans to address the conference at Cannes would disavow the decision of the Reparations Commission. More telegrams followed, with Briand offering reassurances that negotiating points were not agreements and Millerand exhibiting profound mistrust. In the midst of these telegrams, on 8 January, to relax during a Sunday afternoon,

44. J.O.C., Débats, 24 December 1921; J.O.S., Débats, 29 December 1921; *Le Figaro,* 3 December 1921, for the comments about Lloyd George as the *Paris* docked at Le Havre.

Briand accepted Lloyd George's invitation to play golf, a game he had never tried. Photographers snapped Britain's prime minister "tutoring" the French premier on the finer points of gripping a driver. Never mind that—for a while—Briand had beginner's luck, he seemed to be taking instruction from Lloyd George, the scene a perfect symbol of French subservience to the British.

The next day France received bad news from the conference. Without hearing the Germans, economic experts from Italy and Belgium reversed their decision on the Reparations Commission and agreed with Britain that Germany had to be granted at least a partial moratorium for the January payment. With a picture entitled "Leçon de golf" across many front pages, Briand had to explain this fiasco to Millerand, cabling, "I ask you to believe that we have done and are doing everything humanly possible in the present situation to safeguard the interests of France." Millerand did not. He gathered the cabinet on 10 January, the following day, and, with the support of Barthou and Doumer, won a unanimous declaration that to grant Germany a moratorium without seizing territory as a security would violate Briand's pledge before the Chamber of Deputies and that the ministers as a body should debate any project of military alliance with Great Britain before further negotiations took place. As Briand received this humiliating rebuke to his diplomacy from his own cabinet, there was another telegram, from the Foreign Ministry, warning that Poincaré was convening an emergency meeting of the Senate's committee on foreign affairs. The political situation was actually even worse: the committees on finance and foreign affairs of the Chamber met to condemn *any* concession on reparations; the Senate adopted a resolution warning that a military alliance with Britain was not worth compromising French interests. The centrist *Journal des débats* called the proposals under consideration at Cannes "as bad as can be feared." Bainville denounced Lloyd George for making a "sinister farce" of the treaty and French rights. In the inaugural issue of *L'Echo national,* Tardieu editorialized scathingly, "Four days have sufficed for Briand to worsen beyond reprieve the position created during the last year by his policies and to tear up his promises made in December before the Chamber and the Senate." Late that evening, Briand could only reply to Millerand: "Should I or should I not break off talks? If the cabinet wishes to take responsibility for a rupture, I ask you to let me know clearly, that I may leave Cannes, with all of the consequences that will ensue. I trust that the cabinet will weigh the gravity of the situation."[45]

Throughout the next morning, a grim-faced Briand endured patronizing sympathy from Lloyd George. Shortly after lunch, the reply from Millerand arrived with its verdict: if the seemingly inevitable moratorium were not accompanied by ironclad sanctions specific in date and effect pending further German default, Briand was to break off negotiations, the cabinet taking "responsibility for the failure of the talks because it believes France can no longer sacrifice these rights." Briand was not Leygues, not willing to accept dictation of his foreign policy from the Elysée. And he had had his fill of treachery after Berthelot's—betrayal demanded confrontation. Mastering his emotions, he placed the cable in his pocket and announced to the other delegates that "political necessities" forced his return to Paris for forty-eight hours. Although the conference was now in disarray, he must have thought, as he boarded the overnight train, that he would be returning, because he left behind his baggage and his valet.

Perhaps he made the decision not to go back when he reached the station platform in Paris and an aide from the Foreign Ministry handed him the 12 January—that morning's—*Le Matin*. On its front page, he read verbatim excerpts from the cables he had exchanged with Millerand, making public the discord between the president of the Republic and its premier. Briand went immediately to the Elysée palace. After a few contentious words with Millerand, he concluded that their differences could not be bridged but that blame for disclosure of the telegrams belonged elsewhere—to Barthou, he guessed. When the cabinet was hastily assembled, Briand took the measure of the men he had appointed to office and who, with the exception of Loucheur, with him at Cannes, had unanimously disavowed him. Briefly, sharply, he justified his efforts: France alone could not prevent the moratorium, could not prevent the invitation of the Bol-

45. Suarez, *Briand,* 5:352–94, the quotations from 382 and 394; Oudin, *Briand,* 428–33; *L'Oeuvre,* 12 January 1922, published a detailed account of the 10 January cabinet meeting, obviously provided by one of the participants; *Le Figaro,* 11 January 1922, for the committee meetings; J.O.S., Débats, 10 January 1922; *Le Journal des débats,* 7 January 1922; Bainville in *La Liberté,* 7 January 1922; Tardieu in *L'Echo national,* 10 January 1922. A note on the usage of "Russia": the name Union of Soviet Socialist Republics (U.S.S.R.) was not adopted until 30 December 1922.

sheviks to the economic conference, now set for Genoa; was it not better, therefore, to make the best of things by siding with Great Britain and obtain the military alliance France had sought since the Versailles Treaty? Reversing themselves completely, the ministers then voted, again unanimously, to endorse this diplomacy, which was the basic line Briand had followed for twelve months. Were they so craven that they could not stand against him in his presence? Or was their vote sheer hypocrisy because they believed him already beaten? For Briand, the distinction was meaningless, and he declared, "Anyway, I shall not return to Cannes." As protests for form's sake arose, he sat tight-lipped.

One confrontation remained, with the Chamber of Deputies. Briand left the cabinet meeting for the Palais Bourbon, where the deputies were already discomposed by the revelations in Le Matin. As he entered the Chamber, several pressed around him, one of them, Raoul Calary de Lamazière, of the Bloc national's center, promising to vote against the cabinet. "You won't have to take the trouble," Briand replied. Once at the tribune, he barely concealed his anger and bitterness as he insisted that he ought still to be in Cannes and then made the same defense of his policies as before the cabinet. Daudet threw up his usual cry of "You are betraying France!" This time, Briand only answered wearily, "That's no longer important between us." It was so easy, he continued, for politicians and the public alike to assume that if the ministers did their duty, France would gain all it wanted and deserved. "This atmosphere of error" would have to be abandoned for reality:

I have taken on responsibilities, and I thought I could continue to assume them with all the necessary authority. Well, apparently not. A statesman, at the moment where I find myself and in the redoubtable circumstances our nation traverses, must not advance to combat if he is not certain who will be shooting at him. He expects to be fired on by other countries but not by his own! He must have complete, undisputed authority to realize the task confided to him. I cannot say that at this conference I felt myself granted the moral strength to conduct such difficult negotiations. From what was alleged, from the preparation of resolutions, I felt confidence lacking. So I came here to explain what has been done and why that is so different from what is being said, in order for you to understand the meaning of these talks with a friend and ally. For I persist in considering Great Britain a friend. And I proclaim that at no moment have the interests of France been neglected. And I protest against all that has been alleged of the concessions to which I consented at Cannes to the detriment of the dignity and the interests of the nation. Here is what I have done. Here is where we were when I left Cannes. Others will do better![46]

Having delivered that final line as a mocking challenge, Briand walked out of the Chamber, declining a vote of confidence. How like Lenglen at Forest Hills. As the members of the cabinet followed, Briand waited for Barthou and whispered in his ear, "Tell me, dear friend, how much are thirty pieces of silver worth today?" Enough: after Briand formally resigned as premier, Millerand asked Poincaré to form a cabinet, in which Barthou was made minister of justice and France's delegate to Genoa as a reward for his treachery. Reporters later told Briand that his words so affected the deputies that he might have won a majority, but he brushed off the suggestion, saying that the impact would have quickly *effrité*— crumbled away. He ended the interview with much rancor: "I never knew what it was to row in the galleys of the king, but I now know what it is to row in the galleys of the Republic, and I do not want to continue this toil any longer."[47]

Briand did not believe that Poincaré would do better—or even as well. Betrayed like the Clemenceau he had himself betrayed, he would watch from a distance, from a semiexile, although one not as long or as deep. To console his sixty years, he had a new mistress, but he was tired, his step dragging, his back hunched. He looked after himself poorly: his hair was dirty, his clothes were frayed and ill-fitting, his perpetual cigarette dangled lamentably. The poetess Anna de Noailles saw him about this time at the Hotel des Bergues in Geneva and exclaimed, "If that is not the minister, it's a burglar!"[48]

46. J.O.C., Débats, 12 January 1922; *Le Matin,* 12 January 1922; Suarez, *Briand,* 5:395–417; Oudin, *Briand,* 434–37; Trachtenberg, *Reparation in World Politics,* 211–36.

47. Oudin, *Briand,* 437, for the comment to Barthou; Young, *Power and Pleasure,* 167–68, for a defense of Barthou; *Le Figaro,* 13 January 1922, for Briand's interview.

48. Oudin, *Briand,* 440–42, Noailles quoted on 442.

3

■ ■ ■

La Vie est bête

On 15 January 1922, three days after Aristide Briand walked out of the Chamber of Deputies and power, one day after Raymond Poincaré accepted the invitation of President Alexandre Millerand to take his place, a young woman named Elise Enapluche chose midafternoon at the place Pigalle to strip off all her clothes in freezing weather and shout to the quickly gathered crowd unintelligible comments about the change in cabinets. Several police officers ended the show by wrapping her in a cloak and took her into custody. On 23 January, Edouard Crakowski came home after work to discover that another young woman, his wife, Rachel (née Poznowski), had poisoned herself and their five-year-old daughter. A note she left read: "Neither madness nor sudden impulse. I kill myself having considered carefully. Life is wretched. Oh! God, help me! How kill my daughter? I am almost wild. Will I have the strength? Ten o'clock." To her sister in Warsaw she wrote, "Because life overwhelms me, I have to die; my child must go as well, so that nothing remains after me."[1]

For a certain sliver of French society, the Après Guerre in Paris was jazz, the one-step, cocktails, informality à la mode américaine, the new social prominence of speculators and war profiteers. The whole notion of carefully plotting out the future, a hallmark of the French bourgeoisie, was placed in jeopardy. The destruction of traditional investments sug-

---

1. *Le Figaro,* 16, 24 January 1922.

gested that taking even inordinate risks was a more certain course than hard work. Inflation made saving less attractive than consumption. Traditions declined or vanished. Younger women adopted an androgenous style and prepared for careers, not arranged marriages. The number of prostitutes declined, especially the *poules de luxe*—the grand courtesans—as the retreat of restraints on women meant the advance of casual sex. Formality declined: the "at home" for *dames du monde* disappeared, dinners—and their sauces—were less elaborate, servants became harder to find, invitations were delivered by telephone. The nouveau riche flaunted their insolence and ignorance. One arriviste wife, pleased by the performance of a string quartet she had hired for a soiree, told its members, "With a bit more success, you will be able to enlarge your little orchestra."[2]

For them, life was not bête, except through their own excesses. And for most in France, life was less wretched in many ways than at any time since the war because Paul Doumer, before betraying Briand in December, had presided over the beginning of an economic recovery. During the year, payments toward reconstruction reached their highest level, 17.774 billion francs (for 1920, the total had been 13.084 billion, for 1922, it would be 14.181). That sum provided for the restoration of 43,224 private houses, 5,596 farm structures, 579 public buildings, 501 industrial establishments, 2,807 miles of roads, and 110 miles of railroad. This along with previous efforts since the Armistice, meant that France had rebuilt 117,124 private houses, 16,942 farm structures, 1,486 public buildings, 5,116 industrial establishments, 8,376 miles of roads, and 2,589 miles of railroads. The effect of reconstruction and pensions on the national debt had been stunning, raising it from 175 billion francs at the end of 1918 to 280 billion three years later. In 1913, the national debt had been slightly less than the gross national product; at the end of 1921, it was 270 percent greater. But any fiscal restraint fell before the imperative of restoring the industrial and agricultural capacity of the devastated region. Doumer reaped the benefit: in 1920, exports were only 53.9 percent of imports; in 1921, they reached 86.9 percent.[3]

2. Miquel, *Poincaré*, 416.
3. Sauvy, *Histoire économique,* 1:453, 454, for reconstruction; 1:375–76, for the national debt; 1:297, 477, for balance of payments.

The exchange rate for the franc on currency markets, important for national self-esteem and critical for the eventual repayment of war debts, rebounded substantially. In January 1921, a pound bought 58.16 francs, in December 53.06, a decrease of 8.8 percent; a dollar had been worth 15.77 francs but declined by 19.0 percent to 12.78. As inflation reversed, retail prices fell 18.8 percent: using 1913 as a base 100, their index stood at 384 in January, 312 in December. Wages for the working class dropped in tandem, but less so, the index for them going from 388 to 358, down 7.7 percent. The combination was a welcome appreciation of 7.5 percent in buying power. Reconstruction, some increase in production, and the rise of the franc all made nearly everything more, or at least somewhat more, available. By late February 1921, rationing had ended in restaurants, and lighting in Paris was back to prewar levels. On 1 March, all market controls on coal were lifted. But laws against price gouging, *délit de spéculation illicite*, imposed since 20 April 1916, remained in effect and were used to make an example of several butchers in May. Even rentiers, who rightly thought themselves gouged by the times, felt some relief and could believe a little more strongly that their investments might recover. By December 1921, stocks and bonds paying a variable return rose to 35.9, up 17.3 percent from a year earlier at 30.6—computing their real value adjusted for inflation, using 1913 as a base 100. Those paying a fixed return were at 23.2, up 24.7 percent from 18.6 in December 1920.[4]

Doumer was reputed to be "austere," a description well borne out by his budget-making. Although he spent more money on reconstruction than in 1920—4.690 billion francs more—he reduced total expenditures from 39.644 billion to 32.845 billion, a remarkable and stringent 17.2 percent. All of the new taxes were in force, and they brought in 23.570 billion francs, 1.065 billion more than the year before, permitting Doumer to record a deficit of *only* 9.275 billion francs. But that was a mere 45.9 percent of 1920's 17.139 billion. He would have done even better if industrial production had improved as fast as reconstruction would have predicted, but

4. Sauvy, *Histoire économique,* 1:445, for currency rates; 1:501, for retail prices; 1:511, for wages and buying power; 1:532, 534, for the real value of stocks and bonds; *Le Figaro,* 22, 23, 28 February, 5 May 1921, for rationing in restaurants, lighting in Paris, controls on coal, and butcher price gouging, respectively.

the index stubbornly remained where it had been throughout 1920, in the low 60s, using 1913 as a base 100: 63 in January, 62 in December. Doumer would certainly have achieved an Après-Guerre miracle, running a budgetary surplus, if Briand had done better on reparations. Millerand and Leygues in 1920 extracted 791 billion gold marks (989 billion francs); in 1922, Poincaré would obtain 582 billion gold marks (728 billion francs); for all his maneuvering, Briand managed only 496 billion gold marks (620 billion francs). The difference between his result and Poincaré's, 108 billion francs, would have paid for a great deal and was more than eleven times the deficit. Of course, reparations were trumps in France.[5]

But probably reparations, and for that matter the Upper Silesia question in her native Poland, meant little to Rachel Crakowski. Or to another sliver of French society: their suicides in Paris proclaimed a certain level of desperation that escaped depiction in the improving economic and fiscal statistics and for which the politics of Briand and Poincaré—Elise Enapluche's spectacle aside—had no great meaning. Alexandre Gelle stepped in front of a subway train at the Concorde station. Maximilien Rempallu, a student aged twenty-four, fired a bullet into his heart. Dimitri Boulouris, a fifty-year-old lawyer, Hector Dupuich, a forty-year-old teacher, William Ogiler Hozier, a thirty-four-year-old former lieutenant in the British army, Georges Tillet, a jeweler, Suzanne Dubertha, an actress, Emile Colombe, eighteen, and Charlotte Boileau, twenty-four, shot themselves through the head. Marie Heurtin, Berthe Thomas, Henri Sonie, and the belletrist Jane Chrétien, forty-five, who wrote under the name Simone Bovèse, threw themselves from high windows. Two girls, seventeen and twenty, in the tough working-class suburb of Bagnolet, jumped from the old fortification walls. Henri David and Isaac Fresco, middle-aged wholesale merchants, hanged themselves. For none of them could exact motives be determined.[6]

Other times, the reason—love, or what passed for it—was depressingly

5. Sauvy, *Histoire économique*, 1:513, for the budget; 1:377–90, for taxes; 1:464, for industrial production; 1:452, for reparation totals.

6. *Le Matin*, 3 January (Gelle), 15 April (Boulouris, Hozier, and Sonie), 17 April (Chrétien), 11 May (Dupuich), 8 July (Rempallu), 10 July (girls at Bagnolet), 22 August (Heurtin and Thomas), 23 August (Dubertha), 24 August (David and Fresco), 28 August (Colombe and Boileau), 28 September (Tillet) 1921.

obvious. Danyelle Royer, nineteen, stabbed herself without warning at the apartment of Dr. Maurice Escoffet, forty-five and her mother's physician, whom she had promised to marry. There were rumors that her affections really belonged to a young aviator stationed in Morocco, and she had failed the baccalaureate examination the previous year. Another older-man–younger-woman relationship ended the opposite way. Maurice Minol, thirty-seven, confronted his former fiancée, Berthe Bardet, fired three bullets at her face, and then a fourth through his heart. But an age difference was not essential: René Duclin, twenty-six, shot Marguerite Legloaunée, twenty-four, and then himself, after she broke their engagement. Marie Benest, only sixteen and a bride for a mere eight days, threw herself into the Seine after an argument with her husband. Despite the frigid waters of January, she survived.[7]

There were also straggling victims from the war. A retired Major Eachwind, the only one of ten brothers to survive the fighting, refused to carry on alone. Clément Fitz-Gerald, a mutilé de la guerre from a prominent Irish family, whose father owned an automobile factory in Neuilly, drowned himself in the Seine. A Russian prince, Nikita LaGanoff de Rostowsky, lonely in exile from his country and addicted to morphine, shot himself in the Bois de Boulogne. An anarchist calling himself Jacquelon, convicted along with his mistress in 1918 of intelligence with the Germans, had escaped to Holland. He returned to Paris to take cyanide after leaving a letter declaring his disgust with the world and justice. Charles Paix-Séailles, loosely associated with certain of the *Bonnet rouge* traitors and fortunate to escape their trial with a suspended sentence, shot himself after losing 200,000 francs in a speculation on cacao warrants.[8]

In August 1921, *Le Figaro* published an article on the increasing incidence of suicide, especially among the young, by Raymond Meunier, a psychiatrist well known for his prewar studies of "les âmes en peine"—spirits in torment. He attributed the alarming rise to "precocious perversions, the distractions of contemporary imagination, and the contagion of other suicides possessing easily young brains become more and more susceptible

7. *Le Figaro*, 11, 13 June, 16 July 1921, 4 January 1922, respectively.
8. *Le Figaro*, 26 April (Paix-Séailles), 4, 7 August (Jacquelon and Eachwind, respectively), 29 November (Fitz-Gerald) 1921.

through the effect of the first two causes." Whatever *Le Figaro*'s upper bourgeois readership made of this opaque disquisition, they had a more comprehensible explanation six months earlier in an interview with Marie François Goron, from 1887 to 1894 head of the Sûreté, the criminal investigation bureau of the Paris Police, and since then director of a private detective agency and author of superb memoirs as well as fascinating crime novels. During the war, although in his late sixties, he held an administrative post with military intelligence. Forty years of dealing with criminals convinced Goron that the milieu of the Après Guerre was qualitatively different from that of the past: fathers were absent; mothers were in tears; the bombardment of civilians from the air had produced "a moral disequilibrium greater than is generally understood. The use of the revolver has spread, and often it is the ease of execution that encourages a crime."[9]

Not quite a decade earlier, the notorious Bande à Bonnot had carried out France's first motorized bank robbery—at the Montmartre office of the Société générale on 21 December 1911—when hot pursuit for most of the police meant riding a bicycle. Well-armed and ruthless in shooting witnesses, they were a foretaste of crime in the 1920s. Their closest imitators during the Après Guerre were gangs who after boarding express trains worked their way through the compartments robbing and killing. On 25 July 1921, three bandits riding the Marseille–Paris Limited shot passengers after taking their valuables and killed an agent of the Sûreté générale, the national criminal investigation bureau, "like in the Old West," claimed horrified press reports. Tracked down in Paris five days later, two of them and a police detective were killed in a shoot-out at the place des Ternes, barely a block north of the Champs-Elysées, while the third surrendered in the Latin Quarter. *Le Figaro* took satisfaction that this survivor was already dying from tuberculosis. A lone bandit on the express from Le Havre to Paris in early August was captured on the train by police waiting for imitators.[10]

9. *Le Figaro*, 9 February (Goron), 18 August (Meunier) 1921. For Meunier, see his *Les Ames en peine, les désemparés* (Paris, 1913), *Les Ames en peine, les fous* (Paris, 1913), *Les Ames en peine, les rêveurs* (Paris, 1913). For Goron, see Benjamin F. Martin, *Crime and Criminal Justice Under the Third Republic: The Shame of Marianne* (Baton Rouge, 1990), 58–60.

10. *Le Matin*, 26 July–2, 7 August 1921; *Le Figaro*, 26 July ("Old West"), 1 August (tuberculosis) 1921; for the Bande à Bonnot, see Martin, *Crime and Criminal Justice*, 275–317.

Some spectacular armed robberies of jewelry stores were also reminiscent of the Bande à Bonnot: in Paris, a necklace of ninety pearls valued at 400,000 francs taken from Boucheron's, 650,000 francs worth of precious stones from Lévi's; in Boulogne-sur-Seine, various adornments worth 80,000 francs stolen from the store of a M. Baudet. But more troubling were the routine burglaries and larcenies committed frequently by the young. *Le Figaro*'s Louis Thénet decried this "enfance criminelle" and claimed that in Paris alone, there were seven thousand arrests of juveniles, usually for theft. The trial in October of a gang led by twenty-one-year-old Henriette Miffone—dubbed "la jeune apache"—put a human face on these statistics, even if of "a vulgar and unpleasant ugliness." Too successful too many times before being arrested, she and the mostly younger toughs following her well deserved their reckoning, long sentences at hard labor.[11]

Toward murder, the French public and juries held an ambiguous attitude. The theft of a life, though reprehensible, could arise from a *crime passionnel* and be accorded mitigating circumstances; the theft of property was never excusable: consider Jean Valjean. In January 1921, a Mme de Feuquières was on trial for killing her husband out of jealousy for his alleged affair with Rachel Marais. True, she had "un passé": a previous marriage to an army captain destroyed by "too many trips with a young Italian"; true, despite the claim of firing her pistol in a moment of despair, she pulled the trigger five times. But as her barrister, the distinguished Henri Robert, explained, she was "créole." The jury understood, and she escaped with a suspended sentence. In April, Thérèse Juquelier (née Dehy) shot her husband, Paul, dead after discovering a note "proving" his adultery with a Mlle Proust. She justified herself by the admission of having learned about the infidelity a year earlier and having hoped that it would end. When she found the note, she made accusations to which her husband responded by striking her. Thus she fired in self-defense—and so agreed the judicial officials. Yet how much might be hidden behind the

11. *Le Matin*, 7 May, 20 June, 16 December 1921, for Boucheron, Lévi, and Baudet, respectively; *Le Figaro*, 4 September, 13 October 1921, for Thénet and the description of Miffone, respectively; *La Gazette des tribunaux*, 12–16 October 1921, for the trial of the Miffone gang.

matrimonial veil became obvious when Maurice Barrès revealed a scandal from within his own wealthy family. On 7 June 1920, his niece Suzanne was shot in the face by her husband, Paul Boppe, who then demanded that she call the wound a suicide attempt. She refused, but, pressured by most of her relatives, agreed to report it as an accident if she were granted a separation from Boppe and financial support for herself and their children. Boppe did give her a letter, dated 6 August 1920, acknowledging his guilt and accepting these terms, only to disappear with all the assets he could liquify.[12]

The indulgence granted violence within the family—usually explicable and frequently predictable—emphatically did not extend to violence without, where it struck most often suddenly and was all the more dreadful for its randomness. Irma Sutter, a war widow forty-five years old, was stabbed eighteen times as she closed her stationery store near the Gare du Nord. In always dangerous Bagnolet, Emile Tissier was killed by one of a gang he reported for throwing stones. Jules Bunard, twenty-four, died from a bullet after a dispute at a dance hall. Eugénie Hugen, twenty-nine, was shot dead along a street for reasons unknown. As Alfred Hitchcock once remarked, murder belongs in the home, where the partners in death's pas de deux have at least been introduced. For anonymity itself was frightening, even as it was increasingly characteristic of the Après Guerre. In late August 1921, the pieces of a young woman were found in the Seine, but she was not identified as Marie-Marguerite Berrier, twenty-seven, until nearly a month had passed. The delay was not for want of inquiries from all manner of parents, husbands, and friends. Their pathetic trek to the morgue seeking the fate of someone lost called attention to the phenomenon of an estimated ten thousand women in Paris living under assumed names after deserting a previous existence. Berrier's body was claimed by her mother. Many others were buried unrecognized.[13] Such accounts encouraged a general belief that crime was increasing. Some of the police thought that as well, and about murder, they all were right. In 1913, there

12. *Le Figaro,* 9 January (Feuquières), 15, 16, 28 April (Juquelier), 29 December (Boppe) 1921.

13. *Le Matin,* 9 January (Sutter), 6 June (Tissier), 25 July (Bunard and Hugen), 25 August (woman in pieces), 18 September (Berrier identified) 1921; *Le Figaro,* 29 August 1921, article by Louis Thénet about women living under assumed names.

were 226 cases of unpremeditated homicide (*meutre*), the random, anonymous kind frequently committed in the course of another crime, and 155
of premeditated homicide (*assassinat*), usually for highly personal reasons.
By 1920, the statistics available to readers of the woman-in-pieces story, the
totals were 346 and 177, increases, respectively, of a staggering 53 and still
shocking 14 percent. But otherwise, there was little change from the Belle
Epoque, and grand larcenies even declined from 338 to 321.[14]

One undeniable difference was the spreading traffic in cocaine, which
had begun in the last years of the war. Dr. Maurice de Fleury, one of
France's great neurologists, raised the alarm in *Le Figaro,* warning that "le
coco" was "especially detestable because, not content to lead—like other
illicit drugs—to decadence and renunciation, it breeds wickedness." In a
manner depressingly familiar to Americans late in the twentieth century,
there were reports from the front in a "guerre à la cocaine." It was widely
available in cafes, bars, and nightclubs, the price rising as the hour grew
later. A Dr. Régnier, who abused his status as a physician by providing
cocaine to certain patients, was sentenced to two years in prison, his mistress and accomplice to ten months, and a possibly unwitting pharmacist
to a month. Police patrolman Paul Pinel was arrested for selling cocaine
to a detective posing as a user. Raids rounded up dealers and buyers. At
the beginning of November 1921, a rumor flew that most of this cocaine
was being smuggled from a laboratory in Berlin, permitting further grim
satisfaction that another plague of the Après Guerre had its origin in Germany. The claim had some validity: arrests made at the Gare du Nord on
29 October led to the conviction on 30 December of a certain Kleinmann,
once professor of mathematics in Petrograd, and Gerntsen, formerly of the
Dutch diplomatic service, for acting as the couriers of a Dr. Quillitz of
Berlin and a Count de Buinin of Poland in transporting a kilogram of cocaine to France.[15]

14. France, Ministère de la justice, *Compte générale de l'administration de la justice criminelle* (Paris, 1913, 1920); Marcel Sicot, *Servitude et grandeur policière: Quarante ans à la Sûreté*
(Paris, 1959).

15. *Le Figaro,* 28 June (Fleury), 8, 16, 23 July (Régnier), 25 July, 18 August, 16 September (various arrests), 29 October (Pinel), 1 November, 31 December (Berlin connection)
1921; for Fleury, see his *Manuel pour l'étude des maladies du système nerveux* (Paris, 1904), a
monumental 993 pages.

Blame for yet one more pestilence upon traditional society was placed further east. Late in December 1920, at Tours for the Socialist party congress, the French Left, unified only since 1905, split irretrievably. A relatively "reformist" rump slunk away retaining the name "Socialists," while the "revolutionary" majority accepted the leadership of Moscow, called themselves "Communists," and took possession of the party newspaper, *L'Humanité*. The Bolshevism of unsuccessful strikes and demonstrations in 1919 and 1920 was deploying along the political front. There were immediate efforts to tar them with connections to Germany and Russia, which the Communists obliged by claiming French guilt for the war. The wife of Jacques Sadoul, the officer who had deserted to the Red Army, played her part by demanding a separation of property to protect her interests against a traitor. Conservatives signaled the danger to young minds in the schools by revealing that a teacher at Périgueux was editing and publishing a journal preaching Bolshevism under the title *Prolétaire* and had nearly a hundred subscribers among his colleagues. In the Senate, the aged royalist Dominique Delahaye, a "blasphémateur incorrigible" hated all around for his bigotry, conceded that teachers who died fighting in the trenches were "heroes" but refused this distinction to many of the survivors among them, claiming that fifteen thousand adhered to Moscow's Third International and fifty thousand were members of the Confédération Générale du Travail. Briand's minister of public instruction, Léon Bérard, immediately contested these numbers as fantasy.[16]

Because defamation alone could accomplish only so much, conservatives were overjoyed to exploit revelations of a criminal conspiracy. At the end of January and the beginning of February 1921, detectives in Paris began rounding up Communists for distributing leaflets. The Sûreté had penetrated two propaganda groups, "Proudhon," which concentrated its efforts on workers, and "Clarté," which was aimed at intellectuals. This news drew only minor attention until 5 February and the announcement that three prominent leftists, Amédée Catoné (alias Dunois), former secretary-general of *L'Humanité,* Victor Griffuelhes, former secretary-general

16. *La République française,* 3 January 1921, for Communists and war guilt; *Le Figaro,* 18 January (Mme Sadoul), 2 February (Périgueux) 1921; J.O.S., Débats, 13 April 1921, the characterization of Delahaye by Bérard.

of the C.G.T., and Alfred Clovis Mignot, merely an important labor activist, were under arrest. They had cashed checks totaling 40,000 francs left for them at the American Express office on the rue Scribe by a shadowy Russian agent eventually identified as Alexandre Abramovitch-Zalewsky. To the Sûreté, here was proof that a hostile regime was clandestinely financing propaganda or worse. Even the explanation given by Catoné, Griffuelhes, and Mignot, that the money was to pay the expenses of "communists" "visiting" from other countries, whether true or not, raised the gravest suspicions, and they were charged with "plotting against the security of the state." Tracked to Marseille, Abramovitch-Zalewsky was arrested and returned to Paris along with his wife, Zelma Bertin, and their child. Detectives also ran down two of his couriers, a German, Louis Keim (alias Ker), and a Romanian student named Barber. Within days, the Sûreté had evidence that they had distributed 350,000 francs to various French Communists. A judicial inquiry opened under examining magistrate Louis Jousselin: the proof of the Bolshevik peril appeared at hand.

On 1 March, as the interrogations, searches, and seizures proceeded against Abramovitch-Zalewsky—dubbed the "Eye of Moscow" by the press—and his confederates, the Ministry of Justice began the trial of the ten labor leaders arrested in May 1920 when then-premier Millerand crushed the C.G.T.'s attempt to promote a general strike. Jousselin had also conducted the instruction against them, concluding in their indictment for plotting the overthrow of the state, the same charge alleged against the Abramovitch-Zalewsky conspirators. To many in the government, these men were deserving of condemnation at least as much for their iron allegiance to the Russian Revolution and its spread across Europe as for anything they might have done. The presiding justice, Joseph Marie Drioux, made little pretense of impartiality. The prosecutor, Raoul Bloque-Laroque, was implacable, damning as an intrigue from Moscow the openly avowed plan to spread propaganda, form "soviets," and foment revolution under the cover of labor agitation. But the most notable of the ten, Pierre Monatte, insisted that "a doctrine is not a plot." Testifying for them and for the freedom of expression were Hélène Brion, the teacher given a suspended sentence after her conviction for défaitisme in 1918, and Marc Sangnier, the mystical Christian Socialist deputy long a defender of idealistic causes. The jury sided with indulgence, on 17 March declaring all the defendants not guilty. The verdict boded ill for putting the Eye of Moscow on trial, and on 3 May, Jousselin issued a *non-lieu,* a finding of insufficient grounds to proceed, based on his determination that propaganda was not a threat to the security of the state. As an undesirable alien, Abramovitch-Zalewsky would be expelled, but French Bolsheviks were free to pass out their leaflets.[17]

Great was the disappointment among conservatives. Perhaps coincidentally, Jousselin, whose assignment to these cases as examining magistrate had indicated the favor of high judicial officials, would have to wait five years for his next promotion, until after the election victory in 1924 by the Center-Left Cartel des gauches. In early October, *L'Action française* accused the Communist leaders of simply pocketing Abramovitch-Zalewsky's money, implying that they were as venal as any bourgeois politicians. But perhaps they did not because somebody had to pay for the bomb sent to the American embassy and the others exploded at the Salle Wagram later in the month protesting the sentences for Sacco and Vanzetti.[18]

So often in the Après Guerre, politics led to the bêtises of life. Still later in October 1921, at the congress of the Radical party, Edouard Herriot won cheers when he called for overturning the convictions of Louis Malvy and Joseph Caillaux that stained all Radicals as défaitistes. Malvy had been living in Spain since August 1918, when the Senate as High Court banished him from France for five years because as minister of the interior during the first three years of the war he had been extraordinarily lax toward men and actions later proved traitorous. Caillaux was left to grow sick and infirm behind bars throughout 1918 and most of 1919. When the High Court finally heard his case during the first months of 1920, the senators found him guilty of "damage to the external security of the state," something less than the treason initially charged but défaitisme to be reproved by the loss of political rights for ten years and imprisonment for three, the latter suspended because of the long pretrial incarceration. Malvy and Caillaux before the High Court had been high political theater.

---

17. Kriegel, *Aux origines du communisme,* 2:762–64; the excitement, expectation, and disappointment are readily apparent in *Le Figaro,* 31 January, 1, 4–26 February, 1–3, 8–13, 18 March, 4 May 1921.

18. A.N., BB 6 II, 961, dos. Louis Jousselin; *L'Action française,* 10 October 1921.

As during the Dreyfus Affair, everyone politically aware in France had an opinion, and overwhelmingly in the aftermath of victory, opinions were against them. Now, with the Caillaux verdict barely eighteen months old, was sentiment changing? Was everything open to revision in the Après Guerre? Herriot cautioned that the public was not yet ready for a campaign of rehabilitation, but if Bolsheviks could freely preach their gospel of revolution and soviets, why had Malvy and Caillaux been condemned for wanting peace?[19]

At home in Mamers, Caillaux nursed his health and wrote his own version of défaitisme, *Mes prisons*. His wife, Henriette, found not guilty of murdering Gaston Calmette in 1914 but her private life made a public scandal, typed the manuscript herself. Agents of the Sûreté générale and often journalists, mostly hostile, maintained a constant surveillance. Caillaux retaliated with the trick of walking a large, menacing dog up to them and pretending to let it loose, only to turn around and whistle sardonically as he led the dog away. Even so, he was followed everywhere. Newspapers almost gleefully reported his minor automobile accidents. The Ministry of the Interior was told by its agents that he was cultivating new mistresses even as the wife who had killed for him had her attention fixed on the typewriter. On 16 March 1921, Caillaux spoke publicly for the first time since his trial, before the League of the Rights of Man at Grenoble. Some rowdies from the Camelots du roi, shock troops of the reactionary royalist integral-nationalist Action française, were waiting, and there was a scuffle that nearly got out of hand. A week later in the Chamber of Deputies, Paul Marie Dugueyt, a war hero recipient of the Croix de Guerre with two citations, decried Caillaux's despicable decision to make a speech on the seventh anniversary of Calmette's death and demanded that he be gagged. Marc Sangnier defended unfettered public expression no matter how reprehensible, as he had at the trial of the ten labor activists. "With that attitude, we would have lost the war!" André Tardieu interrupted disgustedly. Always ready with blackmail, Léon Daudet threatened the minister of the interior, Pierre Marraud, with Malvy's fate if he did not act swiftly to silence the "traitor." Perceiving little danger from Caillaux or to himself, Marraud did nothing. Between May and July, Caillaux

19. *Le Figaro,* 29 October 1921.

wrote ten articles for *Le Progrès civique* on financial and economic affairs, but they did not attract much notice. Herriot's comment to the Radical party in October was an admission that Marraud was correct.[20]

Almost exactly four years earlier, Poincaré had pondered who to make premier with the war in the balance, Georges Clemenceau or Joseph Caillaux, the choice between fighting to the finish or asking terms. They had been then the two poles of French politics. Now, they were little more than symbols of a time so recent yet so much the past and almost irrelevant. Caillaux had to console his bitterness with a large dog, memoirs that few read, a speech at Grenoble, hardly a center of political significance. Back from his long trip, back from receiving an honorary degree from Oxford, Clemenceau was regarded almost as a curiosity, perhaps a relic. "I ask only one thing," he told journalists, "that you leave me alone." In October 1921, he agreed to emerge from his Vendée retreat for the consecration of a monument at nearby Sainte-Hermine, where he declaimed a valedictory: "What does it serve to say, 'Our fathers were great men,' if from their tombs they judge us diminished? The poilus know they have nothing to fear from History. But they are 'today'—already I am 'yesterday'—and you are 'tomorrow.' The fallen whom we honor say, 'It is your turn now.' "[21]

This exhortation begged the question "for what"? The road back to a France increasingly recalled nostalgically as la Belle Epoque was destroyed far more completely than the devastated region. If Briand, Poincaré, Millerand, and, in a different way Caillaux, remained from the prewar leadership, other notable figures were gone—or, as Clemenceau put it later, "going away"—in 1921 alone: Joseph Reinach, the great Dreyfusard, Emile Combes, anticlericalist supreme, Maurice Bernard, barrister for the guilty powerful like Henri Rochette, Joseph Caillaux, and Henriette Caillaux, Emile Boutroux, philosopher, teacher of Emile Durkheim and Henri Bergson. Before the war, a "gentleman" with however modest a private

20. Joseph Caillaux, *Mes prisons* (Paris, 1920); Jean-Claude Allain, *Joseph Caillaux* (2 vols.; Paris, 1978–81), 2:283–98; *Le Figaro*, 12 January 1921, for the accidents; A.N., F7 12952 3, "Notes Jean," 29, 30 January 1924, with the reports indicating that the relationships were long-standing since the war; J.O.C., Débats, 24 March 1921.

21. *Le Figaro*, 23 June (degree), 12 September (request for privacy), 3 October (Sainte-Hermine) 1921.

income might plan a career in an honorable but poorly paid profession, as a magistrate or an academic. The ruin of rentiers and the inflation of the Après Guerre, made that choice mean hardships and frequently penury. Lucien Herr, for long the librarian of the Ecole normale supérieure, had to take on proofreading and translations to support the family he recklessly acquired in middle age. Other choices were hardly more sure. As economic competition became keener, small retailers with higher expenses and higher markups fell to department stores: there were 2,127 bankruptcies among them in 1921. The collapse of confidence schemes and speculations filled the newspapers. Proposed solutions to unemployment included the improbable digging of a tunnel beneath the English Channel.[22]

"Tout était à reviser, tout à rapprendre"—everything was open to revision, everything had to be relearned. The telephone system seemed always unreliable. The Sûreté was hiring women as detectives—*policières*—and praising their intuition in solving cases. The ideal of feminine beauty shifted from the fleshy and voluptuous as girls were encouraged to adopt vigorous exercise, as new patent medicines pictured winged Cupid measuring the waist of an attractive woman while warning, "Be careful, Madame, you are beginning to get fat, and to get fat is to look old!" "Le basketball" was touted as the "new sport"—but for the short and individualistic French? Movies, advertisements, and auto shows promoted motor cars as the essence of modern life, while accidents involving them made crossing the street in Paris an adventure and prominent figures, such as Léon Bulot, attorney general of the Cour de Cassation, France's supreme court, died in their wrecks. The grand department store Samaritaine held its annual sale of furs in November 1921—for those women who could afford them. In January 1922, some women who could not began throwing vitriol on new coats in the posh Madeleine quarter. As an appropriate accompaniment to this disarray, the Dada movement, launched at Zurich in 1916, was brought to Paris by the painter François Picabia. Celebrating the cult of the irrational, publishing incoherent mani-

---

22. Antoinette Blum, ed., *Correspondance entre Charles Andler et Lucien Herr, 1891–1926* (Paris, 1992), 202; Chastenet, *Histoire de la Troisième République*, 5:228, for retail stores; *Le Figaro*, 12–13 April (the problem of salaries for magistrates and academics), 19 June (confidence schemes) 1921, 10 January 1922 (tunnel proposal); *Le Gaulois*, 5 October 1921 (confidence schemes).

festos, presenting nonsense poetry and drama, erecting the absurd as a principle of life, its adepts proclaimed that the name and their actions signified the negation of everything. Even the weather was miserable in 1921, hot and humid throughout the summer, then an early snowy winter. More than twenty Parisians were cited for removing too many clothes during the heat, only Elise Enapluche during the cold. With F. Scott Fitzgerald's Dick Diver, so many in the Après Guerre could say, "All my beautiful lovely safe world blew itself up here with a great gust of high explosive love." None of this descended remotely to the depths of wretchedness that tore apart the life of Rachel Crakowski, but it still meant that life was bête.[23]

23. Chastenet, *Histoire de la Troisième République,* 5:316, for the quotation; *Le Matin,* 28 September, 1 October 1921 (telephone problems); *Le Figaro,* 13 July (heat), 22 (physical exercise), 24 (Cupid), 26 (*policières*), 31 (basketball) August, 8–9 October (XVI Salon de l'Automobile), 4 (fur sale), 9 (cold) November 1921, 10 (Bulot), 29, 31 (*vitrioleuses*) January 1922; Mary Louise Roberts, "Samson and Delilah Revisited: The Politics of Women's Fashions in 1920s France," *American Historical Review* 98 (June 1993): 657–84, and *Civilization Without Sexes: Reconstructing Gender in Postwar France, 1917–1927* (Chicago, 1994); Michel Sanouillet, *Dada à Paris* (Paris, 1965); Hans Richter, *Dada Art and Anti-Art* (New York, 1965); Maurice Nadeau, *Histoire du surréalisme* (Paris, 1964); F. Scott Fitzgerald, *Tender Is the Night* (New York, 1933), 57.

4

■ ■ ■

Il court s'abstenir

When old and ill and returned to his native Lorraine, Raymond Poincaré
chose a bedroom facing east, to stare into the distance toward Germany,
to repeat, "They will come again." Death in 1934 spared his witnessing
the fulfillment of this anathema upon France's leadership during the
1920s, above all his own during the Après Guerre. For he did not "do better" than Aristide Briand.

The public Poincaré was the personification of bourgeois ideals: confident, polished, reserved, formal, meticulous, scrupulous, possessed of a
prodigious memory. The private man was brittle, curt, shrill, indecisive,
emotional, beset with doubt. In 1913, immediately before his election to
the Elysée, he nearly withdrew his candidacy for president of the Republic
when he learned how enemies on the Left, Joseph Caillaux foremost,
threatened to damage his support among Catholic legislators by revealing
that his marriage lacked church sanction. During the war years, he preserved his sangfroid only by committing every thought and emotion to
paper, plaguing cabinet ministers with streams of memorandums in his
cramped handwriting. When he needed rest most, worn out at the end of
his septennate, the sudden death of his brother overwhelmed him. To his
sister-in-law he wrote in torment: "I am haunted by the memory of our
poor Lucien. I cannot get used to the idea that I shall never see him again
. . . I was the one who was supposed to go first. I always thought that we
would grow old together, Lucien and you, Henriette and I . . . that we

would spend our future years staying with each other in the Meuse at Tri-aucourt and Sampigny. And now all of that is broken in pieces."[1]

Had it ever been otherwise? Poincaré was born at Bar-le-Duc in 1860, the son of a government civil engineer and bred in the obdurate patriotism of Lorraine that never forgot the humiliation of Prussian soldiers occupying the town for three years after his tenth birthday. Notebooks reveal a childhood and adolescence consumed by the necessity to achieve, lying awake at night worried about small errors in his Latin and Greek compositions, disappointed that he received only the second highest score in German. At the Lycée Louis-le-Grand in 1876–77 as final preparation for the *baccalauréat ès sciences,* he had as classmates Alfred Baudrillart, the future cardinal, and Maurice Paléologue, the future ambassador to Russia and secretary-general of the Quai d'Orsay, but it was Poincaré who won the *prix d'excellence* and carried away first place in philosophy, physics, mathematics, and natural history. In three more years, by 1880, he took his law degree from the Faculté de Droit in Paris, yet he also had managed to complete his required one-year military service (at Nancy, with the Twenty-sixth Infantry Regiment) and to write not only four bad novels but much mediocre poetry—none of it published.

Settling in Paris, Poincaré prepared for a career as a barrister, and like so many of the future *avocats-rois* of late-nineteenth-century France, slipped into politics through journalism, writing for the centrist *Le Voltaire.* In 1887, he was elected to the Chamber of Deputies, where he quickly displayed an unusual grasp of budgetary complexities that would make him minister of finance three times by 1906. But first he was minister of education, in April 1893, when Charles Dupuy made him the youngest—at age thirty-two and eight months—member of a cabinet under the Third Republic. The record would last a single year, until Dupuy made Louis Barthou minister of public works. Formal and aloof, Poincaré had mostly "amis," not "camarades," among the other legislators, with exceptions for Gabriel Hanotaux, Alexandre Millerand, and above all, Barthou, whom he granted the right to *tutoyer.*

The distance and reserve were more than a personality trait. Political life, Poincaré discerned early, was slightly disgusting. For a decade, from

1. Payen, *Poincaré,* 411.

1896 to 1906, he declined every offer of a ministry and twice the opportunity to form a cabinet himself. After sixteen years in the Chamber, he won
election to the Senate in 1903 and found its older members and quieter
proceedings more to his liking. His own faction, the Progressives, moderates belonging to the large centrist umbrella organization the Alliance républicaine démocratique, were too often, he concluded, sterile advocates
of "l'égoisme bourgeois." Government in general he viewed darkly as an
intrigue of entreaties and favors. For refuge, he returned to law, establishing at the Palais de Justice a reputation for probity and eloquence that was
rewarded in his election to the Académie française in 1908. He refused to
lead, but, distressed by the zealotry of both Left and Right—especially in
the Dreyfus Affair—he had no one to follow. "Il court s'abstenir!"—he
runs to abstain—was the mocking jest as Poincaré hurried from the courts
to the Chamber of Deputies during these years not to support, not to oppose, but to vote neither.[2]

The aridity of this life was allayed by the entrance of Henriette Benucci.
As a young girl immediately out of convent school, she consented to an
arranged marriage with an American of Irish descent, older, distinguished, and moneyed, living in Paris. Several years later, bankruptcy sent
him fleeing across the Atlantic. Left behind, she obtained a divorce but
undertook to pay some of his debts by giving private lessons in Italian.
Poincaré fell in love with her from the moment of their introduction, but
characteristically, he hesitated long before asking her hand. Because her
first husband was still alive, marriage in the church was impossible, and
their wedding on 17 August 1904 was at a Paris *mairie*. As a wife, she cos-
seted his sensitivity and made herself a buffer to his brittleness. But the
least chill still sent him retreating to his library, and especially after his
father died in 1911 and his mother two years later, all forms of death affected him deeply. He made a cause of protecting trees. He loved animals
and opposed vivisection. And of his Siamese cats, his collies, and his sheep-
dogs, he asked: "In what way are they lower animals? Is not the instinct
that guides them . . . superior in many respects to our most learned and
subtle reasoning? I discover in them a sense of logic as profound as that of

---

2. Miquel, *Poincaré,* 23–190; Keiger, *Poincaré,* 1–11, 14–102; Payen, *Poincaré,* 9–280,
quotation about the Progressives from 185.

mankind and a refinement of which many among us appear completely incapable."[3]

Yet clearly this marriage provided a redoubt from which Poincaré was willing to sally forth claiming the leadership predicted for him since the early 1890s. In 1906, he agreed to serve as minister of finance in Jean Sarrien's brief six-month cabinet with Georges Clemenceau and Aristide Briand. The following year brought the first of twelve elections to the executive committee of the Paris Bar. At the end of the next came election to the Académie française. When confrontation with Germany during the Agadir Affair created an atmosphere of revived nationalism by the beginning of 1912, Poincaré, the patriot from Lorraine, became an obvious choice to head a cabinet, and this time he did not refuse. A year of his rigor had cabaret singers chanting, "Il a les poings, poings, poings, il a les poings carrés"—"clenched fists" evocative of his policy as well as his name. A year of his rigor also had many of France's political leaders urging that he continue these policies from the Elysée, enough of them to elect him president of the Republic on 17 January 1913.

Yet even this supreme honor was tainted. Clemenceau, champion of legislative dominance, rightly suspected that Poincaré would be no figurehead and well recalled his refusal to serve in the first and only Tiger cabinet after Sarrien stepped down in the fall of 1906. When political threats failed to deter Poincaré's candidacy, and then maneuvers to prevent his election, Clemenceau sent the letter breaking all contact. Clemenceau's opposition was based on principle, Caillaux's on spite, the certainty that his conception of Franco-German amity based on French subservience would guarantee seven years of political oblivion during a Poincaré presidency. Caillaux was behind the blackmail of revealing Henriette's past: not merely the civil marriage but her illegitimate birth and their years of cohabiting before the ceremony at the *mairie*. Poincaré held his Catholic supporters with a frank admission of these facts and a promise to seek church sanction if ever possible. And then kept it: a news photograph published in the United States brought the report that Henriette's first husband had died in 1909; Poincaré's former classmate Baudrillart, as

3. Payen, *Poincaré*, 283–85, 315–22, quotation from 321; Keiger, *Poincaré*, 11–14, 102–5.

yet only a monsignor, verified it and, with the explicit approval of the cardinal-archbishop of Paris, Joseph Amette, performed the religious ceremony in May 1913. Almost as much danger had come from a stunning absence of political sense by his old friend Millerand at the Ministry of War, who on 9 January restored to reserve rank Lieutenant Colonel Mercier Du Paty de Clam, a chief tormenter of Alfred Dreyfus forced to retire from the army in 1900. All of the partially buried passions from a decade and a half earlier burned white-hot for three days, until Poincaré formally disavowed the action and accepted Millerand's resignation.[4]

He endured all this to become, he would say, the "prisonnier de l'Elysée," an admission that he had not magnified the executive. He did try: in 1913, through the cabinet of his political ally Briand and then that of his best political friend Barthou, Poincaré continued the nationalist program by lengthening required military service, but Clemenceau and Caillaux gained a measure of revenge in overthrowing both before the end of the year. And so Poincaré joined with Briand and Barthou to sponsor Gaston Calmette's campaign in Le Figaro to destroy Caillaux: a novel use of presidential power that disgraced its target at the cost of Calmette's life. When the war followed immediately, de facto political power for long resided with the military high command until it became clear that they could only maintain, not end, the stalemate on the western front. Yet neither could the politicians, who to some degree were reduced to national cheerleaders, trying to uphold national nerve and national morale. Not always well: in January 1917, when Poincaré and Briand, France's president and premier, arrived late at Dieppe for a ceremony to award the Croix de Guerre, the rows of soldiers waiting in pouring rain greeted them sullenly, provoking Briand's comment, "If you value your popularity, this sort of thing must not happen again!"[5]

Only one civilian truly dominated the military during the war, Clemenceau, for whom Poincaré had the deepest personal antipathy. In November 1917, the stakes for France were clear, paix défaitiste or guerre à

4. Keiger, Poincaré, 105–50; Miquel, Poincaré, 191–312; Payen, Poincaré, 323–407; Martin, Albert de Mun, 258–64.

5. Poincaré, Au service de la France, vols. 3–8; Miquel, Poincaré, 312–62; Suarez, Briand, 4:119, for the remark at Dieppe.

outrance; as Poincaré put it to Henry Franklin-Bouillon: "It is necessary to choose between Caillaux and Clemenceau. My choice is made." Rejecting Caillaux was easy, accepting Clemenceau difficult: "The Tiger arrives. He has grown stout. His deafness is worse. His intelligence remains intact. But his health? His will? I fear that one or the other has faltered, and I sense more and more the peril of the adventure." Clemenceau won the war his way, negotiated the peace his way, and tolerated no interference. Poincaré departed the Elysée one of the nation's heroes because victory has many fathers.[6]

But like so many in France, that victory for Poincaré was hollow. To the stress of the war years, the frustration of his relative impotence as head of state, and his conviction that the Treaty of Versailles was fatally flawed was added the death of his brother. He had entered the Elysée with a fortune of two million francs from his career as a barrister and had donated almost all of it to charities serving the wounded and the survivors of the dead. He would make another fortune writing for the newspapers and magazines that vied for his opinions, but when he described movingly the plight of rentiers in the altered economic world of the Après Guerre, he understood it firsthand. Elected to the Senate a week before his presidential term ended, Poincaré monitored Après-Guerre policy as chairman of the committee on foreign affairs. In January 1920, he also became the first president of the Reparations Commission but resigned four months later in May to protest Millerand's willingness to settle for 120 billion gold marks. Nevertheless, he did not so much complain about the general policy adopted since 1920 by the cabinets under Millerand, Leygues, and Briand—Clemenceau's conception of Germany contained through Anglo-French partnership was the essence of the treaty—as about their lack of rigor in carrying it through. Poincaré initially had some confidence in Briand, based on long acquaintance with his cleverness. But by January 1922, a year of smooth promises amid eloquent speeches had yielded little more than David Lloyd George's golf lesson at Cannes. As president of the Republic, Millerand wavered in his support. The Bloc national majority was

6. Poincaré, *Au service de la France,* vols. 9–10, the quotations from 9:367, 370; Keiger, *Poincaré,* 151–268; Miquel, *Poincaré,* 362–403. For an extreme example of Clemenceau's unwillingness to accept even suggestions from Poincaré, see Duroselle, *Clemenceau,* 710.

restive if still uncertain. In the cabinet, Barthou, friend of both Briand and Poincaré but aware of the prevailing political wind, provoked an insurgency. Briand knew betrayal well from long experience, and as he had from Jeanne Giraudau eighteen years earlier, he would be the one to go. "Others," he said, "will do better!"

But exactly how "other" could Poincaré be? Incontestably, there was a change of mood, captured in the editorial of *Le Figaro*'s Louis Latzarus: "A man of state has spoken. Best of all, a man. For during the past year, a politician has enchanted the legislature with specious words. . . . Finally, we sense that France has a government worthy of the name." In Germany, Gustav Stresemann, leader of the right-center Deutsche Volkspartei, warned that Poincaré would defend "every comma of the Versailles Treaty with fervor becoming a knight of the Holy Grail." Before the Chamber of Deputies, Poincaré himself was more the legalist than the quester. He was assuming power, he declared, to guarantee respect for the treaty at a time when "shameless propaganda" had slandered France's efforts to gain what was rightfully hers, at a time when Germany was pleading bankruptcy while growing economically more powerful daily. Germany would have to pay reparations because only thereby could France's fiscal house be put in order—and he meant to do that, with his symbol the approval of the annual budget on time, as before the war, "returning to a regularity too long abandoned." France needed allied support for financial controls on Germany and thus would attend Lloyd George's Genoa conference, pending a pledge that no revision of the Versailles settlement could even be discussed. The new discipline also had a domestic front: "My government will tolerate nothing that impairs order or attacks established institutions. We must have an environment of calm as we make critical decisions." To this appeal of union sacrée before the enemy, the Chamber of Deputies responded by voting confidence 472 to 107.[7]

The Chambre bleu horizon, it seemed, finally had a leader to its liking, the personification of its ideas. The acute literary critic Albert Thibaudet noted at this moment, "I do not know what verdict history will render on Poincaré, but if severe—and that does not seem out of the question to

---

7. Latzarus in *Le Figaro*, 20 January 1922; Stresemann quoted in Miquel, *Poincaré*, 444; Keiger, *Poincaré*, 268–73; J.O.C., Débats, 19 January 1922.

me—the flock will have to share responsibility with the shepherd." Yet that did not quite make Poincaré the man of the Bloc national. For he kept on twelve of Briand's cabinet members and, although both declined, offered places to André Tardieu, chief clemenciste, and Edouard Herriot, leader of the Radical party and defender of Caillaux. Before the Chamber, he declared that while he wanted a solid majority for his policies, he cared little about its composition. And thus from the start, he disappointed Tardieu and especially Georges Mandel, who since October had railed at Briand's willingness to stand on a centrist majority that threatened the solidity of the Bloc national by permitting alliances with the Radicals. In ironic contrast to *Le Figaro*'s Latzarus, they wanted a "politician" ruling with a disciplined majority of the Center-Right, while Poincaré preferred to be a "statesman" presiding over a government of national union.[8]

When Briand resigned, Poincaré commented, "The politics of slippage have accomplished their task: there is no longer any treaty." He meant that accommodation since 1919 had brought France to the present pass— Germany in default, Britain hostile, the United States aloof. The most urgent issue was to clear up the debris from the now-wrecked conference at Cannes. There, Lloyd George had proposed a pact under which Britain would defend France in the case of unprovoked German aggression, this pledge vitiated by the absence of any military convention, a duration of just ten years—during which France would be already occupying the Rhineland—and only a promise of consultation if Germany violated the demilitarized zones. In rejecting the offer, Briand reminded Lloyd George about the importance of the Rhineland clauses for the containment of Germany and sought his support for maintaining the postwar boundaries in eastern Europe. Without much hope for progress, Poincaré renewed the discussion because with his principal diplomatic adviser, Emmanuel de Peretti de la Rocca, the director of political affairs at the Quai d'Orsay, he was convinced that France could not remain a great power in the face of German recovery except in close alliance with Britain. The choice was therefore stark: obtain the alliance or prevent the recovery. Their draft of 23 January insisted on a British guarantee of Rhineland demilitarization,

8. Miquel, *Poincaré,* 441–49, Thibaudet quoted 448; Keiger, *Poincaré,* 273–94; Sherwood, *Georges Mandel,* 72–74.

rapid completion of a military convention, to last for thirty years, and—to assuage French honor—reciprocity: France guaranteeing Britain against Germany as Britain did France. Lloyd George and Lord Curzon demurred, claiming that Poincaré was demanding a permanent French presence on the Rhine and hence continental hegemony, underwritten by the British. Yet they held out the possibility of compromise in return for acquiescence at Genoa.

That lure might have attracted Briand but never Poincaré, who saw only danger in a conference devoted to resurrecting Germany and Russia when France had no assurances on reparations and security. Peretti de la Rocca, anti-German and anti-Bolshevik, needed no encouragement to devise complications. On 5 February, Poincaré conditioned French participation on an absolute prohibition against discussions bearing on the peace treaties, insisted that any negotiation with Bolshevik leaders be contingent on their honoring the tsarist debt, asked that invitations be extended to the new eastern European states—mostly anti-German, anti-Russian, pro-French—and called for extensive preliminary reports certain to delay the proposed opening date of early March. Having done this much to undermine the conference in advance, Poincaré declined to represent France at Genoa himself. The trusted Barthou, now minister of justice, would go in his stead with the brief to block anything potentially injurious to French treaty rights.[9]

The foreign affairs committee of the Senate rewarded this new stiffer line toward Great Britain with a resolution of support on 3 February, and the Chamber's committee followed six days later. Jacques Roujon, *Le Figaro*'s foreign policy analyst, led the cheering in the press with a month-long series of columns. Sometimes his language betrayed too precisely the fears preoccupying public opinion: "Does Lloyd George dream of forcing Poincaré to continue the policies of Briand? . . . He endeavors to lock the French government into the provisional accords prepared during the foolish conference at Cannes." But when British acceptance of French conditions for Genoa followed a meeting between Poincaré and Lloyd George at Boulogne on 25 February, he crowed, "At Cannes, under the pretext

9. On these issues, see Walter A. McDougall, *France's Rhineland Diplomacy, 1914–1924: The Last Bid for a Balance of Power in Europe* (Princeton, 1978), 177–88.

of realism, the rights of France were abandoned without their even being defended. The arrival of Poincaré to power has halted this debacle." *Le Temps, Le Matin,* and *L'Intransigeant* published accounts of Bolshevik horrors in Russia that bolstered the official resistance to any concessions. When Louis Loucheur, one of Briand's ministers not retained by Poincaré, broke ranks even slightly during a speech to industrialists at Lyon by suggesting that business might be done with Bolsheviks if the tsarist debt was paid, he was attacked roundly, Roujon ridiculing his "too active imagination."[10]

Poincaré's task of rallying national feeling was simplified by a serious incident involving French troops serving in Upper Silesia as part of an interallied force to maintain order. On 31 January, after confiscating weapons hidden at a house in Petersdorff, a company of the Twenty-seventh Light Infantry battalion was ambushed by a band of German civilians throwing grenades. Three soldiers were killed, twenty more wounded, eight seriously. French military leaders made twelve arrests, among them two local officials, and intensified the search for other caches of arms, in less than a week seizing 46 machine guns, 1,800 grenades, 150,000 rifle cartridges, 50 shells for 77mm cannon, and 400 shells for 105mm cannon—all from Germany. Although Charles Laurent, France's ambassador to Berlin, demanded sanctions, Germany's foreign minister, Walther Rathenau, declined all responsibility for territory not under German sovereignty—and had international law, if not morality, on his side. Poincaré could therefore substitute rhetoric for action when he addressed the deputies on 17 February: the guilty Germans he described as members of the vicious Hofer Freikorps; justice, he insisted, would be carried out by the interallied commission in Upper Silesia; France's dead fallen in the cause of making peace would be remembered, he declared, with "eternal gratitude." An emotional Chamber voted unanimously, 506 to 0, solidarity with these words.[11]

If only reparations were even remotely as simple. On 13 January 1922,

10. Roujon in *Le Figaro,* 29–31 January, 2–3, 5, 8–11, 13–17, 19–24, 26–27 February 1922, quotations about Lloyd George from 21, 27 February; quotation about Loucheur from 22 February. See *Le Temps,* 12, 14, 23 February 1922; *Le Matin,* 25 February 1922; *L'Intransigeant,* 22 February 1922.

11. J.O.C., Débats, 17 February 1922, and press coverage since 1 February 1922.

facing certain German default, the Reparations Commission granted a moratorium on the payment of 500 million gold marks due 15 January, but with important stipulations. Beginning on 18 January, Germany was to make partial payments every ten days of 31 million gold marks, although that meant relief from approximately two-thirds the amount agreed upon only the previous May. And by 28 January, German leaders were to submit a detailed fiscal program to the Reparations Commission by which through guarantees for the budget and for the amount of currency in circulation—meaning the control of inflation and thus the value of the mark on world currency markets—they could meet their further obligations for the year.

Poincaré considered this second proviso vital, for like many in France, he believed that Germany was engaging in a "faillite frauduleuse"— fraudulent bankruptcy: the government encouraged inflation that decreased the value of the mark and so enabled German industrialists to win export markets while making payment of reparations in gold or francs or pounds impossible. Poincaré had to make reparations "possible," and from France's experience since the war he concluded that there were only two alternatives. The first and less contentious was to build on the demand of the Reparations Commission for fiscal restraints. If deflationary policies were imposed on Germany, the mark would strengthen while the industrial recovery, deprived of some export markets, might be curbed. Germany could thereby be "controlled" and, in recognizing its obligations, even begin to cooperate. Then, Poincaré believed, the reparations total might be "mobilized"—Millerand's goal during the diplomatic meetings of 1920—through American loans to Germany once repayment appeared likely. Involving the Americans was now all the more important because during the previous nine months the United States had complicated severely the problems of postwar economic revival. By the Emergency Tariff Act of 1921, the Congress reacted to recession by strictly limiting imports, many of them from Europe. And in February 1922, it created the World War Debt Funding Commission, an undeniable warning that the loans made to France and Great Britain would not be forgiven. To pay the United States, France had to have reparations from Germany; American loans to Germany would make the process considerably easier.

But would the Germans accept further controls and would the Reparations Commission impose them? Whenever such restraints had been considered before, Great Britain described them as "Ottomanization"—a reference to the nineteenth-century impositions by Europeans on the Ottoman Empire—and raised the issue of infringing on German sovereignty. Britain had agreed to the January 1922 conditions as the only means of preventing a declaration of default and did not want to go further. As for Germany, recalcitrance had paid handsomely; why change a winning game? If the Germans resisted and the British refused to follow France's lead, the Americans would never offer the loans. Poincaré knew that he would then be forced to his second and much more dangerous alternative, to coerce Germany by seizing territory and productive guarantees in its industrial heartland, the Ruhr. The British admitted that France would have that right under the treaty if Germany were found in voluntary default by the Reparations Commission, but as Lloyd George had told Briand in May 1921, France would act without British support and risk the end of their partnership.[12]

Ironically, a self-sufficient France had been Poincaré's goal in the peace negotiations, but now, granted the responsibility of action, he recoiled before the implications of standing alone. On 2 February, he met with his successor as France's representative on the Reparations Commission, Louis Dubois, about how best to make Germany attractive to American investment. Three weeks later, before the Chamber of Deputies, he endorsed the idea of an international loan based on German credit. But there was an edge to his words as he reported on the conclusion by the Reparations Commission that the numbers in Germany's proposed fiscal program did not add up to much reform. Sensing that Poincaré meant to blame all the current difficulties on his predecessor, Loucheur interjected that he and Briand had German promises at Cannes in writing. Poincaré replied icily, "The documents that I am aware of do not satisfy me at all." There was also a sharper tone to many of the foreign affairs columns in the Paris press. Lieutenant Colonel Frédéric Reboul in *Le Temps* called for retaining Düsseldorf—occupied since March 1921—and for direct allied oversight in Berlin of the German economy; Jacques Bainville in *L'Action française*

---

12. Trachtenberg, *Reparation in World Politics*, 213–31; McDougall, *France's Rhineland Diplomacy*, 199–200; Suarez, *Briand*, 5:410–11.

agreed. Henry Bidou, formerly of the *Journal des débats,* took over at *Le Figaro* from Roujon in a shake-up following its sale to a consortium led by perfume magnate François Coty and expressed the poincariste position perfectly: "Let's see matters as they are. Germany's design is to efface the clauses of the Versailles Treaty. It is firmly resolved to pay only what cannot be avoided. No doubt is possible. Every concession we make to our former enemy will be followed immediately by new efforts to wrench from us yet another. A settlement is agreed upon, and at once it must be modified. Nothing will ever be concluded."[13]

Although leery of forceful action and closer in spirit to Briand than Poincaré, Dubois did his part by winning a unanimous vote of the Reparations Commission on 21 March to offer the German government a continuation of the partial payment agreement only in return for additional fiscal controls to be accepted by 31 May, above all the imposition of 40 billion marks in new taxes. The British were brought along by the hope of French cooperation at the Genoa conference now scheduled to open on 10 April. Would potential American lenders be satisfied? For the moment, at least, the question was moot because on 27 March, Chancellor Josef Wirth declared to the Reichstag that the controls were unacceptable, and Rathenau, the foreign minister, repeated the rejection two days later. By the time this German protest was formally delivered to the Reparations Commission on 7 April, Poincaré had inadvertently revealed his frustration. During a presentation before the deputies on 3 April of the French strategy for the Genoa conference—after which they rewarded him with a vote of confidence 484 to 78—he permitted Tardieu to goad him into a shrill exchange about the degree to which each maintained a similarity between deeds and words, Poincaré saying from the tribune of the Chamber: "I am older than you, Monsieur Tardieu, and I pride myself on having always conformed my speech to my actions and my votes to my promises. May you be able to say as much when you have arrived at my age."[14]

The portents for Genoa were surely grim and became more so on the

13. J.O.C., Débats, 23 February 1922; *Le Temps,* 11, 16 March 1922; *L'Action française,* 20 March 1922; *Le Figaro,* 10 March 1922.

14. J.O.C., Débats, 3 April 1922; Trachtenberg, *Reparation in World Politics,* 240–42; McDougall, *France's Rhineland Diplomacy,* 201.

eve of the conference when eleven more French soldiers in Upper Silesia were killed investigating a booby-trapped arms cache at Gleiwitz. Poincaré's close friend Alfred Capus, once again editor of *Le Figaro,* tapped the mood even if his language was high-flown: "France, by her resistance to German imperialism and to Russian barbarism, maintains alone the peace she is accused of compromising. Her rights are the rights of mankind. To incarnate a higher civilization is her historical role, and she plays it this time before a malevolent gallery with more integrity and brilliance than ever." At Genoa, Barthou resorted to earthy metaphor, but the sentiment was the same: "It is humiliating for a French statesman to see himself constrained to repeat on all occasions that France is resolutely pacific. We are placed in the situation of a wife entirely faithful to her husband whose constancy is systematically questioned. In the end, she revolts, and how can she be blamed?" When Lloyd George opened the conference by claiming that there were no more victors or vanquished, only Europeans who had to work together for the good of all, he seemed to justify the French sense of standing alone: what, after all, did the Versailles Treaty, its war-guilt clause, and reparations mean without winners and losers? But even Lloyd George had to profess astonishment when Grigori Chicherin, Soviet commissar for foreign affairs, countered the demand that the Bolsheviks assume the tsarist debt with one for reparations because of Western support for White forces during the civil war. The failure of the conference was manifest less than a week after it began when Rathenau slipped away with Chicherin to Rapallo on 16 April to sign the pact of the outcasts, announcing trade agreements and the mutual renunciation of civil and military claims; secret provisions allowed Germany to breech allied demilitarization rules by hiding outlawed armaments on Russian soil. Clearly, Bolsheviks and Germans had long been negotiating this alignment, which made nonsense of the premise behind the Genoa conference. Although Barthou proposed packing up immediately, the discussions limped on hopelessly until 19 May.[15]

15. *Le Figaro,* 12, 14 April 1922, respectively, for Capus and Barthou; see generally Carole Fink, *The Genoa Conference: European Diplomacy, 1921–1922* (Chapel Hill, 1984), and Stephen White, *The Origins of Detente: The Genoa Conference and Soviet-Western Relations, 1921–1922* (New York, 1985); for reaction to the Rapallo pact, see Pertinax in *L'Echo de Paris,* 18, 20 April 1922; René D'Aral in *Le Gaulois,* 17 April 1922; Edmond Laskine in *La*

As if Poincaré's first alternative were not already sufficiently beleaguered, five days after the Rapallo pact the World War Debt Funding
Commission officially asked the French government to submit a plan for
repaying the nearly 20 billion francs owed on American loans. The moment had come for unveiling the second, to encourage through its likely
consequences some revision in the current impasse and, if not, to serve as
fair warning when it became French policy. On 24 April, speaking at Bar-
le-Duc in symbolically charged Lorraine, Poincaré challenged his presumed allies and partners with a bluntness not heard from a French leader
since Clemenceau. The Versailles Treaty, if enforced, he began, would
guarantee France reparations and security, but French efforts to do so
were unjustly regarded as "imperialism." Whether this ill will of her allies
came from simple but prolonged misunderstanding or from a selfish willingness to surrender French rights in the quest for some new vision of
peace, France might henceforth have to act alone, as was her right under
the treaty, to undertake seizures against which there was no appeal if the
Reparations Commission found Germany in default. The Rapallo pact, he
predicted—correctly—had secret military clauses that were "a direct menace against us"—the very equilibrium of Europe was at stake: "France,
which sees clearly the peril of tomorrow, will try to convince the allies that
the best means of avoiding that is to have confidence in us and never to
respond with feebleness to attempts at intimidation. As for France, we are
resolved to preserve what we have been given in a treaty for which our
heroes paid with their blood."[16]

Behind Poincaré's brave words lay the great French fears of the Après
Guerre, of an impoverished France facing a revived and vengeful Germany alone, fears that a single fortnight—Genoa, Rapallo, and the American debt demand—evoked as the apparition of a terrible future. First
would come financial and economic humiliation. Without reparations,
France could not honor her war debts. Without reparations, the double
budget—"ordinary expenses" covered by receipts, "extraordinary expenses" covered eventually by reparations—was a confidence scheme: the

---

République française, 18, 22 April 1922; Bainville in *L'Action française,* 20, 22 April 1922;
Bidou in *Le Figaro,* 18, 20 April 1922.

16. Much of the speech is reproduced in *Le Figaro,* 25 April 1922.

loans used to fund restoration would have to be repaid either through heavy additional taxes or through inflation. Poincaré's minister of finance, Charles de Lasteyrie, was presiding over the continuation of a genuine economic revival begun under Paul Doumer, but he recognized its fragility, recognized that it depended on the faith that reparations would be paid—somehow.

That faith and more than three years of recovery were bringing results that even a rentier could cheer. Wholesale prices for 1922 would be down only another 5.1 percent and retail prices just 1.0 percent (using 1913 as a base 100, their indices went from 352 to 334 and from 312 to 309, respectively), but since 1920, the declines were 35.8 percent and 22.3 percent. By December 1922, stocks and bonds paying a variable return reached 45.0, up a handsome 25 percent over the year and nearly back to their levels at the end of the war, computing their real value adjusted for inflation, using 1913 as a base 100. Those paying a fixed return fared much less well, standing at 24.5, yet that was an increase of 5.6 percent and marked the highest level fixed returns would ever reach. Committing 14.181 billion more francs to the devastated region restored 37,278 private houses, 3,488 farm structures, 864 public buildings, 345 industrial establishments, 475 miles of railroad, and, spectacularly, 5,339 miles of road. The deflation owed much to this reconstruction of industry and infrastructure: as availability improved, prices dropped. Industrial production, which, using 1913 as a base 100, was only 62 in December 1921, rose to 78 by June and 88 by December, a gain of 41.9 percent, by far the best performance since the war. The balance of trade remained static—a deficit of 3.177 billion francs compared to 1921's 3.097 billion—but both exports, 27.217 billion francs, and imports, 30.394 billion francs, were up from 25.244 and 28.341, respectively, an indication of increasing prosperity. Another was the clamor against the income tax, its progressivity biting sharply as incomes rose. The economic revival was also reflected in the exchange rate for the franc, which improved 8.1 percent against the pound from December 1921's 53.06 to May 1922's 48.76, and nearly double, 14.2 percent, against the dollar, 12.78 to 10.97.[17]

17. Sauvy, *Histoire économique,* 1:495, for wholesale prices; 1:511, for retail prices; 1:532, 534, for the real value of stocks and bonds; 1:453–54, for reconstruction; 1:464, for industrial production; 1:477, for balance of payments; 1:445, for currency rates. On the income

But the exchange rate reflected even more the perception of France's likelihood of collecting reparations: the franc down as Briand foundered in November and December, the franc up with Poincaré—and essentially beyond the power of the French government to influence. This reality could provoke profound pessimism. "We stand before the abyss!" despaired Henry Bérenger, the Senate's floor leader for the budget, at the end of March. Another senator, Hugues Le Roux, suggested that the ambitious might do well to leave a tired France for the colonies. Lasteyrie had the sense to maintain his sangfroid. Poincaré did as well and added the speech at Bar-le-Duc to warn of the consequences if Germany did not conform to the requirements of the Reparations Commission by 31 May. His friend and ally Capus at *Le Figaro* chose to see this as a resolute position: "As soon as we invoke our rights in a voice that no longer trembles and with gestures that do not fumble, we will see an end to the moral isolation of France." But Tardieu in *L'Echo national* more acutely derided, "If Poincaré has a policy, nothing prevents him from declaring it." For almost exactly a year earlier, there had been the confrontation with Germany over accepting the final total of reparations: threats from the French, complaints from the British, protests, obstruction, and finally uncooperative compliance from the Germans—how was Poincaré different from Briand? What had changed except the loss of twelve months?[18]

Tardieu's cynicism seemed well founded. In mid-May, through its minister of finance, Andreas Hermes, the German government declared its inability to make reparation payments and its unwillingness to impose the reform program of the Reparations Commission, new taxes, reducing domestic expenditures, and preventing the flight of capital abroad. Before the House of Commons, Lloyd George recalled the indulgence shown France after 1815 and suggested applying this precedent to Germany. Poincaré replied before the Chamber of Deputies that France was defending rights and principles, not seeking revenge. At the last moment, facing

tax, see *L'Intransigeant,* 15 February 1922, denouncing "inquisition fiscale"; *La Libre parole,* 29 May 1922; *Le Figaro,* 8 June 1922.

18. J.O.S., Débats, 27 March 1922, for Bérenger; *L'Intransigeant,* 8 March 1922, for Le Roux; *Le Figaro,* 2 May 1922, for Capus; *L'Echo national,* 1 May 1922, for Tardieu.

a declaration of voluntary default and uncertain of the consequences, Germany "agreed" to enact the required reforms.[19]

This historical encore provoked two wise, prophetic, but largely ignored commentaries. The first came from Clemenceau, who on 27 May dedicated a memorial at the Lycée de Nantes, where he had schooled, to its faculty and students lost in the war. "I used to be very young myself, last century," he began. "Back then, boys were not very considerate: their noses were insolent, their mouths caustic, their eyes filled with big dreams—but they became men." He counseled them—it was almost his refrain—that "life is a perpetual struggle" and that "of a soldier's courage, there is no need to teach you—you have it already, it belongs to your race; but you must have that for which there are no ceremonies, no flowers, you must have civic courage." He had one final injunction for them: "We are going to leave each other for always, me to die, you to live and to prepare the life of France. Farewell my dear friends. I am grateful that for this instant you have wanted to hear my words; but now forget me, roll up your sleeves and make your destiny." At the banquet afterward, although he intended to say nothing more, the emotion of the past conspiring with the present compelled him: "I did nothing extraordinary. I said some fine words. Perhaps I did do something, but all of us did our best. Today, we must spend every bit of our energy to preserve the peace. But there is a limit where I stop: Better to die with honor than to live in shame. We have no need to live in glory, but we want to live in honor." The second, far different in tone, came the following day from Jacques Bainville, writing in *L'Action française*, "Regarding 31 May, let us dispose of a widely held error: the occupation of Germany does not mean that the Germans are going to pay, that we will get money; it means, to the contrary, that the moratorium granted Germany will be prolonged."[20] One assessment of Poincaré might be that his moralism was not as fervid as Clemenceau's and his analysis not as frigid as Bainville's.

19. See general press coverage, 19 May–1 June 1922; J.O.C., Débats, 31 May 1922, for Poincaré.

20. *Le Figaro*, 28, 29 May 1922, quotes Clemenceau's remarks at Nantes; *L'Action française*, 28 May 1922, for Bainville.

In late spring 1922, this judgment was premature by at least a year. The question at hand was what had changed in twelve months, and the answer—even Tardieu agreed—was a great deal. Most obviously, an American loan to Germany was finally under serious consideration. On 24 May, a so-called bankers' committee led by the Francophile John Pierpont Morgan convened in Paris. Tardieu addressed them that day during a discussion of foreign policy in the Chamber of Deputies to evoke the threats of economic disaster, revolution, and future war stalking Europe, to ask that they propose new solutions because "merely invoking the treaty is no longer sufficient . . . life must go on, even as a river flows." No public figure in the United States was more in sympathy with the French position than Morgan, and he also recognized clearly that reparations were the great apple of discord between France and Great Britain, threatening the entente that he considered "the pivot of civilization." Yet Morgan had to tell Poincaré that any loan to Germany was contingent on the French agreeing to a drastically reduced total for reparations—and even then, the mistrust provoked by the Rapallo pact would make lenders require a high interest rate. Given the new pressure on war debts, the sums already expended on reconstruction, and the likely effect on the stability of the franc, Poincaré flatly refused to accept any substantial reduction. And if he had, the Ruhr magnates, enriching themselves through the fall of the mark, would have pressured the German government to refuse the loan. When the bankers' committee adjourned on 1 June having accomplished nothing, some commentators claimed that French positions had been successfully defended. Only Bainville, his vision cold and clear, saw that the time was not far when financial distress would force France to endure whatever terms the bankers set.[21]

Another change was some erosion among his own majority in Poincaré's image of inerrancy. After traveling through Germany in early 1922, Marc Sangnier, the prominent social Catholic who had been elected as a member of the Bloc national, spoke before the Chamber on 24 May about

---

21. McDougall, *France's Rhineland Diplomacy,* 201–4; J.O.C., Débats, 24 May 1922; Bainville in *L'Action française,* 5 June 1922; for other comments on the failed loan, see Pertinax in *L'Echo de Paris* and D'Aral in *Le Gaulois,* 7 June 1922, and Bidou in *Le Figaro,* 8 June 1922.

his vision of a durable peace and his fear that Poincaré had "rather discouraged Germans of goodwill." Poincaré replied quickly, "I have always sought to get along with Germans who are resolutely pacific," and he accused Sangnier of having been "too friendly" toward his recent hosts. Stung, Sangnier attempted a recovery: "I believe that I have acted in the interests of humanity and out of profound patriotism." But Henri Rillart de Verneuil, an infantry officer twice wounded and five times decorated, lashed back, "Give your speech at Chemin des Dames and at Verdun!" Still angry a week later, Poincaré interrupted his dissection of German character based on the Genoa conference to chide Sangnier for having been duped during his trip. When Sangnier dared to respond, "There are peace-loving elements in Germany to whom we should extend our hand," Poincaré cut him off sharply, "Am I belligerent in claiming only what is due us?"[22]

The next day, Briand all but answered that question in a speech before his constituents at Nantes. He remained within the Bloc national, but as he defended his cabinet's policies, he drew a subtle distinction between himself and Poincaré. "The disastrous year of the Briand ministry—as some call it—did not lack vigor. That year, the allies unanimously agreed upon the German debt; the French position on Upper Silesia prevailed; the three river port cities of the Ruhr were occupied; Germany paid a billion gold marks, handed over 30,000 cannons, 160,000 machine guns, several million pieces of ordnance, dismantled all of its fortresses under the inspection of the military control commission; and harmony among the allies was preserved. . . . If that record merits a trial before the Senate, then so be it! I will appear with the legitimate pride of a man who has maintained around his country the sacred battalions belonging to the nations of victory." That, for Briand, was the critical factor: Poincaré risked the grave danger of isolation by alienating Great Britain. Already, fixation on reparations and every paragraph of the treaty made France appear pedantic and mean. Why were the new nations of Poland and Czechoslovakia attracted to France? "Because she is the country of the Revolution, of liberty, of the future, and not the France of the cemeteries!" The differences between Briand and Poincaré were thus far more of style than of sub-

22. J.O.C., Débats, 24 May, 1 June 1922.

stance, more of approach than of issues—because the alternatives were so limited. But as a warning, and to keep the record clear, Briand drew his distinction.[23]

Far more serious than a few restive figures within the Bloc national was the renewed confidence of the Radical party, another change from only twelve months before. In January 1922, the Sûreté générale reported that Caillaux was planning a political comeback through the construction of a leftist alliance based on popular discontent with the efforts to enforce the Versailles Treaty and on the view that Poincaré presided over "a ministry of reactionaries." In February, Herriot spoke at Marseille and Lyon to the most enthusiastic Radical rallies since the 1919 elections, and in March at Tour, where he laid out a program clearly distinct from that of the Bloc national: the rehabilitation of Caillaux and Louis Malvy, a ¿ax on capital, "the progressive reconciliation of yesterday's enemies" (meaning Germany), and "the establishment of international relations with states regarded as in default to the entente" (meaning Russia). In late May, on the same day Sangnier affronted Poincaré, Herriot argued his party's foreign policy and dared to defend Malvy's name. Moderate and conservative newspapers reacted predictably. Emile Buré dismissed the speech as "humbug, sophistry, confusion." Tardieu denounced "the Caillaux party, which has changed its leader but not its spirit, which has only one goal, the exploitation of the Republic." The reaction was so strong that it betrayed the fear of a Radical resurgence.[24]

Or more precisely, the reaction betrayed the fear that Radicals could create an alliance of the Left, a Cartel des gauches, that would be a formidable opponent for the Bloc national in the next legislative elections. Perhaps it would be more than formidable: 1919 was the only victory for a Right-Center coalition in France since 1871 and owed much to the disorganization then of the Left. Rejecting all "bourgeois" parties, the French

23. Suarez, *Briand*, 5:423–24, quotes from the speech; for commentary, see Georges Bonnefous in *La République française*, 5 June 1922; and *Le Figaro*, 7 June 1922.

24. AN, F7 12951, "Notes Jean," P 42, 5 January 1922; P 248, 19 January 1922; *Le Figaro*, 1, 2, 27 March 1922, for campaign rallies—the newspaper held a grudge; J.O.C., Débats, 24 May 1922; Emile Buré in *L'Eclair*, Tardieu in *L'Echo national*, 25 May 1922; see also Arthur Meyer in *Le Gaulois*, Louis Latapie in *La République française*, and Joseph Denais in *La Libre parole*, 25 May 1922.

Communists excluded themselves from any cartel, but as in 1919, their tactics and propaganda, their "Bolshevism," influenced the opinion held by moderates and conservatives of everyone outside the majority. Poincaré as premier galvanized both: he was the personification of the Chambre bleu horizon, and he was "Poincaré-la-guerre." For that was the vicious title, often chanted as a refrain, that the Communists and some of the Socialists awarded him because, they claimed, he failed to prevent war in 1914 and then gloried in its results. No matter how often he produced documentary evidence to refute their charges, they invented new ones. The most repellent was using a photograph taken of Poincaré as he visited a military cemetery, sunlight in his face causing him to squint and thus seeming to smile. The Communists printed thousands of copies as postcards with the caption, "Riant dans les cimetières" (Laughing in the graveyards).

The climax of this vilification—somewhat reminiscent of the campaign supported by Poincaré against Caillaux—came in early July, beginning with a speech before the Chamber of Deputies by Paul Charles Couturier, known as Vaillant-Couturier. Like Rillart de Verneuil, who rebuked Sangnier, Vaillant-Couturier had served as an infantry officer and was twice wounded; unlike him, he embraced Bolshevism after the war, won election as a Communist deputy from Paris, and was currently under investigation for spreading antimilitarist propaganda to recruits. His courage proven incontestably on the battlefield, he had earned the right to be heard by the Chambre bleu horizon, and his accusations were incendiary:

I speak today not only because we accuse Poincaré of certain responsibilities in the origins of the war but because we judge that his presence at the head of France is not a guarantee of peace in Europe. . . . We accuse him of having been the man about whom the desires of revenge crystallized among the wildest of the nationalists. We accuse him of having been what [Jean] Jaurès hoped he would not be, the president of reaction and war. . . . For us, Poincaré represents all that is baleful about nationalism before and after the war. Today, his politics lead us to isolation, to bankruptcy, to new wars. . . . The era of new policies may arrive soon, perhaps, but the first condition is that Poincaré, who bears a portion of the responsibility, who has acted without doubt in accord with his conscience, but from whom the universal conscience will demand an accounting, retire into the shadows, from which as the leader of the war he should never have emerged.

The peroration was crushing: "In vain, you will seek to vindicate yourself; in vain, you will be applauded, acclaimed by this Chamber . . . because for many former soldiers at last realizing the truth, you face a terrible accounting as Poincaré-la-guerre."[25] But in these concluding words, Vaillant-Couturier tipped his hand: Poincaré merely personified the real target, which was the Bloc national-la-guerre.

The majority immediately presented a united front. Poincaré replied first, damning the Communists for "the most abominable, the most anti-patriotic of campaigns. . . . At the moment when Germany seeks to shake the foundations of the Versailles Treaty, to throw off its responsibilities in the war, my duty as witness to the events as they transpired is to say that all these charges are false." He brought with him critical documents, which he used to excellent effect, stumbling only once, when he could not resist pointing out the failure of the Communists to produce their own evidence, calling that "joining cowardice to the lie" and giving Vaillant-Couturier the chance to riposte, "I laugh at the accusation of cowardice, I who was fighting the war while you could not even make the peace!" But this retort fell hollow because Poincaré turned to the photograph. Although here was the shabbiest and most transparent of lies, he felt compelled—despite having been president and premier—to offer an explanation: "I had sun in my eyes and so was squinting. I add that despite the intensity of the sun, my head was bare, sufficient proof, I believe, that when I am in a cemetery, like all the French, I have respect for the dead." Ever so briefly, he revealed the brittle, defensive private man. Then, he recovered the polish: "It is shameful and contemptible that this campaign has been encouraged by a few misguided Frenchmen. But the country as a whole, with invariable good sense, has already rejected it as an outrage to truth and as an offense to the nation." Any who did not, he excluded from "the national community."[26]

René Viviani made the same point far more eloquently. Since his em-

25. J.O.C., Débats, 4 July 1922; Miquel, Poincaré, 450–53.
26. J.O.C., Débats, 4 July 1922; Miquel, Poincaré, 453–54.

barrassing trip with Briand to Washington, he had declined into neuras-
thenia and near political obscurity. But in the summer of 1914 he had been
premier, and he insisted now on his own responsibility for the decisions
during those critical days at the beginning of August. His most vivid
memory was announcing the declaration of war before the Chamber of
Deputies and making an appeal with Poincaré for a union sacrée. "Then,
[Albert] de Mun, representing the past, and [Edouard] Vaillant [whose
name Couturier had taken], representing the revolution, these two old
men went one to another. That day, we escaped from the quarrels of parties and rose above factions. Remember that day always, and renew your
vow of fidelity to the nation!" Wild applause, cheers, and cries of bravo
erupted everywhere but from the Communist seats—and subsided only
for the deputies to vote 445 to 29 in favor of *affichage,* that Viviani's words
be posted throughout France.

Yet even then the Communists had not had enough. Their leader, Marcel Cachin, complained that the union sacrée Viviani praised was the facade behind which France sacrificed peace for tsarist ambitions. As Poincaré once again took out the documents, Briand intervened, recalling that
the Germans had argued Cachin's thesis of French-Russian culpability at
London in March 1921, until he and Lloyd George thoroughly discredited
it. Poincaré then recounted how France had done everything possible to
avoid the "frightful catastrophe" of war, even assuming the risk of with-
drawing troops six miles from the frontier to avoid provoking an incident:
so clear was French innocence that Socialists, including Jules Guesde and
Marcel Sembat, did not hesitate to join union sacrée cabinets. The mention
of these names seemed to free the non-Communist Left from any inhibi-
tions about openly standing with the Bloc national. Paul Painlevé, the last
premier before Clemenceau and a prominent Radical, praised Poincaré's
diplomacy before and during the war. Léon Blum, the new leader of the
Socialists, disavowed any connection to "Poincaré-la-guerre" and denounced "fake postcards contrived by the Communists." To complete the
rout, a motion by which "the Chamber rejects and stigmatizes with all its
scorn the campaign of calumny organized for the benefit of Germany de-
sirous of escaping its responsibility for the war" passed 532 to 65.[27] The

27. J.O.C., Débats, 5–6 July 1922.

Bolsheviks were thoroughly beaten back, the honor of Poincaré, of the Bloc national, of "France," upheld, but such a debate would have been barely imaginable a year earlier.

So a great deal had changed in twelve months—serious proposals regarding an American loan, the stirring of challenges from the Left, hints of doubt within the Bloc national—but primarily because the fundamental issues—reparations, war debts, relations with Great Britain, with Germany, with the United States—remained intractable. Poincaré's sterner version of Briand's approach was in a shambles by mid-April, and at Bar-le-Duc, he threatened to act alone. Despite Tardieu's derision, Poincaré was hesitantly, reluctantly, embracing his second alternative—less hesitantly after the failure of the bankers' committee. On 7 June, he testified in secret session before the Senate's committee on foreign affairs that the intractable issues could be mastered through a single intrepid stroke. He accepted Morgan's analysis that American banks would not lend to Germany without French sacrifices and drew the conclusion that France would lose reparations in either case. If denied loans, Germany would clamor for an ever-longer moratorium while encouraging the fall of the mark to win export markets. If granted the loan, Germany would recover rapidly while France would be faced with the enormous burden of paying herself for war debts and reconstruction. To compel Germany to honor the treaty and to shock Great Britain and the United States into recognizing the French dilemma, a resort to military force was imperative: France had to occupy the Ruhr.

Here was the ultimate touchstone of the Bloc national at least since Briand proposed "sending the constable" in April 1921 but deferred to Lloyd George's objection. Most recently, even before the bankers departed Paris, Adrien Dariac, chairman of the Chamber's finance committee, submitted a report arguing that only a seizure of the Ruhr could guarantee reparations and coal deliveries. Poincaré had already asked for contingency plans from André Maginot, the minister of war, and from General Joseph Degoutte and Paul Tirard, the military and civilian heads of the Rhineland occupation, respectively. To ensure a legal basis for action, France had to wait for the Reparations Commission to declare Germany in voluntary default, but when that moment came—and Poincaré was in no doubt that it would—France would seize the entire Ruhr valley and hold it as collateral until Germany *paid*—promises would no longer be sufficient. To cover the expenses of occupation, France would confiscate customs receipts and take temporary possession of German state mines and forests in the Rhineland.[28]

Poincaré provided the details of his new policy only in secret; publicly, he merely hinted, using language similar to that at Bar-le-Duc. On 29 June before the Senate, he accused the German government of a self-induced fiscal crisis that it could solve by taking seriously the promises made to the Reparations Commission. France would take action only in strict adherence to the treaty, but "when a treaty gives us the right to take sanctions, I will not permit that right to be diminished." Great Britain and the United States had to recognize that "to leave France foundering in misery would be to give Europe a mortal wound." Poincaré spoke only five days after the assassination of Walther Rathenau, who had signed the Rapallo pact and delayed as much as possible the adoption of the Reparations Commission reforms—shot dead by a German nationalist fanatic for not having done even more. With the blood of his foreign minister barely wiped up, Chancellor Wirth blamed the demands imposed on Germany by the treaty. When Emile Buré in *L'Eclair* wrote that Rathenau's death proved the worst about the Germans, he was referring to those who would murder and those who would exploit murder. In this context, the Senate gave Poincaré a unanimous vote of confidence. A week later, that sense of revulsion contributed to the overwhelming support he received in the Chamber of Deputies during the angry debate with the Communists.[29]

The best adversaries live down to their depiction. During the Bastille Day parade at Longchamps, Armand Naudin, the new Paris prefect of police in office only five days, received a literal baptism of fire from Charles Bouvet, a member of the Jeunesse communiste (Communist Youth), who thought he was shooting at President Millerand. When arrested, Bouvet claimed that he only meant to create an incident, yet he was armed with an automatic pistol and twenty-nine bullets. On 20 July, Com-

---

28. McDougall, *France's Rhineland Diplomacy,* 214–18.

29. J.O.S., Débats, 29 June 1922; Buré in *L'Eclair,* 27 June 1922; see also D'Aral in *Le Gaulois,* Bainville in *L'Action française,* and Capus in *Le Figaro,* 25 June 1922; Laskine in *La République française,* 26 June 1922, and Bidou in *Le Figaro,* 27 June 1922.

munist leaders Vaillant-Couturier and Cachin were indicted, as expected, for antimilitarist agitation. When a lower tribunal convicted them eight days later, the judges upheld France's traditional tolerance for dissidence by imposing a fine of merely 500 francs. Even so, Vaillant-Couturier and Cachin, purposely not taking the point, appealed—and lost.[30]

For all that, the Bolsheviks barely made the front pages because on 12 July, Germany demanded a complete moratorium for the cash payment of reparations until the end of 1924. In public, Poincaré's response was restrained. As he dedicated a memorial on 16 July at Joncherey near Belfort to Corporal Jules André Peugeot, France's first casualty in 1914, killed on 2 August by fire from a German patrol penetrating the border before war was even declared, he could easily have sounded the tocsin. Instead, he simply repeated the imperative that Germans recognize their responsibilities for the war and thus for reparation: "We want to crush no one. We have only two modest ambitions, to be indemnified for the damages we have suffered and to be sheltered from new attacks." Prominent editorialists were equally measured. But secretly, Poincaré directed that the contingency planning begun in June be quickly completed. Momentum was driving him toward the Ruhr as other strategies failed. The fiscal reform program of the Reparations Commission was now in effect, but the value of the mark declined even faster. Worth 85 to the dollar in August 1921, falling to 300 in April 1922, it plunged to 670 by the end of July, with the trajectory ever downward. In Poincaré's view, the only alternative left before occupying the Ruhr was to demand the "livraison des gages"—Germany's handing over material pledges such as state-owned mines.[31]

The British reaction to the demand for a moratorium was utterly different. Briefly, there was talk of abandoning the Rhineland, rumor of which provoked Capus to fulminate: "That would be a definitive renunciation of all payment and flight before the enemy. From then on, all the power that Britain might conjure would not delay for one hour the ruin of our nation, and we would quickly see victory obliterated beneath the

---

30. See Le Figaro, 15, 16, 21, 29 July, 8–9 August 1922.

31. For Poincaré at Joncherey, see Le Figaro, 17 July 1922; for the editorialists, see Bainville in L'Action française, 9 July 1922, and Bidou in Le Figaro, 14 July 1922; for Poincaré on the Ruhr and alternatives, see McDougall, France's Rhineland Diplomacy, 218.

feet of new hordes." What the British did propose was not much more welcome. The "Note" of Arthur James Balfour, secretary of the exchequer, announced Britain's willingness to establish a payment schedule for war debts due the United States but argued as preferable that the United States forgive the British debt in return for Britain's forgiving all war debts due her and all reparations from Germany. Here was another example of Lloyd George's grand schemes for restoring international finances and trade—and also an example of blatant moral extortion. The United States was asked to absolve its debtor because its debtor would absolve others; the United States refused with ill grace. And France, although not mentioned in the "Note," was being asked by implication to give up all reparations from Germany in return for a cancellation of war debts. Poincaré and Lloyd George had agreed to a meeting of the reparations powers—Great Britain, France, Belgium, and Italy—in London to discuss the moratorium demand, but they were agreed about little else.[32]

How little, they made no attempt to hide: on 26 July, Poincaré addressed a letter to the German government threatening to apply sanctions "immediately and automatically" for failure to pay reparations; a week later, Lloyd George told the House of Commons that Germany must not be pressed to "despair." When the conference opened in London on 7 August, Poincaré proposed a stern program of material guarantees in return for a moratorium: the Reparations Commission should expropriate the state-owned mines in the Ruhr to guarantee required coal deliveries; the state forests in the Rhineland should be seized and all German exports taxed 26 percent to generate reparation payments; the Reichsbank should come under direct allied supervision to ensure compliance with the fiscal reforms; and the territory under occupation should be made a separate customs zone. His reference unmistakable, he asked that *France* not be pressed to despair: "We are ready to work for the reconstitution of Europe which would be made impossible by the collapse of France if we are not reimbursed for our expenditures." Unmoved and unconvinced, Lloyd George countered that the moratorium be granted without conditions. He especially rejected the economic segregation of the Rhineland, which

32. Capus in *Le Figaro*, 27 July 1922; McDougall, *France's Rhineland Diplomacy*, 218–22.

would force the payment of tariffs on goods within Germany and might encourage the small Rhenish separatist movement that the French intermittently supported. When Poincaré insisted, Lloyd George threatened, as he had to Briand in May 1921, to sunder the entente. From Paris, Millerand telegraphed the cabinet's unanimous backing for Poincaré; that was matched by the British cabinet's unanimous backing for Lloyd George. Although the Belgian premier, Paul Theunis, tried in vain to mediate, the conference ended after a week with Great Britain and France so far apart that the name "Fashoda"—where their empires collided in 1898 at the headwaters of the Nile—was spoken.[33]

In Paris, the mood was nervous and defensive. The 14 August *Le Figaro's* headline warned of "Le Risque"; the 15 August *Le Temps* bannered "Le 'Deadlock' Continue!" A large crowd hailed Poincaré as a hero on his return at the Gare du Nord. The cabinet, meeting at Rambouillet with Millerand, again declared its unanimous approval. Most of the conservative or moderate editorialists insisted, like Capus in *Le Figaro,* that "all interpreters of French opinion applaud the posture assumed at London." But *La Victoire's* ardent nationalist Gustave Hervé cautioned: "Lloyd George will pass. Let us guard preciously the British alliance." And Briand worried about long-term damage to the entente from such open disagreement.[34]

Poincaré clearly did not. On 20 August, when he dedicated a memorial at Triaucourt in the Meuse, he spoke of German atrocities during the fighting, not to remind the French—who did not need reminding—but the British, who had been spared what the Germans did to civilians, "murders, pillage, arson, the bombing of open cities, poison gas: all contrived in an effort to obtain through terror a victory they despaired of winning on the battlefield." The following day, he returned to Bar-le-Duc and, in a speech overflowing with frustration, took up again the arguments he had made at London: Great Britain admitted that Germany had

33. McDougall, *France's Rhineland Diplomacy,* 222–24; Trachtenberg, *Reparation in World Politics,* 249–75; the votes of confidence were reported widely in the press, see *Le Temps,* 11 August 1922.

34. *Le Figaro,* 14 August (headline), 17 August (for Capus) 1922; *Le Temps,* 15 August 1922, for headline and Poincaré's arrival; *La Victoire,* 15 August 1922, for Hervé; *L'Action française,* 15 August 1922; Suarez, *Briand,* 5:425–27.

failed to make coal deliveries, to pay reparations, and to control inflation, yet was willing to grant a moratorium that would cause grave harm to France; to gain France's consent, Great Britain was willing to threaten demanding payment of French war debts. "I hardly need to say," Poincaré pledged, "that we will not accept being placed in such an anomalous position." France asked instead material guarantees for payment of reparations, yet to exploit Britain's willful misunderstanding, German propaganda "accuses us of wanting to reduce their nation to slavery or even to annihilation. We have never had, and we do not have, such absurd schemes." Although these words and especially the lecturing tone went over badly in Germany and Great Britain—for Poincaré was clearly addressing Britons as well as French—he cared only about the French reaction, and that remained as strongly positive as immediately after his return from London.[35]

But there had been exceptions then to the chorus of approval, and there were some now, asking how tensions in the entente were to be transformed into gains for France, asking whether the contentious language was a bluff. Always a thorn, Tardieu patronizingly counseled Poincaré against any more speeches: if the strategy was an allied accord on French terms, further antagonizing exchange was counterproductive; if the strategy was to seize material guarantees, action had to replace words. In essence, Tardieu was repeating his May Day derision—"If Poincaré has a policy, nothing prevents him from declaring it." Four months later, Poincaré had a policy, but he had not decided the very question Tardieu posed: the risks either way were staggeringly high. Because Poincaré was still running to abstain, Pertinax's dismissal of "collective action" by the allies against Germany was a more dangerous jab—not just because it threatened to reduce his running room but because it anticipated a development under way.[36]

With no decision about the moratorium forthcoming at the level of

35. *Le Figaro,* 21, 22 August (for quotations from Poincaré's speeches), 23 August (for a compendium of press reaction in Germany and Great Britain) 1922; see praise for the speeches from *Le Temps, Le Figaro, L'Homme libre, L'Avenir,* and *L'Action française,* 22 August 1922.

36. *L'Echo national,* 23 August 1922, for Tardieu; *L'Echo de Paris,* 21 August 1922, for Pertinax.

prime ministers, the Reparations Commission on 19 August sent two of its financial experts, Sir John Bradbury of Great Britain and Eugène Mauclère of France, to sound out their counterparts in Berlin. Initially, the Germans asked for a remission of payments through December 1924 but quickly retreated to December 1922, along with the promise to make the required deliveries in kind of timber and coal. Bradbury wanted the elimination of all conditions. Mauclère insisted on the surrender of state mines and forests, and Poincaré made clear to Dubois, France's representative on the Reparations Commission and its president, that this position was the minimum acceptable. When the commission met to vote on 31 August, Dubois did win the defeat of Bradbury's proposal, but the best he could do otherwise was a vote extending the status quo: fiscal reforms, deliveries in kind, and partial payments in gold. Even that agreement was modified to Germany's advantage: the partial payments would be due monthly, not every ten days, and through December could be made in bonds, redeemable in gold after six months, to be secured by Reichsbank reserves. Although the other three representatives appear to have been influenced by the collapse of the mark—from 350 to the dollar when Rathenau was assassinated to 2,000 on the day of the vote—Poincaré blamed Dubois's timid diplomacy. This defeat for French policy came immediately after the American secretary of the treasury, Charles Evans Hughes, made clear in his letter of 23 August that the United States expected war debts to be paid whether or not reparations were in moratorium. So much, as Pertinax had said, for collective action. Poincaré's running room was now dramatically reduced.[37]

The contingency planning he had ordered also pressed him toward the Ruhr. Jacques Seydoux, under secretary for commercial relations at the Ministry of Finance, predicted that the German government would offer no resistance and that occupation expenses could therefore be kept to 125 million francs, while exploitation of the industries would yield upward of 850 million gold marks—a profit of at least 400 percent. Lasteyrie was much less optimistic, expecting that the operation would do no better than pay for itself. He feared the effect of France's going alone on the value of

37. *Le Temps* and *Le Figaro*, 20 August–1 September 1922, provide detailed reports about the Reparations Commission; McDougall, *France's Rhineland Diplomacy*, 226–27.

the franc, over which the government had no control; but without a resolution of the reparations question, the franc was certain to weaken, and heavy new taxes could not be avoided. Although prepared for some initial protests and demonstrations, Maginot, Degoutte, and other military officials anticipated no more difficulties than in the Rhineland. To lead the technical experts, Tirard designated Emile Coste, an inspector general of mines in the Ministry of Public Works, who argued for treating the Ruhr and the French zone of the Rhineland as a single economic unit, implying that France meant to stay. The German government would have to negotiate seriously or risk the threat of partition.[38]

If these assessments were correct, the danger of seizing the Ruhr lay only in the effect on France's diplomatic position. For Poincaré, that was exactly the point: the wartime allies were already completely at odds. Over the next ten days, like the brilliant barrister he was and armed with moral certainty in his case, he laid claim with sustained eloquence to the right of independent action. On 1 September in the official reply to the Balfour "Note," he bluntly reminded the British government that war debts and reparations were not commensurable, not to be treated merely as debits and credits on an accountant's page. Had Great Britain forgotten that the debts were incurred in the common effort of victory and that the reparations had been imposed to restore damage inflicted by their common foe? In language chosen to shame, he concluded, "We ask to be treated as we treat our fellow allies: we do not ask repayment of war debts, for we recognize that, morally and materially, such a request would be inadmissible, and we would never even consider making it." Two days later, Poincaré unveiled a memorial at Honfleur to the historian Albert Sorel, recalling "his admiration for the genius of France, his pride in our triumphs, his tenderness for our illusions, his compassion for our adversities"—and his warnings about the threat from Germany. For these Germans, "with their mania for inverting roles, accuse us of imperialism at the very moment when we have given proof to the world of our patience and moderation, while they raise anew the chant of their 'Deutschland über alles' to the dignity of a national anthem. Let us reread Sorel and remain prepared to

38. Trachtenberg, *Reparation in World Politics*, 275; McDougall, *France's Rhineland Diplomacy*, 225–26.

defend our rights!" Then, on 10 September, Poincaré spoke at Meaux, near where the two critical battles of the Marne had been fought and won, the first preventing German victory in 1914, the second ending the last German advance in 1918. "Already eight years have passed, and the work begun in September 1914 is not yet finished! The more time passes, the better we understand the military importance and the moral significance of these two great battles. We all fought for the same cause, for deliverance from German imperialism. . . . We must end the provisional nature of this victory. By consent or through force, Germany must fulfill its obligations. Before the battlefields of the Marne, let us swear to obtain justice."[39]

"Il faut que, de gré ou de force, l'Allemagne remplisse ses engagements": these words at the Marne were Poincaré's clearest threat of independent action. If they were regarded at London as more bluster à la Briand, they quickly gained a nonrhetorical complement. On 14 September, Poincaré assembled the cabinet for a comprehensive discussion of foreign policy. Dubois was summoned to explain his failures and, because of them, afterward dismissed. To have a legal basis for occupying the Ruhr, France needed a vote by the Reparations Commission that Germany was in voluntary default. For this vital responsibility, Poincaré trusted no one more than Barthou—based on thirty years of *tutoiement,* betrayal of Briand, and obstruction at Genoa. The announcement on 5 October of his appointment as Dubois's replacement, and therefore president of the Reparations Commission, was an unmistakable warning. When the moment came, entering the Ruhr could best be justified by the argument that France acted reluctantly after the failure of other alternatives. In mid-September, Poincaré looked unseemly eager, and he therefore sought opportunities for a public pose of moderation.[40]

Clemenceau provided the first, drawn from his exile in the Vendée by the open quarrel among the allies whose cooperation the Versailles Treaty presumed. When the *New York World* asked him to comment, he responded with the extraordinary proposal of going personally to the United

39. *Le Temps,* 1 September 1922, for the reply to the Balfour "Note"; *Le Figaro,* 4 (for the remarks at the Sorel monument), 11 (for the speech at Meaux) September 1922.

40. *Le Temps,* 15 September, 6 October 1922; see the editorial by Eugène Lautier in *L'Homme libre,* 14 September 1922.

States—at the age of eighty-one—"candidly to say what, in my opinion, are the rights and duties of each people in the alarming world crisis unloosed by the war, where the common victory has made all the allies jointly responsible for the future." The United Press immediately questioned whether he was implying that America had failed in these responsibilities. Clemenceau could have uttered his reply during the debate ratifying the treaty: "I consider that America accomplished magnificently its duties of solidarity during the war, but peace being the goal of war, the duties of solidarity for each are not exhausted by the settling of terms in which one of the parties disinterests itself. I believe that if solidarity had continued among America, France, and Great Britain, the current crisis would have been avoided, and that it cannot be resolved without renewing that solidarity." To the *London Times* asking the same question about British responsibilities, he answered that without the entente, Europe faced "a general conflict with inevitable ruin for the entire world." The major American East Coast newspapers, including the *Philadelphia Ledger,* the *New York Tribune,* and the *New York Times,* applauded Clemenceau's almost quixotic decision to cross the Atlantic. They recognized a good story when they saw it coming because the reaction on Capitol Hill was distinctly cool. Senator Gilbert Hitchcock of Nebraska, a member of the foreign affairs committee, chose this moment to denounce the French use of black Senegalese troops in the Rhineland as an offense to German racial sensibilities. His fellow senators Thomas Watson of Georgia and William King of Utah warned that not even a "tiger" could hope to change the American position on war debts. For Poincaré, however, Clemenceau's quest was a chance to back away slightly from his harshest words by joining in the call for recovering the spirit of the wartime alliance among the Western democracies.[41]

A second chance to pose as a moderate came when the legislature reconvened in October after its summer recess. Poincaré sought to define the terms for domestic policy in a speech at Sennes (Vosges), inviting into his

41. Clemenceau's replies to the *New York World,* the United Press, and the *London Times* were reprinted in Tardieu's *L'Echo national,* 10, 11, 13 September, respectively. See the reaction of the French political world in *Le Temps, Le Figaro, L'Eclair,* and *Le Petit parisien,* 10–14 September 1922; *Le Figaro,* 14, 18 September 1922, reported the attitude of the American newspapers and the comments of the senators.

majority everyone committed to "respecting republican institutions, restoring our financial position, inspiring public administration with its duties to the state, fortifying in all the notions of order and method, and up-
lifting an exhausted France"—the agenda as broad as it was vague.
Although calling for a certain national rigor, he was appealing to the
broad center of French politics, not just the Bloc national, and reaching
out toward the Radicals, whose support he would want for the maintenance of national consensus if he seized the Ruhr. They had rallied to him
during the "Poincaré-la-guerre" debate in July, but he worried at their
leftward drift. Herriot traveled to Russia in mid-September, the first non-
Communist French politician to do so, and in the weeks following, there
were rumors that although the Communists would remain outside any
formal alliance of the Left, they might cooperate with it by mutually with-
drawing weaker candidates to improve the chance of stronger ones against
the Bloc national. For the first time during the Third Republic, a two-
party alignment—however much cobbled together from factions—
appeared possible: Cartel des gauches versus Bloc national.[42]

Tardieu and Georges Mandel believed that such a clear-cut choice
would add discipline to political parties and that on this basis, the conservatives could repeat their 1919 victory in 1924. Poincaré felt less certain,
but, more important, those elections were a year and a half away, during
which time he would need a union sacrée. He was, moreover, tempera-
mentally opposed to closing alternatives and had spent his career in the
Center. Capus reflected not just the current political line but the essence
of his longtime friend when writing in Le Figaro that Poincaré tried to
stand above terms like Right and Left. Poincarisme is usually equated with
nationalism, but it was frequently a careful balancing, as when Lasteyrie
declared before the Paris Chamber of Commerce, "The government is
resolutely opposed to any policy of inflation . . . but that is not to say that
we are partisans of brusque deflation." Another was Poincaré's own reply
to Albert Favre, a former cabinet official under Clemenceau, who accused
him of encouraging harsh editorials against Lloyd George in the Paris
press. Poincaré had always criticized the policies, never the man, and he

42. Le Figaro, 18, 22 September (Herriot's trip to Russia), 2 October (Poincaré at
Sennes) 1922.

insisted on the distinction: "You accuse deceitfully, because no one more than I regrets these personal attacks on the head of a foreign government. If it were up to me, they would never have appeared."[43] Yet even as Poincaré was playing the moderate, the political constellation of Europe altered dramatically and suddenly to the benefit of independent French action.

The Near East was in flames. To force Turkish acceptance of the harsh Sèvres Treaty, British, French, and Italian troops occupied various portions of the Ottoman Empire, and Lloyd George encouraged Greece to seize Eastern Thrace and part of Asia Minor. Under Mustapha Kemal, Turkish nationalists took up arms in resistance, eventually halting the Greek advance in late summer 1921. Recognizing the power of Kemal's appeal, France and Italy had withdrawn their troops from Asia Minor the previous March, but Lloyd George, pursuing control of the straits through British influence in Greece, held on until the complete rout of Greek forces in mid-September 1922. When he appealed to Poincaré, to the Italians, and to the British Dominions for joint action against the Turks, he found no support. At the conference of Moudania in early October, the Sèvres Treaty was set aside, Kemal regaining Eastern Thrace and all of Asia Minor in return for accepting the neutralization of the straits under international control.

On 19 October, eight days after the Moudania convention, Lloyd George resigned after almost six years as prime minister. The formal reason, the withdrawal of the Irish Unionists from his majority, derived from domestic politics, but his prestige had been seriously eroded by the collapse of British policy in the Near East and by the sense of impending new crisis in Germany, where the mark, already at 2,000 to the dollar on 31 August, fell to 3,050 six weeks later. Because the fiscal controls imposed by the Reparations Commission were obviously without effect, France had impeccable grounds to ask for stronger sanctions. Although Andrew Bonar Law, the leader of the Conservative party, who became prime minister on 23 October, appeared more willing than Lloyd George to take a firmer attitude toward Germany, any controversial policy that his cabinet might

43. Sherwood, *Georges Mandel*, 72–76; *Le Figaro*, 6 October 1922, for Capus on Poincaré and Lasteyrie before the Paris Chamber of Commerce; J.O.C., Débats, 12 (Poincaré and Favre), 20 (Mandel on political divisions) October 1922.

adopt had to await the outcome of parliamentary elections on 15 November. While British decisions were placed in abeyance, power shifted in Italy, where Benito Mussolini was made premier on 31 October, after his Fascist leagues convinced King Victor Emmanuel III of their popular support by the March on Rome. Though not especially friendly toward France, Mussolini did not hide his disdain for Germany and his willingness to support a declaration of voluntary default. Belgium had already moved toward the French on seizing productive guarantees. That gave Barthou a majority in the Reparations Commission no matter what position Britain took. And would the inexperienced Bonar Law dare to threaten the end of the entente as Lloyd George had? Events had moved Poincaré's way. But before acting, he had to wait for the most advantageous moment.[44]

The interim also allowed a last girding for battle. Appallingly insensitive to the calendar, Mandel chose 10 November—the eve of Armistice Day and its remembrance of shared sacrifice—to offer denunciations of insufficient zeal. Because some moderates in the Bloc national refused to sever all links to the Radicals, he castigated them as unworthy of membership in the majority. Poincaré replied first with ridicule, thanking Mandel for excluding him from the denunciation: "I was somewhat reassured, saying to myself, he won't kill me this time!" Mandel wanted government by a tightly disciplined core; Poincaré preferred a broad consensus, the exact limits of support varying with the issue. For Mandel, the ideal was Clemenceau's reading out of the défaitistes in 1917; for Poincaré, the ideal was the union sacrée of 1914. The former defeated the Germans, but only because the latter had stopped them cold. All the tradition of the Third Republic lay on Poincaré's side, and he reasserted it now as he had a month earlier. All except the Communists were welcome: "The cabinet asks the support of all good citizens for the work of national reconstruction and social peace, excluding only those who seek reform through revolt and disorder."[45]

44. McDougall, *France's Rhineland Diplomacy,* 230–33, is a superb brief analysis of how the French interpreted these changes.
45. J.O.C., *Débats,* 10 November 1922.

At this moment of gathering crisis, the Radicals eagerly accepted the invitation during a series of dramatic legislative debates that reached a climax on 17 November before the Chamber of Deputies. As the "barrister for slandered France," Poincaré was making his case yet again. Ten days earlier, Loucheur had argued that a choice had to be made between a Germany representing no threat but unable to pay reparations and the converse. Poincaré refused to recognize the dilemma:

> If we had to choose between being paid or having security, I would, like Loucheur, take security, but I do not want to have to choose. France has up to now given superhuman proof of patience and moderation in this question of reparations. More than anyone else, we suffered for the common cause, our armies holding the longest and most exposed front and suffering dreadful losses. France must be indemnified, but for that we are dependent on our allies, always faced with being in the minority on the Reparations Commission. Before us, we have a Great Britain saying, "Look at Germany—it is broken!" That is a negative policy which cannot persist longer. We will not accord a further moratorium without taking guarantees, and we will not gain control over German finances without a certain coercion. To those ends, we will hope to regain the sympathy of our allies that came to our aid in other tragic hours.

At Bar-le-Duc twice and in dedicating monuments, Poincaré had made the threat of independent French action, but not so specifically and never before the legislature. There could be no doubt that he was stepping across a self-imposed boundary. Some Communists and Socialists took the rostrum to speak against him. Vaillant-Couturier uttered an insult at his desk inaudible to most of the Chamber but heard by Gaston Vidal, one of the cabinet under secretaries, who then had to be restrained from responding with a punch. On the Far Right, Daudet proffered his own brand of calumny: "For three years of war, the politics of France under Viviani, Ribot, Briand, and Painlevé were those of Caillaux and Malvy—partisans of Franco-German rapprochement. If I had been in power, I would have had them shot, with a smile on my lips!" Daudet stood with Poincaré, but even after those words, the Radicals did so as well, giving him an overwhelming vote of confidence 461 to 71.[46]

On the following day, 18 November, the *Paris* docked at New York, and Clemenceau returned to the United States, where he had taught French and made a schoolgirl his bride more than five decades earlier. He came to tell Americans what they seemed to have forgotten, making the arguments he had made since 1918, but unlike his old antagonist Poincaré, he did not speak as a polished barrister. About Clemenceau there was ever something elemental, emotional, charismatic. At New York, Boston, Chicago, St. Louis, Indianapolis, Dayton, Baltimore, Philadelphia, and Washington, his language flayed, and for that he made no apologies:

> America played a great part in the war, in the armistice, in the treaty. But if we had known that four years later the promises made to us would still be unfulfilled, we would have fought all the way to Berlin. I felt from the day of the armistice that Great Britain was no longer with us. And you—you have left us as well. You mixed your blood with ours. You do not have the right to leave us this way without trying to help. At the peace conference, wanting to surround myself with safeguards, I asked for the Rhine frontier. Lloyd George offered me the guarantee of Great Britain and of the United States if I renounced it. I did renounce it, but the promises have not been kept. If these guarantees existed, we could be certain that Germany would not attack us, and Germany could be certain that we would not attack, because we would not risk losing our friends. We are in the gravest of crises. You swore before the world that you would issue your guarantee. You proclaimed it in the treaty. I ask you, why did you go to war? Was it to help others preserve democracy? What have you gained? You accuse France now of militarism, but you did not do so when French soldiers saved the world. There can be no doubt that Germany is preparing a new war. Nothing can stop that except a close entente among America, Great Britain, and France.

The few thousand Francophiles who came to see and hear him at each speech needed no conversion. Congress and the White House could not be

---

46. J.O.S., Débats, 9 November 1922; J.O.C., Débats, 7, 10, 17 November 1922; "barrister for slandered France" by Henri Vonoven, *Le Figaro*, 18 November 1922.

converted. For the rest of Americans even aware of his visit, Clemenceau was much admired for what he had done, for what he had been—but as a relic from the past with little relevance to the present. Although his reception was markedly different from that given Briand a year earlier, Clemenceau's trip was equally a political failure.[47]

But Poincaré had not been counting on the Americans, and he had given up counting on the British. His conviction in the Germans' recalcitrance was confirmed by their request on 13 November for a renewal of the 1922 payment terms through 1923 and by the formation of a new cabinet on 21 November under Wilhelm Cuno, a shift rightward because for the first time since the Armistice the Socialist party was not included. Two days later, Poincaré met with Theunis and his foreign minister, Henri Jaspar, who pledged Belgian support in the Reparations Commission. Poincaré could run to abstain no longer. On 27 November, at a cabinet meeting in the Elysée palace with Millerand and Ferdinand Foch, he proposed that France occupy the Ruhr as soon as Germany could be found in default. Barthou explained that because Italy and Belgium would vote with France on the Reparations Commission to deny extension of the 1922 terms, Germany would owe 500 million gold marks on 15 January 1923. Its almost certain failure to make that payment would cause the declaration of default. Around the table, Lasteyrie alone raised a warning, that the franc could collapse if the British or the Americans chose to apply pressure in opposition—but without reparations, the franc would collapse anyway. The decision was made. On the day before, Poincaré had dedicated another monument, this one at Bouligny-les-Mines in the Meuse, and had obliquely revealed his intention: "Before the end of the year, France and her allies are going to face the most serious of foreign policy crises. They will have to take important decisions on which our future will depend."[48]

47. See the reports in *Le Figaro,* 23, 26, 30 November, 4, 10 December 1922, respectively, of Clemenceau's speeches at New York (21 November), Boston (24 November), Chicago (28 November), St. Louis (3 December), and Washington (9 December). Almost the only historical account is David S. Newhall, *Clemenceau: A Life at War* (Lewiston, N.Y., 1991), 492–96.

48. McDougall, *France's Rhineland Diplomacy,* 237–39; *Le Figaro,* 27 November 1922, for Poincaré in the Meuse.

At the beginning of November, Henri Vonoven took over as editor of *Le Figaro* when Capus died suddenly of typhoid fever. His first spectacular coup was reporting the essence of this cabinet meeting the very next day in his editorial. Better-known columnists such as René D'Aral, Edmond Laskine, and even Bainville mistrusted their usual government sources and also disregarded the allusion at Bouligny. Perhaps they were led astray by Poincaré's willingness to discuss options with Bonar Law in London from 9 to 12 December. But after the clear failure of this meeting, there were such open predictions of French action that Poincaré felt constrained to dampen the wildest rumors. France was not, he insisted before the Chamber of Deputies, undertaking military operations. Nor was the entente at an end: if, to enforce the treaty, French engineers and customs officials had to be sent into the Ruhr, "we will hold a place for the engineers and customs officials of our allies." Before the Senate, he elaborated: "There may be differences of opinion between ourselves and our allies, but we will take care that these are not transformed into discord. We will know how to preserve intact the bonds which unite us and which spring not only from a brotherhood of arms but from the same faith in justice and liberty." The deputies voted confidence 512 to 67, the senators unanimously, by show of hands.[49]

At least two old wise men had misgivings. Clemenceau arrived at Le Havre aboard the *Paris* on 20 December. His chief disciples—Tardieu, Mandel, Edouard Ignace, General Henri Mordacq—were there to welcome him home. A crowd of journalists were also waiting, to ask about an interview he gave that was published a week earlier in the *New York World.* "I fear the Ruhr," he had told Walter Lippmann. "The German workers would make nationalist strikes. Shall we send in French soldiers against them?" Many in France interpreted his words as undermining Poincaré, and Daudet condemned them in the Chamber. At dockside before climbing into a car, Clemenceau clarified his statement: he did not mean that he was *opposed* to entering the Ruhr, only that he was *hesitant* to

49. *Le Figaro,* 28 November, 13 December 1922, for Vonoven; *L'Action française,* 8 December 1922, for Bainville; *La République française,* 11 December 1922, for Laskine; *Le Gaulois,* 11 December 1922, for D'Aral, 14 December 1922, for Meyer; *L'Homme libre,* 13 December 1922, for Lautier; *L'Echo de Paris,* 14 December 1922, for General Edouard de Castelnau; J.O.C., Débats, 15 December 1922; J.O.S., Débats, 21 December 1922.

do so because of potential strikes. However tempered, here was a warning. Another came the following day from Alexandre Ribot during Poincaré's triumphal Senate session: "I would watch with some anxiety France entering the Ruhr alone."[50]

French exasperation had been heard before: words were not deeds. Did the British and the Germans recognize from all of Poincaré's signals that he had finally drawn a line? Pertinax and Tardieu thought not, and they were proved correct. The general assumption was that the decisive moment would come in mid-January. Instead, a German government determined to call Poincaré's bluff provoked the confrontation before the end of the year. The issue was reparations in kind of timber: France was to be delivered 55,000 cubic meters of sawed wood by 30 September and 200,000 cubic meters of telegraph poles by 30 November. The dates passed, the deliveries were seriously deficient, but the Reparations Commission gave Germany until late December to fulfill the requirement. In previous years, small discrepancies had been ignored and might have been again—timber mattered less than coal and much less than gold marks. The discrepancy for 1922 was enormous: one-third (20,000 cubic meters) of the sawed wood and two-thirds (135,000 cubic meters) of the telegraph poles. On 26 December, the Reparations Commission voted three to one, France, Belgium, and Italy against Great Britain, to declare Germany in voluntary default. Both Great Britain and Germany were astonished at the audacity. Poincaré now had a legal basis for seizing material guarantees. If France failed to act, the entire Versailles settlement would be placed in doubt. If Poincaré declined the role he had written for himself, he would be harried from public life, branded a liar, a fraud, a coward. France had to enter the Ruhr, and Poincaré had to lead her there. Abstention was no longer an option: "If I do not attempt the task myself, someone else will be entrusted with it—and do it less well."[51]

50. Clemenceau's comment from the interview published in the *New York World*, 13 December 1922, is quoted in Newhall, *Clemenceau*, 494; *Le Figaro*, 21 December 1922, described Clemenceau's homecoming; Ribot spoke briefly before the Senate: J.O.S., Débats, 21 December 1922.

51. *L'Echo national*, 25 December 1922, for Tardieu; *L'Echo de Paris*, 26 December 1922, for Pertinax; Chastenet, *Histoire de la Troisième République*, 5:101, for Poincaré's comment; McDougall, *France's Rhineland Diplomacy*, 239–41; Trachtenberg, *Reparation in World Politics*, 275–89.

5

■ ■ ■

Les Jeux sont faits

The Germans called Raymond Poincaré's bluff and then were astonished that he did not back down. In January 1923, with the full support of Belgium and a token presence from Italy, France went into the Ruhr—not alone as Alexandre Ribot had feared—to seize productive guarantees. When the strikes Georges Clemenceau had warned of brought chaos and violence, French and Belgian engineers took over the railroads and the mines. Breaking the German will to resist took more time and money than even the most pessimistic had predicted, but by the fall, the occupation was actually turning a modest profit. And Germany was on the brink of national disaster—the mark attaining hyperinflation, the government in Berlin reeling under threats by separatist movements and extremist groups from the Left and Right. Poincaré appeared to have won. On 23 November, the Chamber of Deputies endorsed his foreign policy by the overwhelming vote of 500 to 70, an even greater majority than the 478 to 86 he received on 11 January, when on announcing the decision to enter the Ruhr he called for a demonstration of unity. Yet only ten days earlier, the prominent Socialist Alexandre Varenne had boldly—and correctly—predicted to the Chamber that Poincaré and the Bloc national would lose the legislative elections scheduled for the following spring. Poincaré had shouted back: "Wait! Don't sell the bear's skin while the bear is still alive. It has claws to defend itself!"[1] Still alive, obviously, but the bear—

1. J.O.C., Débats, 11 January, 13 and 23 November 1923.

Poincaré's cabinet—had one foot in a steel-jawed trap, the failure of the Bloc national to recognize the economic realities of the Après Guerre. When had the meticulous Poincaré taken a false step? From the beginning?

After the Reparations Commission declared Germany in default on 26 December 1922, Andrew Bonar Law, Britain's prime minister, attempted to forestall French action by calling for a conference in Paris of the reparations powers—Great Britain, France, Belgium, and Italy—at the beginning of the year and promising British support for coercive measures if Germany failed "again." Given Britain's record since May 1921, Poincaré was disdainful—and rightfully—because when the meeting convened on 2 January, the official British position had become granting Germany a four-year moratorium in which to reestablish its finances and requiring a unanimous vote for the imposition of sanctions. Poincaré replied that he would forgo military occupation only in exchange for material guarantees (various taxes and assessments from the Ruhr and the Rhineland as well as deliveries in kind) worth a billion gold marks a year, strict control by the Reparations Commission over Germany's fiscal policy, and a declaration that any failure of compliance would mean automatic and immediate military occupation of the Ruhr as well as the imposition of a customs border between all regions under occupation and the rest of Germany. When Paul Theunis, the Belgian premier, sided with Poincaré, Bonar Law retreated gingerly by acknowledging a parting of ways on reparations but insisting that preservation of the entente between France and Britain was not in jeopardy. Since 1919, Poincaré had called for a self-sufficient France: now he would be forced to prove that he had been right.[2]

Louis Barthou, president of the Reparations Commission and one of the few *en tutoiement* with Poincaré, reassured the mass readership of *Le Petit parisien* about the future of the entente: "Two travelers having journeyed together across the country and finding themselves before a forest, one wants to take the path to the left, the other the path to the right, but they will meet up again on the other side." Emile Buré, writing in the moderate *L'Eclair,* predicted, "Today, Poincaré has the support of all the French." Or at least most: from the Left, *Le Radical* praised "the clarity and firm-

2. McDougall, *France's Rhineland Diplomacy,* 242–49; Trachtenberg, *Reparation in World Politics,* 275–90; for a biographical overview, see Keiger, *Poincaré,* 294–307.

ness of Poincaré." Even the captious André Tardieu joined the chorus: "Henceforth, France no longer has a choice." In secret session, the cabinet voted on 3 January to occupy the Ruhr, and military leaders were given a week to make final preparations. On 11 January, three French combat divisions, a battalion-sized Belgian force, an Italian team of industrial technicians, and engineers from the Rhineland's Mission interalliée de contrôle des usines et des mines (MICUM, the Interallied Control Commission for Factories and Mines), entered the Ruhr. Four days later, they had spread throughout this heartland of German industry.[3]

The occupation force had barely crossed into the Ruhr when Poincaré appeared before the Chamber of Deputies to seek a broad and public endorsement for his decision. The most sensitive point was the break with Britain, which he justified by insisting that the "entente cannot survive unless each, in certain circumstances, retains complete freedom of action." When he asked for a vote of confidence that would demonstrate national unity and resolve, there was tumultuous applause and then a series of disconcerting incidents. When Léon Blum, the leader of the Socialists, requested that Poincaré reply to questions, a Bloc national deputy cried out, "Go eat sauerkraut!"—presumably an accusation of pro-German bias. One of Blum's followers yelled back, "And you, go eat shit!" After the session was briefly suspended, Poincaré answered by declaring that he had said all that needed to be said. At that, a third Socialist, Jean Erlich, proclaimed his support for the cabinet, whereupon Paul Vaillant-Couturier, Poincaré's Communist antagonist from the previous summer, shouted "Traitor! Judas!" and threw a few coins to symbolize pieces of silver. The session was suspended a second time, but afterward, Poincaré won the day. By an overwhelming voice vote the deputies censured Vaillant-Couturier and then formally approved the occupation of the Ruhr 478 to 86.[4]

But if Poincaré was looking for a union sacrée, it was already beyond his grasp. The day before, ten prominent Communists had been arrested, and others, including party leader Marcel Cachin, were being sought for having traveled to Essen in the Ruhr and there urged resistance to French

3. Barthou interviewed in *Le Petit parisien,* 7 January 1923; Buré in *L'Eclair,* 4 January 1923; *Le Radical,* 6 January 1923; Tardieu in *L'Echo national,* 3 January 1923.
4. J.O.C., Débats, 11 January 1923.

troops. The decision to charge them with "plotting against the security of the state" was made at a midnight meeting among the minister of justice, Maurice Colrat, the minister of the interior, Maurice Maunoury, the director of the Sûreté générale, M. Durand, and the public prosecutor of Paris, Théodore Lescouvé—and therefore with Poincaré's full approval. Because Cachin and any other deputies involved could be arrested only if the Chamber lifted their parliamentary immunity, Poincaré was risking a divisive fight over "political liberties" in order to make examples. Further danger lay in the news that the United States was using the Ruhr occupation as an excuse to withdraw its last troops from the Rhineland, ending any pretense of cooperation under the Versailles Treaty. And, only slightly overshadowed by all the other news, there was the cabinet's proposal, made by the minister of finance, Charles de Lasteyrie, to cover the budget deficit through the imposition of a "double décime," a 20 percent increase in all direct levies except the income tax. These issues had the potential to create unpredictable fissures in the grand majority Poincaré had just achieved.[5]

Whatever tactics Poincaré might have adopted to deal immediately with these threats he was forced to delay because the Ruhr spun out of control. Lasteyrie alone among the ministers, Clemenceau alone among the "wise men," had predicted trouble—and they alone were right. General Joseph Degoutte and Paul Tirard believed that they could simply extend their military and civilian administration of the Rhineland into the Ruhr as they seized material guarantees, the coal tax, profits from state forests, and customs receipts. The German government under Chancellor Wilhelm Cuno, appearing shocked that France could not be antagonized forever, reacted initially by refusing to deliver any coal due as reparations and by calling for "moral demonstrations" against the occupiers. Workers in the Ruhr had sterner ideas, striking in the mines and on the rails, leaving French troops in control of coal at the pithead but without a means of moving it to France. Emboldened by example, Cuno made such "passive resistance" official policy on 16 January and terminated all reparations

5. *Le Figaro,* 10–11 January 1923; *Journal Officiel,* Chambre des Députés, Documents parlementaires (hereinafter cited as J.O.C., Documents), no. 5432, 1923, for the initial proposal of the double décime; Schuker, *End of French Predominance,* 42–47.

payments in cash or in kind. If the French wanted to exploit the Ruhr, they would have to do it themselves, at enormous cost yet uncertain gain.

But once committed, Poincaré was always dogged, as the Germans would discover again. By unilaterally ending all payments, Cuno handed the Reparations Commission the opportunity to declare Germany in general default on 26 January—Great Britain merely abstaining. France then had a legal basis for more repressive measures. In the French and Belgian zones on the left bank of the Rhine, Tirard's Rhineland Commission became the de facto government, assuming virtually all executive, legislative, and judicial powers. Across the Rhine in the Ruhr, Degoutte imposed Tirard's policies by military decree. France's goal of isolating the occupied territories from the rest of Germany physically as well as administratively was accomplished by the end of March. Officials of the German central government were expelled. Means of transport by water, rail, or road were subject to license. All exports from the occupied territory to the rest of Germany were prohibited, and even travel was severely circumscribed. Acts of sabotage against the occupation were tried by court-martial; sabotage of rail lines or rolling stock was made punishable by firing squad.

Much the most difficult and costly task was to restore coal deliveries, the absence of which was calamitous to the French economy. In the face of German passive resistance, the French and Belgians had to assume complete control of the world's densest rail net, to establish the so-called Régie, from the term for a government-directed enterprise. After assessing the situation firsthand, Yves Le Trocquer, the minister of public works, described to reporters on 7 February a disorganization so complete and methodical that French workers were able to get only nine trains out of the Ruhr to Aachen in the Rhineland during the previous two days. Belgian and French transportation officials responded by taking "possession définitive" of the railroads running through their areas of occupation in both the Ruhr and the Rhineland. Although unenthusiastic, Bonar Law on 17 February consented to their controlling the short stretch of an important trunk line from Düsseldorf to Aachen that crossed briefly into the British zone near Cologne. The Régie was formally declared on 1 March, with Henri Bréaud, deputy director of the French national railroad system, at its head, a work force from France and Belgium, and an initial budget of 60 million francs. The expense was unanticipated, but with coal

moving again—even slowly—French industry could survive and the occupation would eventually pay for itself.[6]

These first six weeks established the pattern for Poincaré's policy in the
Ruhr, relentless yet measured. Certainly, the Germans howled—never
more so than against French use of "black" colonial troops—and won
some support in Great Britain. But when David Lloyd George sought a
condemnation of French action by the House of Commons, the Bonar
Law cabinet defeated the motion 305 to 196. Poincaré knew well that
eventually the question of reparations and war debts would have to be resolved through agreements with Britain and the United States, and for
that matter with Germany, and knew well that the occupation of the Ruhr
was a means to this end, not the end itself. Of extreme solutions, Poincaré's own advisers were full: Jacques Seydoux, already wrong in predicting no German resistance, argued that now in the Ruhr, France might remain indefinitely. Le Trocquer, proud of having created the Régie, wanted
to maintain it permanently. Tirard schemed for a Rhineland largely autonomous from the rest of Germany. André Maginot, the minister of war
and a mutilé de la guerre, submitted a plan on 31 January calling for intentional damage to the Ruhr that would make it Germany's "devastated region." Emmanuel Peretti de la Rocca at the Quai d'Orsay, who closely
shared Poincaré's thinking, ironically annotated one such proposal, "Ad-
mirable projet, si l'Angleterre n'existait pas!" The tone Poincaré did want
to project was caught exactly by Barthou in a speech before the Société des
conférences on 19 January, "If the hour of the bailiff has been delayed,
should one be astonished that it is inexorable?" and also by General Degoutte, who told reporters on 30 January: "We will do whatever is necessary, with whatever means are necessary. Nothing will divert us from our
task. The fate of Germans is in their own hands."[7]

Yet because the extreme solutions—however absurd—circulated
widely, and because as early as 22 January, Tardieu began attacking him

6. McDougall, *France's Rhineland Diplomacy,* 256–59; *Le Temps,* 7 February 1923, for
Le Trocquer's news conference at the Quai d'Orsay; report of government intentions, *Le
Figaro,* 25 February 1923.

7. Trachtenberg, *Reparation in World Politics,* 295–98; McDougall, *France's Rhineland
Diplomacy,* 259–64, Peretti de la Rocca quoted 262; *Le Figaro,* 20 January (for Barthou), 31
January (for Degoutte) 1923.

in *L'Echo national* for coddling Germany, Poincaré had to speak himself. But not before the legislature: to do so would imply a willingness to accept interpellations with the risk of inflaming political passions as he was forced to justify every action taken. Thus far, the Bloc national agreed, on 1 February easily defeating—485 to 71—a motion by the Socialists and some Radicals calling on the cabinet to hold a debate about the Ruhr. Better, Poincaré thought, to address the annual banquet of the Association des journalistes républicains three days later, with no questions allowed. "As for us, what do we want? Two things only: to be indemnified for our ruins and to be attacked no longer. . . . It will not be we who will yield. . . . For what is at stake is the future of France and the peace of Europe. And this peace, in which we ask not a square centimeter of German territory, this peace, in which we seek only our reparations and our security, we are resolved to establish finally on indestructible foundations."[8]

In deciding to avoid the Chamber of Deputies, Poincaré had rightly interpreted 1 February as a sign of danger. The Socialists he had never counted among his supporters, but the Radicals, although not members of the Bloc national, he wanted in a broad majority of union sacrée. And he had good reason by now to believe that they would not be. On 11 January, when Poincaré announced the occupation of the Ruhr, forty-six Radicals, led by the head of the party, Edouard Herriot, abstained in the face of a clear call for national resolve. The following day, Edmond Du Mesnil, editor of the party newspaper *Le Radical,* described this abstention as a "forfait"—failure of duty—and "imbecility": "French interests are involved; the government is grappling with the foreigner. The problem of reparations, which tears at the entrails of the country, might be assuaged by this vote. At such a moment, on such a subject, abstention is inconceivable. No electoral finesse, no political casuistry: a plain and sincere vote—for or against!" But after a ferocious internal debate, political casuistry became the Radical position, Herriot announcing on 17 January that they favored economic sanctions against Germany but not military ones and so, while they would not oppose Poincaré, they would not support him.[9]

If that language sounded much closer to opposition than support, the

---

8. J.O.C., Débats, 1 February 1923; *Le Figaro,* 5 February 1923, printed the speech.
9. *Le Radical,* 12, 17 January 1923.

proof came quickly. On 15 January, a specially constituted Chamber committee chaired by clemenciste Edouard Ignace recommended unanimously that the deputies strip Marcel Cachin of his parliamentary immunity. When the Chamber as a whole took up the issue three days later, Colrat, Poincaré's minister of justice, was at pains to emphasize that the vote was not on the question of guilt. Cachin was predictably indignant that he might be called to account for defending the German working class against French—presumably capitalist—nationalism. And who should support that position but Ferdinand Buisson, for long a power in the Radical party, insisting, "The Chamber is on the road to ruin if it permits this prosecution to go forward." With most of the Radicals joining the Socialists and the Communists, the final vote was only 371 to 143. As it was announced, the Communist deputies began singing the "Internationale." On the other side of the Chamber, many members of the Bloc national replied with the "Marseillaise." Between them, the Radicals held silence, but in doing so made their separation from Poincaré obvious.[10]

A union sacrée could not even be generated to honor a Third Republican eminence, Théophile Delcassé, more than anyone else the architect of the Triple Entente, who died on 22 February. At a grand state funeral, Poincaré eulogized him as one whom all generations hence would recognize as a great Frenchman. But when the Chamber took up the apparently innocuous vote of paying for these ceremonies, the Communists launched an unexpected attack. Delcassé, they claimed, "compromised the safety of the world with his foreign policy." "Delcassé knelt at the feet of the tsar!" The Radicals were nonplussed. Delcassé had been one of their worthies, and because of that Herriot was floor leader of the proposal, but the politics of "no enemies—or at least not many—on the Left" had to be considered. And so Herriot's tribute lacked a certain ardor: "It is not a question, in honoring the man, to grant our assent to all his ideas, but Delcassé was a parliamentarian in all the sense of the term, a man of state whom we should salute. Let us not trouble by our quarrels the benevolent peace of his death." The vote was 484 to 73, the only opposition from Communists and Socialists, but as an expression of national gratitude, the debate was humiliating to Delcassé's memory.[11]

10. J.O.C., Débats, 18 January 1923.
11. J.O.C., Débats, 9 March 1923.

In hindsight, the date on which Poincaré's chance for a broad republican majority disappeared was 22 January, when a twenty-year-old anarchist named Germaine Berton went to the headquarters of the royalist
party, the Action française, where its newspaper, *L'Action française,* was
edited. There, she assassinated Marius Plateau, the head of its street bul-
lies, the Camelots du roi. Daughter of a teacher in Puteaux, tubercular,
with an arrest record for theft, she claimed to be avenging the deaths of
Jean Jaurès—shot dead by a nationalist fanatic on the eve of mobilization
in 1914—and Miguel Almereyda, the editor of *Le Bonnet rouge,* who committed suicide in 1917 while awaiting execution as a German agent. Because Charles Maurras and Léon Daudet, the party's leaders and editors
of the paper, proved inaccessible, she had to make do with Plateau. Not a
few thought about Henriette Caillaux's murder of Calmette. Berton
turned the pistol on herself in an ineffectual effort at suicide and later told
authorities, "I hope that you will let me die in tranquillity." Tranquillity
would be in short supply for everyone, and she would decide soon enough
that she wanted not only to live but to be exonerated of her deed.[12]

Judicial authorities now had a second politically charged case to balance. The first had been entrusted—with much trepidation—to Louis
Jousselin. Among the examining magistrates in the Paris prosecutorial office he had the most experience dealing with left-wing conspiracies but
with a conspicuous lack of success. His investigation into the role of the
Confédération Générale du Travail in the 1920 general strike and into the
propaganda campaign led by the "Eye of Moscow" had led to not a single
conviction. This latest "Communist Plot" appeared utterly straightforward—Frenchmen in collusion against their government's foreign policy
with Germans—involving simply the apportionment of blame among the
various Communist politicians, labor leaders, and journalists, nearly all of
whom Jousselin knew from previous interrogations. Beginning with
vigor, he immediately issued an arrest warrant for the party's leader,
Cachin, thereby requesting that the deputies lift his parliamentary immu-

---

12. Almereyda was the alias of Eugène Bonaventure Vigo. The press reports on the
shooting were extensive: see, for example, *Le Temps* and *Le Figaro,* 23 January 1923. For
this and the rest of the story of the royalists, see Eugen Weber, *Action Française: Royalism
and Reaction in Twentieth-Century France* (Stanford, 1962), 136–47.

nity from prosecution. When that followed, Cachin, expecting no favors, awaited the police with his valise packed for a sojourn in detention. For him and most of the others arrested, that lasted until 7 May.[13]

Jousselin spread his net broadly, until the initial ten names had become nearly fifty. From that, he worked back downward to thirty principal figures in the French Communist movement, fourteen of them in critical positions: Cachin (president of the party), Albert Treint (secretary-general of the party), Louis Keim (known as Ker) and Louis Sellier (both from the editorial staff of *L'Humanité*), Gaston Monmousseau (secretary-general of the C.G.T.), Georges Cazals (secretary of the C.G.T.), Marie Guillot (treasurer of the C.G.T.), Pierre Provost (secretary of the Jeunesses communistes), Charles Piétri (secretary of the Syndicat des instituteurs libres), Edmond Lartigue (secretary of the Fédération postale unitaire), Georges Marrane (secretary of the Fédération de la Seine), Charles Hueber (secretary of the Fédération communiste du Bas-Rhin), Maurice Pacquereau (secretary of the Fédération communiste de Seine-et-Oise), and Jules Massot (secretary of the Syndicat des métaux de la Seine). But what had they actually *done* to "endanger the security of the state"? Certainly, they had—verbally—encouraged the German working class to resist French occupation of the Ruhr. Certainly, the Germans had resisted, more passively than actively, though they did not appear to need the invitation of Communists from France to do so. How was this conduct any different from that of the C.G.T. in May 1920 or the Eye of Moscow in early 1921? The spreading of such propaganda might be considered reprehensible and the ideas behind it more so, but while French Communists had *encouraged,* they had carefully refrained from *acting.*[14]

A conviction in criminal court could be difficult to win, making a trial politically risky, especially coming after the acquittal of the C.G.T. leaders. The cabinet and Lescouvé had an alternative, to try the thirty before the Senate, sitting as Haute Cour (High Court of Justice) under Article 12 in the Constitutional Law of 16 July 1875, by which it could judge any person charged with an attempt against the security of the state—meaning cases

13. *Le Figaro,* 21 January 1923.
14. Leaks from the course of the investigation appeared in the press: see, for example, *Le Figaro,* 26–28 January, 1–2, 6 February, 16 March, 6, 8–9 May 1923.

involving "political justice." A decree from the president of the Republic was required, but Alexandre Millerand was more than willing. Boulangism deflated when the mere threat of an Haute Cour trial led its poltroon leader, "le brav' Général Georges," to seek exile in 1889. Any threat of insurrection during the Dreyfus Affair ended when the senators convicted Paul Déroulède and his amateurish circle of conspirators in 1899. Défaitisme lost its appeal after they found Louis Malvy guilty in 1918 and Joseph Caillaux in 1920. Why not similarly cripple French Communism, blameworthy above all of disdaining the Bloc national's image of France? Why not: because the Bloc national reigned in the Chamber, not in the Senate. This detail escaped Colrat, Lescouvé, and even Poincaré.

Shortly after 2 P.M. on 24 May, the president of the Senate, Gaston Doumergue, a long-standing pillar of the Radical party, formally read Millerand's decree convoking the senators as the High Court. A roll call revealed that twenty-six of them, about 10 percent, had concluded that absence would be easier to explain than any vote. Lescouvé then presented the *réquisitoire,* the summary of the government's case: that the thirty defendants had engaged in "machinations and intelligence with agents of a foreign power to the end of engaging it to commit hostilities against France or of procuring the means for it to do so." When he finished at nearly 4 P.M., a closed debate began about procedures for hearing the evidence, but after three and a half hours more, the session—and the trial—ended because by a vote of 145 to 104 the senators declared themselves "incompetent" to hear the case. Juridically, they had decided that the charges did not meet the constitutional definition for judgment by the Haute Cour. Politically, they had administered a stunning blow to Poincaré and the Bloc national.[15]

The news reached Poincaré just as he completed a confident appearance before the Chamber. Vincent Auriol, second only to Blum among the Socialists, had complained that French strategy in the Ruhr was contradictory and confused, for how could ruining Germany save reparations? Auriol's words were not an interpellation because the Bloc national had successfully postponed indefinitely debate about the Ruhr occupation, and

15. J.O.S., Débats, 24 May 1923; *Le Temps, Le Figaro, L'Echo national, L'Humanité,* 25 May 1923.

nothing constrained Poincaré to reply. But he did so, serene in his sense of embodying the nation's will and assuming that the Senate was simultaneously administering a stern rebuke to the Communists for opposing it: "France is not at all in a hurry. She can wait and wait patiently until Germany comes to its senses. . . . We entered the Ruhr to be paid and for no other reason, so let there be an end to these lying accusations. We are the surest friends of peace, because peace is meaningless when treaties can be violated shamelessly while the world looks on with indifference." The applause that followed included even the Socialist seats. And thus it was with stupefaction that Poincaré learned the ruling of the Haute Cour. With the entire cabinet, he immediately set off for the Elysée to resign and changed his mind only after forty-five minutes of entreaties from Millerand. Poincaré was not one to abandon his post at a moment of danger, but he rightly considered the Senate's action close to a vote of no confidence.[16]

What had gone wrong? Having spent more than a dozen years in the Senate (from 1903 to 1913 and since 1920), Poincaré had taken its loyalty for granted. He should not have. The system of répartition proportionnelle applied only to the Chamber of Deputies, and in the January 1920 voting that had returned him to the Senate seat at the Palais Luxembourg, the Radicals, moderates for the most part, had maintained their control. Elected indirectly, the senators bowed to the tradition of letting the Chamber—as the expression of direct universal manhood suffrage—set the political tone, which for more than three years had been that of the Bloc national. But a warning sign had come early in 1923. Léon Bourgeois, president of the Senate since 1920, stepped down in mid-February, tired and increasingly preoccupied by his devotion to the League of Nations. The senators elected in his place Doumergue, a conservative Radical, yet known for his links to Caillaux—a caillautiste. The conservative press took notice, *Le Gaulois* writing that here was "a retreat, a regression in the march toward a better and freer future." *Le Figaro*'s Henri Vonoven saw it as the political system readjusting its equilibrium after a shift to the right and cautioned of the import.[17]

16. J.O.C., Débats, 24 May 1923; press coverage, 25–26 May 1923, especially *Le Temps* and *Le Figaro*.

17. J.O.S., Débats, 22 February 1923; *Le Gaulois* and *Le Figaro*, 23 February 1923.

What energized this readjustment was above all the reaction of the extreme Right to the murder of Plateau. When the first arrests were made of French Communists for their actions in the Ruhr, *Le Radical* indignantly editorialized, "We refuse to concede that Cachin, Monmousseau, and their friends can have any accomplices, openly acknowledged or not, within the ranks of republicans." Less than two weeks later, Berton shot Plateau. Without question, the extreme Left seemed the danger. There was even some slight sympathy for Plateau, a violent man who had survived the war badly maimed. That lasted only long enough for his Camelots to mete out retribution by sacking the offices and printing shops not of Communist, Socialist, or anarchist newspapers but of the moderate *L'Oeuvre* and *L'Ere nouvelle*—because their opposition, more reasoned, had greater effect. If the Camelots did nothing so outrageous for some weeks afterward, Daudet, for whom vituperation was second nature, made the pages of *L'Action française* a weapon of assault by issuing an open invitation for any vengeance wreaked in Plateau's name.[18]

Unwisely, the government, through Maunoury, the minister of the interior, and Armand Naudin, the Paris prefect of police, took no overt steps to check this provocation. That circumspection profoundly worried moderates, who had the recent example of Benito Mussolini's Fascisti with which to compare the Camelots and gratuitously offered an opening to criticize the cabinet because the suspects in the "Communist Plot" and Germaine Berton were all under arrest, but no one from the Action française. On 23 March, with Cachin and his valise in detention, one of his lieutenants, André Berthon, shouted across the Chamber of Deputies at Poincaré: "You are Daudet's prisoner! I wonder what blackmail he exercises against you?" As Poincaré vividly protested, Daudet leaped from his seat and interrupted, "I forbid you to accuse me, you, the lawyer for Bernain"—a reference to Berthon's defense of Mme Bernain de Ravisi, accused but never tried on charges of treason. "Why should I extort the premier? It is you who are the master blackmailer, an agent of Germany and Moscow!" But Berthon continued, "The country asks itself, remembering the campaign by which some tried to attack you in the months which pre-

18. *Le Radical,* 11 January 1923; *L'Action française,* from 23 January through mid-March 1923.

ceded your election as president of the Republic, whether Daudet is not attempting a maneuver of the same sort today." He was recalling the sordid rumors about Henriette Poincaré in December 1912 and implying that there was more yet to whisper. If he meant to incite an intemperate reply, he succeeded. "You are an abominable scoundrel!" Poincaré cried out at Berthon. And then addressing the Chamber as a whole, he spoke with icy disdain: "This man has dared to pretend that dossiers compromising to me or my family have been compiled and that I fear their being made public. He has lied!"[19]

The cheers for Poincaré from all but the Communist seats and the contemptuous boos for Berthon, many of the deputies shaking their fists at him, demonstrated how poorly the opening had been exploited—this time. Soon enough, the chance came again, the Action française willfully raising fears that the Bloc national saw no enemies to the right. On 10 May, a band of approximately forty Camelots attacked Caillaux as he walked in Toulouse. That these young toughs beat up a man sixty years old with their fists and canes, leaving his head bloody and left arm smashed, was entirely appropriate to Daudet, and he said so not merely in his newspaper but before the Chamber of Deputies the following day. That much was to be expected. But with the Radicals outraged at the assault on their former leader, Maunoury should have understood that a similar degree of outrage was required from him, if only to indicate a separation from Daudet, and he failed to do so. When Herriot formally asked what steps the government would take in reaction, Maunoury replied only that justice would proceed as usual. Auriol interjected that such an unconcerned response was insufficient and that the entire domestic policy of the cabinet was now in question. That condemnation served as Daudet's cue. Why, he asked, did Caillaux deserve such solicitude? "The violence did not begin with us. It was Caillaux's wife who in 1914 began things by murdering Calmette. And Marius Plateau is dead at the instigation of caillautiste newspapers!" No one from the cabinet called him to order, and the Chamber adjourned in chaos. Over the next two weeks, the justice promised by Maunoury did begin to take its course. By 23 May, six of the Camelots in Toulouse had been identified and arrested, but the damage

19. J.O.C., Débats, 23 March 1923.

from the 11 May Chamber session could not be undone. Only one day later, the senators voted against trying the thirty Communists.[20]

Although public prosecutor Lescouvé vowed to take the case to criminal court, the Senate's refusal incited the Action française to exemplary action against the principle of free speech—especially criticizing France—that seemed the ideological justification. An appropriate occasion was quickly presented by a meeting on the evening of 31 May to protest the Ruhr occupation. Separate bands of Camelots roughed up and smeared with printers' ink three of the scheduled speakers before they could even attend: Marius Moutet, a Socialist, and Maurice Viollette, a Radical, both of them fair game merely by political affiliation, and Marc Sangnier, the social Catholic manifestly too full of Christian kindness for Germans and Communists. But this time the Action française had gone too far. Sangnier and Moutet were deputies, Viollette a former deputy; they were not Caillaux, disgraced by his conviction for défaitisme, as if that were sufficient reason for battery. Just how much too far could be guessed from Vonoven's editorial in the sometime-friendly Le Figaro: "By striking Sangnier, Moutet, and Viollette yesterday evening, the Camelots du roi have just done great harm to their party, the nation, and the Chamber." Definitive proof would come from the deputies.[21]

When the Chamber convened on 1 June, Maunoury was finally ready to display outrage: "Violence of this sort is intolerable, and we will not tolerate it. If some ruffians can lurk amid the shadows to ambush political adversaries and so prevent their speaking in public, that would mean the end, little by little, to all the liberties constituting the patrimony of the Republic." The government, he announced, had already issued warrants for the Parisian leaders of the Camelots du roi and was examining documents suggesting the existence of a "royalist plot." Herriot quickly endorsed this statement, but when he started to add his own commentary, "In the name of republicans, of all republicans, I say to you that we have had enough," Daudet interrupted with "You had Plateau murdered!" That brought the

20. Le Temps, Le Figaro, L'Action française, 11–24 May 1923; J.O.C., Débats, 11 May 1923.

21. Le Temps and Le Figaro, 1–2 June 1923, Vonoven's "Contre les Royalistes" from 2 June.

slamming of desks and epithets from all but the deputies of the Far Right: "Bandit!" "Coward!" "Blackguard!" "Scum!" "Extortioner!" "Get out!" "Take your filth away from here!" When Daudet was shouted down, Herriot continued to cheers: "Democracy has a case of the nerves! Its attachment to order and its confidence in the law should not be taken for weakness. Why have those defiling the Republic gone unpunished? The moment has come to take a position on one side or the other." To emphasize Daudet's isolation, Emmanuel Brousse of the Bloc national took the tribune: "I protest energetically against the detestable actions of a few fanatics. The Republic can live only in order and calm. The security of citizens must be assured. Violence is not fitting in this country, for France is not ripe for 'fascism.' " After the speeches, the deputies needed no vote to demonstrate the opprobrium into which they had cast the Action française and its spokesman. What they did vote on was confidence in the cabinet, with the result, 379 to 191, the measure of how the treatment of political violence left and right had eroded its majority.[22]

During the next two weeks—even though France had yet not overcome German passive resistance in the Ruhr and was struggling to make the occupation pay—Poincaré's broad majority began to ravel seriously. Tardieu's contribution to the dramatic session on 1 June had been typically caustic, "A government must govern—say so, if you think that's the case." But in accusing the cabinet of indecision about how to confront the violence of both extremes, he seized upon, with his usual acuity, a point of weakness and sensitivity. The following day at Nantes, Aristide Briand gave another of his speeches drawing the distinction between himself and Poincaré, this time with a slightly sharper edge. The Chamber had, he rejoiced, overwhelmingly denounced the violence of the Camelots, but somehow the royalists had been led to believe that they could act as they pleased. In the elections less than a year away, "all republicans, from the most moderate to the most advanced, must band together, every member of the republican family, everyone who is a 'blue' [in French politics, the color of republicanism] stand fast and fight against everyone who is a 'white' [the color of monarchism]—fight, that is to say, on the terrain of ideas, with courtesy." Briand was envisioning a broad majority but one

22. J.O.C., Débats, 1 June 1923.

clearly leftward of the Bloc national: including the Socialists and excluding anyone even sympathetic to the Action française. In 1919, he had carefully positioned himself on the left edge of the Bloc national; for 1924, he appeared to be choosing the right edge of a Cartel des gauches. Eleven days passed before the next political body blow, Jousselin's decision on 13 June—over Lescouvé's energetic objection—to dismiss all criminal charges against the thirty Communists.[23]

To present a united front during the foreign policy crisis created by the Ruhr occupation, Poincaré had sought to minimize disputes over domestic policy by adopting centrist positions generally acceptable both to most of the Radicals and to the Bloc national. The "Communist Plot" and the "royalist plot" from the extremes of Left and Right threatened to spike this strategy because they incited partisan debate and would spread the political opportunism adopted by Briand at Nantes. After Jousselin's *non-lieu* and facing the trial of Caillaux's attackers near the end of the month, Poincaré recognized that formal discussion of domestic issues could not be put off, and he announced that he would accept interpellations on 15 June. Sensing that the cabinet's hand had been forced, public anticipation was so great that the galleries of the Chamber were surcharged, and some thousands waited outside after being turned away. The thunder against Poincaré's broad centrism began from the right edge of the Bloc national, as Jean Ybarnégaray, a personal friend of Daudet, accused the Left of dreaming up a royalist plot in order to claim that they had saved the country from such a threat and to justify organizing a Cartel des gauches against the Bloc national in the next election. Poincaré, he insisted, had to choose: "For your majority, either you will embrace as many elements as possible, and thereby deprive it of meaning and significance, or you will impose strict and clear limits, from which you will gain new strength to pursue your politics of security and reparations." The thunder then rolled through the moderates, with Charles Bellet attacking the left wing of the Bloc national for sliding toward the Radicals—the Radicals "who welcome the singing of the 'Internationale' here in the Chamber, yet consider the 'Marseillaise' a reactionary hymn. Enough of that! The government

23. J.O.C., Débats, 1 June 1923; *Le Figaro,* 3 (Briand at Nantes), 14 (Jousselin) June 1923.

must decide whether to stand with those who serve it or with those who do not, even as they take every advantage."

Poincaré could already count losses to his majority on the Left, and now demands were being made on the Right. Accepting them meant adopting the clemenciste position of Tardieu and Georges Mandel, of seeking to create a clear divide in France between Right and Left and therefore relying on a relatively small, tightly disciplined, majority—relying, in 1923, on a majority clearly of the Right. Accepting them meant abandoning his own preference, the tradition of the Third Republic for governing by presiding over a large, somewhat amorphous majority of the Center that shifted slightly to the left or right on each issue—governing, in 1923, with a union sacrée. Poincaré was not ready to give up on that. In a carefully worded speech, he tried to stanch defectors on both sides by staking out for himself the moral high ground of impartiality and patriotism and then demanding a majority "républicaine et nationale" to defend it. For the assaults from the Left and the Right were not simply political violence but subversion of the republican regime, and "the government, while permitting parties the greatest freedom of the press and of legal propaganda, will in the event of violence, of crimes and misdemeanors, show itself inexorable in the defense of public order, whether the attacks are committed by the royalists, the Communists, or by anyone else." The rest of his domestic policy was defined by the course of his long career as a moderate: the laic laws enforced to the letter, but the Vatican embassy retained; the political rights of government employees *(fonctionnaires)* limited by a requirement to show respect for the state; the prefects ordered not to interfere in elections.

Emphasizing his position in the Center, Poincaré recalled how at his urging the obdurate Marxist Jules Guesde and the courtly Orleanist Denys Cochin both served in wartime cabinets. "I dreamed this union sacrée that was our strength might be prolonged," but now not everyone was welcome: the extremist parties—he meant the Action française, the Communists, and perhaps the Socialists—he did not want in his majority because they were not "républicaine" or not "nationale" or not either. To the Action française, Poincaré insisted that support for the Ruhr occupation was not enough. To the Socialists and some Radicals, he declared that belief in class warfare or a willingness to compromise with its adherents was too much. Everyone else was invited to join him, and "if this majority is ready to follow us, we ourselves are ready to blaze the way." But such a majority was not willing to follow him. Poincaré's words, although seemingly even-handed, appealed only to the Bloc national. Most of the Radicals sat ominously silent, well aware that their election tactics had just been proscribed. On the motion of confidence, Poincaré prevailed 354 to 161, but he had lost more than a hundred votes since January, and the Radicals were now willing to oppose rather than merely abstain—even with France in the Ruhr. Afterward, Ernest Lafont of the Communists declaimed that the Bloc national was "dead, well dead, despite what Poincaré has been able to say. . . . The cabinet is composed only of reactionaries. You protect the elements hostile to the Republic." Although a harangue, these words captured the essence of the vote: the left wing of the Bloc national had fallen away, and Poincaré was forced back upon support increasingly weighted toward the Right. Instead of reviving a union sacrée as he had hoped, the session of 15 June was the opening shot of the legislative election campaign.[24]

Further salvos quickly followed. On 20 June, at a party meeting in Paris, Herriot lectured on political arithmetic and logic. By labeling 175 of the deputies voting for Poincaré as "droites"—rightists—he reduced the cabinet's total of "true republicans" to 179, a minority compared to the 182 Radicals and Socialists either opposing or abstaining—thus Poincaré should resign. But because he surely would not, the three Radicals he had included in his ministry should do so or risk being drummed out of the party. Albert Sarraut, the minister for colonies, and Paul Laffont, the under secretary for PTT (Postes, télégraphes, et téléphones), were holdovers from Briand's ministry, and Poincaré had added Paul Strauss as minister of public assistance (Hygiène, assistance, et prévoyance sociale) to prove his bona fides in seeking broad support. In demanding that they choose their fate, Herriot decried their having been recruited "for the work of reaction." Great, then, was Radical annoyance at the response to this *chantage:* from Sarraut, "I continue to stand beside the great republican who is Poincaré"; from Strauss, "I remain proudly a member of the Poincaré government, the politics of which I approve without reserve";

24. J.O.C., Débats, 15 June 1923. See Weber's assessment in *Action Française,* 145–47.

from Laffont, "It will be the honor of my life to have been the co-worker and friend of one who is the firmest of republicans and the greatest of Frenchmen."[25]

The Radicals found more resonance by concentrating on right-wing violence. On 22 June, Gustave Laroque, the examining magistrate for the attack on Sangnier, Moutet, and Viollette, ordered three Camelots—the only ones clearly identifiable—before district court *(tribunal correctionnel)* for trial on assault. Spectacularly, and perhaps evidence of heightened concern in the cabinet, he added the charge of complicity against the founder and animator of the Action française, Charles Maurras, ideological father of integral nationalism. At their trial five days later, they offered no defense, only a justification, and Maurras proudly testified, "I am the only one guilty, and I demand the responsibility for this act which I consider useful and honorable." The judges took him partly at his word, imposing a sentence of four months in jail for Maurras, three and two months for the Camelots. A week later on 5 July at Toulouse came the similar trial of the Camelots accused of beating up Caillaux. Again, of the many involved, only a few had been conclusively identified, and again, their leader, a certain Ebelot, took pride in his action, telling the court, "That evening, my duty accomplished, I went to bed joyful." He received a sentence of three months in jail, the others one month, suspended. Despite the injuries and the invitation to conduct politics through street battles, justice in both Paris and Toulouse decided not to err on the side of severity. And even then, Maurras at least, and perhaps the others as well, contrived to avoid serving their minimal sentences. Good for them, but here was additional fodder for Radical propaganda.[26]

Was there anything behind the Camelot violence beyond a taste for brawling and the motive of revenge after Plateau's murder? Certainly, the evolution and attitude of the Radical party, symbolized by its ambiguous position on the Ruhr occupation, excited the worst fears among the Right, whose gains of influence and respectability had come in direct proportion

25. *Le Radical* and *Le Figaro,* 21–22 June 1923.
26. *La Gazette des tribunaux,* 23, 28 June, 5, 8 July 1923. Weber, *Action Française,* 147, n. j: "There is no record that Maurras ever served this sentence; amnesties always seemed to save him in time."

to Radical losses. Now, after bowing to Poincaré throughout 1922, the Radicals were restive, staking out a position apart from—if not yet clearly opposed to—the cabinet, talking up a Cartel des gauches for the 1924 elections, no longer ashamed to claim Caillaux and Malvy. On 14 March before the Chamber of Deputies, Daudet warned that if France was still in the Ruhr when legislative elections were held, a victory for the Left would mean an accommodation with Germany—just as Caillaux had tried in 1911. At the end of the month, Gustave Hervé betrayed the worry of conservatives when he editorialized in *La Victoire,* "If domestic peace reigns since the abortive general strikes of 1920, if Germany eventually pays reparations in full, the country will owe it—we must keep repeating until the next election—not to the friends of Cachin, Blum, Caillaux, and Herriot, but to the much maligned Bloc national." The Radicals proposed, however, to run on different issues. The *Journal des débats* reported that Herriot was using the establishment of the Vatican embassy—never mind Briand's support for it—to revive the anticlericalism that had been the cement for prewar alliances of the Left. Malvy had returned to France from his exile in Spain to a warm reception. And at the beginning of May, brazenly courting the Socialists, Herriot proclaimed in *Le Radical,* "Radicalism, having exhausted its political platform, will henceforth be 'social' or it will not be." Was the attack on Caillaux one week later merely coincidental?[27]

Yet such frustrations acted out, and then punished gingerly, only gave substance to the accusation that the axis of the Bloc national and of the Poincaré cabinet was too far to the right. Conservatives who were more moderate had to put the case more moderately, as *Le Figaro*'s Henri Vonoven began to do in late summer: "The propaganda against the Cartel des gauches is easy to organize in a country where patriotism remains intact and judgment always alert." As allies of the Socialists, the Radicals will be "the auxiliary force charged with demolishing and undermining for their electoral allies the existing social institutions, which they claim to support. They will be the sappers of the collectivist regiment." Facing the challenge of the Ruhr occupation, "will we tremble at the thought that the Radicals

27. J.O.C., Débats, 14 March 1923; *La Victoire,* 30 March 1923; *Le Journal des débats,* 12 April 1923; A.N., F7 12952 1, "Notes Jean," P 1956, 3 May 1923; *Le Radical,* 3 May 1923.

will denounce us as reactionaries?" And when at Creysse on 10 October the Camelots got around to assaulting Malvy, Vonoven denounced the attack as "intolerable" but suggested "reading again the decree" of the Haute Cour from 7 August 1918, all the better to understand why Malvy would be so despised and what the Radicals were defending.[28]

There was ample room for this commentary because the principal political figures were holding their fire, awaiting the outcome in the Ruhr as France's strategy entered the endgame. Finally, Germany reached the breaking point and on 26 September formally announced the end to all passive resistance. At least for the present, Poincaré had won, but he had few illusions about the future and not the slightest inclination to gloat. Four days after the German capitulation, speaking at Saint-Mihiel, where the fighting had been extraordinarily fierce during the war, he warned that "the work of tomorrow is more difficult from what we have already accomplished. . . . France does not yet have the victory guaranteed her by the treaties, but she will have it. We have sworn that to you, and we will keep our oath." The next day at home in Bar-le-Duc, he was still more blunt: "Our labors are not finished, and now is not the moment to fold our arms or sulk at the task." No one could mistake his continuing appeal for a union sacrée. Briand scurried to claim credit for supporting Poincaré's Ruhr policy, at Guérande (Loire-Inférieure) on 7 October, insisting, "When the government is grappling with problems of this sort, the duty of every Frenchman is to rally around it and to give whatever aid possible in the accomplishment of the task." But to make certain that the manner of his own cabinet's demise was remembered, he added, "Do not expect me to oppose the acts of my successors, who are doing their best to overcome the difficulties which they face, and of which, I cannot forget, I myself knew all the treacheries." No one could mistake how Briand was typically hedging his bets, as he balanced between staying within the Bloc national and not—just as he had abstained on 15 June.[29]

And then on 14 October, Alexandre Millerand exploded the "Bombe d'Evreux," a speech in which neither union sacrée nor hedging of bets had any place. Since his election to the presidency of the Republic in Septem-

---

28. *Le Figaro,* 25, 31 August, 13 September, 11 October 1923.
29. See verbatim extracts in *Le Figaro,* 1, 2, 8 October 1923.

ber 1920, Millerand had chafed at playing the traditional nonpartisan head of state. Although the deputies rebuffed his effort to direct foreign policy from the Elysée by overturning the Georges Leygues cabinet in January 1921, he pressed the prerogatives of the presidency to the limit during the Cannes negotiations a year later and certainly did not oppose the maneuvers that persuaded Briand to resign. Of Poincaré's foreign policy, Millerand had no complaint, but as one of the organizers of the Bloc national, he was uneasy about seeking a broad consensus that blurred ideological lines. For Poincaré to seek a union sacrée made sense while the outcome of the Ruhr remained in doubt, and Millerand had made the same plea as recently as 23 September, when he spoke at Rambouillet to dedicate a war memorial: "All that for which the dead died must be realized. . . . France first will be our guiding principle as it was for them. We will make the peace as they won the war . . . we will remain fraternally united and to the end, no matter what happens, firm in our resolutions. Assembled around the flag, we will maintain a vigilant guard to prevent divisions or discouragement, to extinguish all brands of discord, and to rekindle, wherever it threatens to die out, the sacred love of country." But now that the Germans had given in, the forthcoming legislative elections had to be considered, and Poincaré's words at the end of September implied a certain tendency not to take political advantage of foreign policy—depriving the Bloc national of its trump card. If Poincaré appeared reluctant to lead his majority into the elections, Millerand was not. He had meant what he said at Ba-Ta-Clan in November 1919, and now he had the opportunity to prove it.[30]

The speech at Evreux (Eure) was a bombshell. For a president of the Republic even to address political controversies publicly was a dramatic departure from tradition, to take a clearly partisan stand on them extraordinary. And dangerous: Millerand was violating the unwritten rules of the presidency, acting more like a premier even as Poincaré was assuming an almost presidential demeanor. To leave the political invisibility of the Elysée was to make himself a highly visible target. At Evreux, Millerand all but dared the opponents of the Bloc national to aim at him. When he

---

30. Farrar, *Principled Pragmatist,* 328–60; for the Rambouillet speech, see *Le Figaro,* 24 September 1923.

called for a "union des bons citoyens" to "pursue social progress in an atmosphere of calm and hard work," there was little doubt who he considered "good citizens" and who not. When he declared the war and German
recalcitrance afterward proof that the "pacifists were wrong," everyone
recognized the reference to défaitisme. When he adopted the program of
natality associated with Catholic conservatives, "avoir des enfants et faire
des hommes"—have children and make men—he was placing himself in
their midst. When he proposed revising the constitution "to give the government more stability and economic interests additional guarantees," he
was not appealing to the Left. And when he concluded that such revisions
would generate "a political life more social and national, more devoted to
the prosperity and grandeur of the homeland," Radicals and Socialists
heard the leader of the Bloc national speaking, not the president of the
Republic.[31]

Provocation breeds provocation: by making himself a target, Millerand
ensured that he would be shot at. The firing began in earnest when the
Radicals held their annual party congress in Paris less than a week later.
The speech at Evreux, they claimed, was "unconstitutional." It was a new
Seize Mai, referring to the contest for power between President Patrice de
MacMahon and the Chamber of Deputies that began on 16 May 1877, with
his demand that a premier with a working majority resign and then his
invocation of the constitutional provision permitting, with the consent of
the Senate, dissolution of the Chamber and the calling of new elections.
And it would end the same way: when the elections supported the Chamber, MacMahon resigned—although nearly a year and a half later—and
no president since had dared another confrontation. Until then, "the Republic was in danger," and its safety could be ensured only through a victory the following spring by a Cartel des gauches, ranging from such deputies of the Center as Gaston Thomson, Louis Loucheur, and Charles
Dumont, who were sometime supporters of the Bloc national, to the Socialists of Léon Blum, whose moderation in comparison to the Communists made them appropriate partners. Herriot also sponsored a resolution
denying the vote of any Radical to a cabinet not supported by a majority
of this "republican Left."

31. See the text of the speech in *Le Temps,* 15 October 1923.

If the proposed membership for the Cartel des gauches was now defined and thereby also its ambition—"to bring down the Bloc national and prevent the growth of Communism"—the alliance was not yet created. The final manifesto of the congress made clear that it was to be essentially on Radical terms: "To our left, the pact depends on our neighbors as much as on ourselves. To our right, there are excellent republicans whose sincerity and service we do recognize . . . to them, as well, we offer our hand, but it is in their interest as much as ours to avoid any misconceptions." And these terms were, as a minimum, retention of the income tax, support for the eight-hour workday, defense of *laïcité* by suppressing the embassy to the Vatican and by refusing authorization of any religious congregations to remain in France, and endorsing the League of Nations as the best means for settling international disputes—therefore disavowing the "unilateral" Ruhr occupation. This last was the most controversial because many of the Radicals were decidedly uneasy about condemning the cabinet's foreign policy, especially with the outcome potentially successful. Socialist criticism of them for not opposing what their spokesman Jean Longuet called "the detestable adventure of the Ruhr" made some concession mandatory if the Cartel were not to be stillborn, but the wording was sufficiently vague to blame the lack of "interallied accords" more than the "Ruhr operation" itself. Enthusiasm for the League of Nations was also hardly absolute. When the historian Alphonse Aulard, a decidedly left-wing Radical, proposed submitting the question of the Ruhr and the entire enforcement of the Versailles Treaty to the League, Herriot quickly opposed the idea. Henry Franklin-Bouillon, who had gained some experience in diplomacy as Poincaré's emissary to Mustapha Kemal during 1921, added, "I am a great adversary of the Versailles Treaty, but I tell you, do not tear it to pieces!"[32]

"Tous ensemble!"—All together!—was the slogan the Radicals wanted for their Cartel des gauches, but could they bring together an electoral alliance ranging from the right wing of their party to the left wing of the Socialists, expressed by the phrase "from Gaston Thomson to Alexandre Varenne"? What did they share besides a common opposition to the Bloc national and a desire to exercise power? There was anticlericalism and

32. *Le Radical,* 17–21 October 1923.

thus the revival by the Radicals of an issue settled before the war—even Clemenceau's old newspaper, *L'Homme libre,* wondered at the emphasis. There were scores to settle and thus the acclaim for Caillaux—absent because the sentence of the Haute Cour deprived him of his "political rights" for ten years—as "un grand républicain, un grand Français, victime des nationalistes." There was a certain conception of the regime—embodied in the phrase "republican Left"—that took offense at Poincaré's attitude toward power, and much more so Millerand's. And that seemed all. By contrast, the Bloc national could hold high the progress of reconstruction in the devastated region, the steady recovery of the economy, and, at last, the teaching of a stern lesson to the Germans. These accomplishments had not come as fast as French voters had hoped in 1919 or as fast as Bloc national candidates had promised, but the success, in the face of enormous difficulties domestic and foreign, was undeniable. Conservatives warned of complacency but felt confident.[33]

That was Poincaré's attitude when he spoke on 4 November at Tulle (Corrèze) and on 17 November before the Comité de commerce et de l'industrie in Paris, four days after his exchange with Varenne in the Chamber about "selling the bear skin." Although he denied that the electoral season had opened, he laid out a domestic program that was vague yet consciously and carefully differentiated from that of the Cartel. The defining spirit of his policy would be the "maintenance of republican laws, applied precisely and defended against the adversaries of our institutions"—by which he meant to insist on his own republican credentials while situating himself in the broad Center, with the unnamed "adversaries" to the extreme Left and the extreme Right. In the best republican tradition he was a "laic," but the *laicité* of the state did not require a new round of anticlericalism. Instead, France needed the "religious peace" that would come through "respect for belief," retaining the embassy to the Vatican, and tolerance toward at least some of the religious congregations, especially the nursing convents—the appeal to Catholic conservatives was

33. On the revival of anticlericalism, see the comments of Lautier in *L'Homme libre,* 22 October 1923. Vonoven's editorial in *Le Figaro,* 25 October 1923, is typical of the cautious but unapprehensive reaction to the proposed Cartel; see also *Le Journal des débats, L'Echo de Paris, L'Eclair,* and *La République française,* 23–26 October 1923, for a similar response.

obvious. There would also be "administrative reforms" and new "economies," never the language of the Left. Yet even as he attacked the Cartel
program through indirection, he called for the kind of broad majority he
had always cherished. Side by side, he had worked with Frenchmen of
goodwill across the political spectrum, from Guesde to Cochin, and in between, Millerand, Briand, Delcassé, as well as prominent Radicals like
Théodore Steeg, Jules Pams, Jean Dupuy, and Louis-Lucien Klotz—
"without the slightest discord." The omission of Caillaux and Malvy was
pointed, but also that of Clemenceau, Tardieu, and Mandel. "To the task
all together"—Poincaré used "tous ensemble" almost in derision of the
Radicals—"with reverence for all republican institutions and laws: a politics for the nation, of revival, reparations, and security."[34]

The Ruhr was Poincaré's justification for staking out the political high
ground. Over protests and fears, foreign and domestic, he had with great
sangfroid carried off an undeniable triumph. Although mistaken in failing
to foresee the passive resistance and its initial chaos, Poincaré rightly recognized that the German position would become untenable as the French
took over the work and guaranteed the transportation of coal through the
Régie. For the government of Chancellor Cuno, underwriting the resistance by paying the lost wages of the workers and the lost profits of the
industrial magnates when revenue, tax and otherwise, from the Rhineland
and the Ruhr was going to France, not Berlin, meant a recourse to printing money, in large quantity and without backing. The inevitable result
was hyperinflation of the mark beyond European imagination, approaching one trillion percent. When the currency became as worthless within
Germany as without, Cuno had the rare and unenviable privilege of
watching from the seat of power the disintegration of his nation. Social
and economic crisis spawned riots and labor strife throughout the country.
The Communists were a threat to seize power in Saxony and Thuringia,
the as yet little-known National Socialists to do so in Bavaria. Renewed
agitation for separatism or at least autonomy grew in the Rhineland. Appeals to Great Britain were fatally flawed by Germany's status of voluntary default. Bonar Law had decided to give Poincaré the chance to prove
the French position on reparations, thus the accommodation for the Régie.

34. See the excerpts and analysis in *Le Figaro,* 5, 18 November 1923.

Although he resigned on 22 May—mortally ill, he died on 30 October—and the new prime minister, Stanley Baldwin, was more strictly neutral, that did Germany no good. By 13 August, Cuno had had enough and stepped down.

How close had Germany come to catastrophe? Theunis, Barthou, and the French ambassador in Berlin, Pierre de Margerie, considered that his successor, Gustav Stresemann, might be the last hope for a settlement short of violence. From the first, Poincaré had imposed as a precondition to any negotiation that Germany recognize the legality of the Ruhr occupation and formally end all passive resistance. On 1 September at Stuttgart, in a clumsy effort to exploit the fear of what might happen next, Stresemann sought to outflank this ultimatum by proposing talks among the "Rhine-interested" powers. Poincaré refused on 9 September, Baldwin did so as well after a quick trip to Paris on the nineteenth, and on the twenty-first, Theunis made the rejection unanimous. Recognizing that his independent options were exhausted, Stresemann then decreed passive resistance over and, on 26 September, revoked the legislation granting it formal support. Negotiations were now possible, but what kind? At the moment of seeming triumph, Poincaré appeared to hesitate before the possibilities.

One alternative was to gamble that Bismarck's achievement of German unification could be undone, that some form of Rhenish separatism would create an independent, or at least largely autonomous, Rhineland. To do so would risk all for the policy of self-sufficiency: against such a weakened Germany, France could stand alone, while extorting "reparation" payments through continued occupation of the Ruhr. Then and later, Poincaré was accused of seriously considering the proposition, the evidence coming from France's "benevolent neutrality" in late September and then through October when the disparate separatist groups in the Rhineland launched a series of bloody demonstrations and attempted coups. On 23 October, the lead editorial in *Le Figaro,* which always reflected Poincaré's thinking, was entitled "The Rhenish Republic: The Movement Expands." Two days later, *Le Temps,* almost the semiofficial newspaper of the cabinet, defended "Notre politique rhénane"—Our Rhenish policy. In the Rhineland, Tirard was given permission to explore possibilities with local notables. In fact, there were no possibilities: the adamant opposition of

Great Britain, the less adamant opposition of Belgium, the incapacity of separatist leaders, and the utter lack of popular support meant that the separatist movement collapsed by December. Poincaré might have dared greatly through open intervention. Or he might have refrained charily through complete abstention. Instead, he merely acquiesced in the course of events.[35]

A second alternative, said to be favored by Millerand, was a variation on French self-sufficiency, to strike an independent deal with Germany. Like the tentative wager on Rhenish separatism, such an agreement, by dispensing with interallied coordination and dependency, would be as revisionist of the Versailles Treaty as any German recalcitrance since 1919. However tempting to eliminate British interference in what the French saw as their critical national interests, this path was perilous. For the Stresemann cabinet to negotiate exclusively with Poincaré would mean the Germans had, against all evidence, decided that they could expect a better deal from France than from the reparation powers as a group. Assuming that an arrangement could be reached under those circumstances, France alone would have to enforce it if Germany recanted, and what alternatives—short of war—were left with the Ruhr occupied? The cost was also certainly a final break with Britain. Yet Poincaré hinted at retaining the option. On 16 November, he proudly announced to the Chamber of Deputies that while the direct expense to the French government of the Ruhr occupation had, as of 30 September, reached nearly 700 million francs, income from various receipts was more than 1 billion francs: "We therefore have the right to congratulate ourselves about the results obtained." A week later Germany appeared to admit the point that French coercion could turn a profit. On 23 November, the Ruhr industrialists signed an agreement with MICUM to restore full production as rapidly as possible and from that to make deliveries to France and Belgium, for which compensation was to be paid by the German government; the occupation would be relaxed in return for willing compliance.[36]

35. *Le Figaro,* 23 October 1923; *Le Temps,* 25 October 1923; McDougall, *France's Rhineland Diplomacy,* 299–311; Trachtenberg, *Reparation in World Politics,* 309–15.

36. J.O.C., Débats, 16 November 1923; McDougall, *France's Rhineland Diplomacy,* 298, 337; Trachtenberg, *Reparation in World Politics,* 315–30.

Yet however appealing these alternatives might be to the only partially repressed desire of the Bloc national to wreak vengeance on Germany and to the humiliating memories Poincaré himself retained from his boyhood, they had to be discarded in favor of a third, return of the problem to the Reparations Commission now that the German government was presumably willing to act in good faith. That much beyond question Poincaré had achieved in the Ruhr, and in his careful, legalistic fashion, he would adhere to the letter of the treaty. Character and mentality aside, Poincaré was constrained by a problem nothing he did in the Ruhr could solve, war debts owed to Great Britain and the United States. Squeezed hard enough and long enough, the Ruhr as a productive guarantee *might*—assuming the French had the will and the strength to do so—produce sufficient payments to cover both reconstruction and war debts. But what if the "Anglo-Saxons"—as the French had taken to calling the British and American governments collectively—would not wait? In a secret session of the Senate's foreign affairs committee on 17 May, Auriol had asked why the cabinet had not negotiated with them over war debt payments, to which Poincaré replied testily, "Because I *have* negotiated with England and the United States for a long time on the debts and have obtained, as you know, no favorable response from either."[37]

If the Anglo-Saxons were unwilling to wait, they could make unacceptable demands on the French currency. The value of the franc, already depressed to approximately one-third its 1913 level against the dollar and the pound, was, in fact, artificially high, given the continuing deficits of the budget combined with the consequent recourse to ever more borrowing and the vast increase to the amount of currency in circulation. Already, the French economy was under additional pressure. Despite the best efforts of French and Belgian workers and the relatively smooth operation of the Régie, passive resistance had sharply reduced coal shipments. Even by November, France was receiving from the Ruhr only two-thirds of what the Germans had supplied as reparations in kind during 1922—and therefore roughly half the amount formally required. The difference in coal supplies had to be made up through purchases on the open market, most often from Great Britain, where the weakness of the franc elevated the price substantially.

37. Quoted by McDougall, *France's Rhineland Diplomacy,* 278.

Poincaré recognized the danger but also the opportunity in returning to the Reparations Commission. Warren G. Harding had died suddenly on 2 August, and the new president, Calvin Coolidge, was being urged by Andrew Mellon, the secretary of the treasury, to favor greater American involvement in Europe. Baldwin had come to Paris for brief talks with Poincaré on 19 September, the first meeting of the entente's prime ministers since January. The diplomatic climate seemed different, and the German capitulation brought France new respect. Poincaré was referring to both changes when during one of his monument speeches, on 7 October at Ligny-en-Barrois (Meuse), he addressed the Anglo-Saxons: "Some of our friends repeat to us, 'You are wrong to bind yourselves obstinately to the Treaty of Versailles. It is unenforceable.' How can we not reply to them: 'If it is unenforceable, why have you signed it? Why did you draft the essential clauses?' As for us, we believe that once reciprocal engagements are undertaken none of the parties may withdraw unilaterally, and we hold fast, today as yesterday, to what we have been promised." With that firm warning in place, on 19 October he accepted a British proposal that a committee of experts, acting in the context of the Reparations Commission and including representation from the United States, take up the question of German payments.[38]

But even as Poincaré accepted the principle of the committee, he tried to limit its competence. The experts were not, he insisted, to alter the May 1921 total for reparations, not to grant Germany a moratorium, not to question *whether* Germany could pay, only *how*. When speaking at Sampigny (Meuse) on 28 October, he claimed that those prerogatives belonged entirely to the Reparations Commission, over which Barthou presided, and "we cannot accept that the commission be dispossessed or that it be superseded by an entity where our influence, already inferior to our interest, would be further reduced. The limit of our concessions has been reached. We will not go further. . . . What do we ask of our allies? Only that they observe the treaty they signed with us." And having acted in ac-

---

38. Poincaré's speech quoted by *Le Figaro,* 8 October 1923; McDougall, *France's Rhineland Diplomacy,* 294–99; Trachtenberg, *Reparation in World Politics,* 330–35; on these issues and the foregoing discussion of alternatives, see Jon Jacobson, "Strategies of French Foreign Policy After World War I," *Journal of Modern History* 55 (March 1983): 78–95.

cordance with the treaty when occupying the Ruhr, France would not relinquish her guarantees "avant d'avoir touché le montant de nos réparations"—before having received the total amount of reparations. France would leave the Ruhr when Germany *paid,* not when Germany *promised* to pay.[39]

But by entertaining, too long, alternative possibilities, especially Rhenish separatism—what he called keeping his options open—Poincaré disastrously undermined with the other reparation powers France's achievement since January. If he stood on the treaty, if he stood on the precedence of the Reparations Commission, he needed their votes. And how far he might be from having them now, compared to the beginning of the year, was demonstrated in mid-November, when Crown Prince Wilhelm, designated a "war criminal" by the Versailles Treaty, left the Hohenzollern exile of Doorn, Holland, and took up residence on his personal estate at Oels, in Silesia. Confirmation was not long in coming that Stresemann had personally consented to his return. Poincaré demanded sanctions for this violation of the treaty, but he found support not even from Belgium. When Britain made clear that any action by France alone carried a price, he agreed that a simple letter of reprimand would suffice. Recognizing reality, Poincaré then retreated on the question of what powers to grant the experts. Two committees would be formed under the general chairmanship of Charles G. Dawes, Chicago financier, brigadier general during the war, director, in 1921, of the Bureau of the Budget, and Coolidge's vice-president from 1925 to 1929. One committee would advise how best to restore Germany's fiscal stability and thus the voluntary resumption of reparations. The other would seek an international loan to assist in this stabilization. Poincaré continued to insist that the Reparations Commission had the right to accept or refuse the recommendations, but if a majority wanted a broad mandate for the experts, the same majority was likely to approve their work. France would then have to abide by this decision—or go it alone in the Ruhr.[40]

39. *Le Figaro,* 29 October 1923, printed the speech.

40. For the crown prince episode, see the tempest in the Paris press, especially *Le Temps* and *L'Echo de Paris,* 10–13 November 1923; for Poincaré's strategic retreat, see McDougall, *France's Rhineland Diplomacy,* 335–38.

So Poincaré's year on the brink had not changed the fundamental question present since the peace conference. But perhaps the terms of asking
were now different. Germany was learning the price of defiance. The
United States was coming back to Europe. Britain was no longer indispensable to continental stability. France was regaining her nerve. Or at
least that is what Poincaré told the Chamber of Deputies on 23 November.
France could, if she chose, stand with her allies in executing the treaty but
now with greater respect and upon a more compliant Germany. Or France
could stand alone, relying on the MICUM agreement to remain in the
Ruhr for as long as necessary. Poincaré contrasted this new independence
with the work of his predecessors: Clemenceau, on Tardieu's advice during the peace conference, and Briand, as premier, had bound France
through the quest for an unworkable collective security, but now, "if tomorrow we have to defend ourselves, we do not have to wait on the convenience of anyone." The entente was important, and he would strive to
maintain it because "I have always believed that its rupture would be a
misfortune for France, for Britain, and for European peace." Yet "we are
keeping our guarantees. We are ready to act in concert with our allies. We
wish that the crisis in Europe not be prolonged and that Germany regain
its equilibrium. We have every reason to avoid an armed conflict. We ask
only that our friends help us to consolidate the peace." Briand defended
himself discreetly, and Poincaré replied likewise, as if recalling their long
years together. Not so Tardieu: he launched into a diatribe against Poincaré, calling him inferior to Clemenceau in every way, and against his fellow deputies, castigating their lack of unity when the issue was the "mutilation of French rights." Trembling with anger, Poincaré fired back, "I do
not know whether what you intended to accomplish today was for politics,
but I know that it was not for the nation!" That insult sealed the overwhelming vote: 500 to 70. The Bloc national could vote for Poincaré's occupying the Ruhr. The Radicals could vote for Poincaré's returning to negotiation. All but the Communists and a few Socialists could vote for
Poincaré's "national performance."[41] And perhaps he had come close to
changing the terms for France's foreign policy dilemma. But even as they
voted, everyone in the Chamber, most of all Poincaré, was aware that all
the gains of the year were potentially at forfeit to the state of the franc.

41. J.O.C., Débats, 23 November 1923.

Frenchmen, so the adage goes, vote with their hearts on the left but their pocketbooks on the right. And that was the basis of Varenne's prediction on 13 November, for as the Cartel des gauches was laying claim to the hearts, the Bloc national was losing the pocketbooks. Inflation had returned with a vengeance. From December 1922 to December 1923, retail prices rose every month, 17.8 percent for the year, and wholesale prices climbed 28.1 percent, promising worse for 1924: using 1913 as a base 100, the indices were 309 to 364 and 334 to 428, respectively. The news was by no means all bleak. Industrial production had nearly recovered from the war, almost reaching the 1913 level by the end of the year—the index going from 88 to 98, a gain of 11.4 percent. The increase in production meant greater exports, by an astonishing 52.7 percent, from 27.217 billion francs to 41.554 billion, and nearly offset the coal purchases from Britain that pushed imports up 43.0 percent, from 30.394 billion francs to 43.473 billion. That left the trade deficit at only 1.919 billion francs, the best since the war, with exports 95.6 percent of imports. Because the good times for industry led to higher wages for industrial workers, the effect of inflation on them, though psychological, was blunted: the index of their buying power remained unchanged from December 1922 to December 1923.[42]

As earlier, since the end of the war, the inflation hit hardest on government workers, whose salaries were not increased, and rentiers, whose sense of relief at the improvement of their investments by the end of 1921 was, two years later, mixed with renewed frustration. In December 1923, the index of stocks and bonds paying a variable return—computing their real value adjusted for inflation, using 1913 as a base 100—stood at 54.6, up 52 percent, from 35.9 in December 1921, a mirror of the industrial recovery. But those paying a fixed return had fallen to 19.2, a decline of 17.2 percent from 23.2. The rentiers had believed Poincaré their savior, but they pointed at the value of the franc as proof that he had failed them. In December 1921, a pound bought 53.06 francs, in December 1922, 63.74, and in December 1923, 82.92—a collapse of 56.3 percent. For the dollar, the figures were equally depressing: 12.78, 13.84, and 19.02—48.8 percent.

42. Sauvy, *Histoire économique,* 1:501, for retail prices; 1:495, for wholesale prices; 1:464, for industrial production; 1:477, for the balance of payments; 1:511, for wages and buying power.

And why not: the amount of currency in circulation had increased from 36.459 billion francs to 37.755 billion; the budget, 9.275 billion francs out of balance in 1921, now had a deficit of 11.806 billion. Briand and Paul Doumer had not gone into the Ruhr, but they appeared to be fiscal paragons in comparison.[43]

Such a judgment against Poincaré and Lasteyrie was unfair at least by half. The enormous expenses incurred by, and the paucity of return from, the Ruhr occupation were the result of German resistance. Within France, the reconstruction was an economic, political, psychological, and perhaps above all, moral imperative, even though it devoured almost a third of the budget. In 1923 alone, the restoration of 96,620 private houses, 54,830 farm structures, 2,996 public buildings, 1,239 industrial establishments, 6,579 miles of road, and 240 miles of railroad was completed—at an expense for the year of 12.461 billion francs. That made the total since the Armistice 250,992 private houses, 75,260 farm structures, 5,346 public buildings, 6,700 industrial establishments, 20,295 miles of road, and 3,304 miles of railroad—and 66.355 billion francs.[44] In both the Ruhr and the devastated region, Poincaré and Lasteyrie had their eyes fixed on the long-term rehabilitation of French finances—and they were correct. For the short term, to cover the deficit, to provide against surprise costs in the Ruhr, and to shore up the franc against hostile speculation, they had proposed the double décime—and again, they were correct. But unlike in the Ruhr, on the new taxes, Poincaré blinked.

When Lasteyrie formally proposed the double décime before the Chamber of Deputies on 11 January, he called it a temporary expedient for the duration of the Ruhr occupation, which was beginning that very day. Already, Louis H. Aubert, widely respected for the rigor of his economic analysis, had written in *Le Figaro* of the need for this sacrifice. Yet only four days later, a delegation of deputies from one element in the Bloc national, the Entente républicaine démocratique, complained to him that the Chamber was in no mood for any tax increase, least of all one striking so heavily across the board. To match Aubert, they enlisted François Pon-

43. Sauvy, *Histoire économique,* 1:532, 534, for the real value of stocks and bonds; 1:445, for exchange rates; 1:525, for currency totals; 1:513, for the budget.

44. Sauvy, *Histoire économique,* 1:453–54, for reconstruction.

cet to write a long attack in *L'Opinion,* which appealed to middle-class business owners. All manner of legislative tactics could also be brought to bear, harassing and frustrating Lasteyrie with delays. The "Communist Plot" and Camelot violence were divisive enough as Poincaré tried to gain control of the Ruhr against German resistance. To risk splintering the Bloc national over taxes ran directly counter to the effort to create a union sacrée. Lasteyrie quickly comprehended that priority for the double dé-cime had been lessened and that it could by no means be the basis for a vote of confidence.[45]

Upon becoming premier, Poincaré had made a point of insisting that the annual budget be approved "on time," meaning at least by the end of the preceding year. Yet the habit of not doing so was now so much in-grained since the war that neither Lasteyrie nor the senators and deputies took him seriously, and Poincaré himself was preoccupied by foreign af-fairs. When the Chamber finally gave its assent to the budget for 1923 on 26 January, the deadline was already four weeks in arrears, and the Senate had yet even to begin its consideration. The deputies made their initial case against new taxes by claiming new economies, taking aim at the easi-est target, fonctionnaires—government workers—fifteen thousand of whom were to be eliminated by the end of the summer. But they did not stop there: when the Chamber began a two-week debate about tax policy in late February, Emmanuel Brousse, who would denounce Daudet on 1 June and was an important figure in the Bloc national, called for the clos-ing of schools, courts, and prisons that were not being "fully utilized." To raise money, he was ready with a detailed proposal for a national prize lottery—which won applause long and loud. Louis Loucheur, who had the prestige of an industrial fortune to go with his service beside Clem-enceau, declared that the value of the franc depended less on the state of the budget than on confidence in the nation—an optimism not shared by any trained economist but cheered by the deputies. Even a lone Commu-nist weighed in, Charles Baron wanting to tax "big automobiles" instead of tobacco, "the sole pleasure of the poor."[46]

45. J.O.C., Débats, 11 January 1923; Aubert in *Le Figaro,* 10 January 1923; report of the delegation, *Le Temps,* 16 January 1923; Schuker, *End of French Predominance,* 47.

46. J.O.C., Débats, 26 January (1923 budget approved, 480–84), 20 (Brousse and Baron), 27 (Loucheur) February 1923.

These schemes were peripheral to the principal exchange, between Lasteyrie and the spokesman for the Chamber's budget committee, Maurice Bokanowski, along with the—inevitable—acerbic general condemnation from Tardieu. Because the sentiments of the Bloc national were reflected by the budget committee and its sentiments by Bokanowski, his words represented the current legislative possibilities. And according to him, such possibilities did not, indeed should not, include the double décime. Instead, the Ministry of Finance could solve the deficit simply by tightening its enforcement of the income tax. The great loophole was its evasion by the holders of bearer bonds because the coupons they clipped and deposited were not traceable. Bokanowski estimated that 8 billion francs of income thereby went unreported and untaxed—more than enough to cover the committee's latest estimate of 1923's deficit, between 1.2 and 1.8 billion francs. Placed on the defensive by these statistics and forced to admit that tax inspectors lacked the power to examine bank records, Lasteyrie could only whine that Bokanowski was wrong to harp on tax evasion because "France should not be portrayed as a nation of frauds." The Ruhr occupation would, he claimed, balance the budget *eventually*, through the taking of material guarantees, but until then, the double décime was, however unfortunate, necessary. For Tardieu, the welter of conflicting figures, the confusion of proposals singular or prosaic were easy to ridicule—in *Le Figaro*, Vonoven called him "a mordant polemicist who has found a good subject"—while never declaring a plan of his own. The most painful sting of his caustic words came when he mockingly asked why Lasteyrie did not pose a vote of confidence on the double décime and then answered by predicting he could not win. The words stung because Lasteyrie knew just that, the proof coming on 8 March, when the Chamber voted 315 to 243 its preference to cover any deficit through further loans, not new taxes.[47]

After this lackluster performance, Lasteyrie retreated to his offices on the rue de Rivoli to wait for the Senate—and wait. By 1 June, without a budget for the year in sight, Vonoven observed with some rancor that the bombast and ill will of the Chamber and the Senate might set a new

47. J.O.C., Débats, 22 (Bokanowski), 23 (Bokanowski and Lasteyrie) February, 1 (Tardieu), 8 (vote on covering the deficit) 1923; *Le Figaro,* 2 March 1923.

record for delay. But was delay any worse than the report of the Senate budget committee, finally issued on 8 June, which projected a *surplus* of nearly 900 million francs for 1923—by the legerdemain of moving 3 billion francs in short-term floating debt from the current budget to the status of long-term loans recoverable through reparations in 1924? The Senate as a whole then blithely adopted this charade on 26 June by a vote of 303 to 2. In agreement on almost nothing else, Herriot and Tardieu both editorialized against this "hérésie budgétaire." Poincaré and Lasteyrie had by now reached the point of utter exasperation, having first proposed the 1923 budget on 31 March 1922, almost fifteen months earlier. Because reconciling the Chamber and Senate versions still remained, they decided on a drastic procedure. The deputies and senators would be asked to extend the budget for 1923 to cover 1924 as well, thus creatively making orthodox the heresy voted by the Senate, as well as eliminating having to begin immediately the tortuous task of budget-making all over again for the next year. With only a little embarrassment, Lasteyrie explained that "given the late date, the budget of 1923 has, in reality, become the budget of 1924." Exhausted from the rancor, the Chamber and the Senate both agreed on 30 June.[48]

Of course, with the "budgetary heresy" of the Senate now official national policy, belief in legerdemain, not additional tax receipts, had to generate confidence in the franc. But on currency markets, "léger" was correctly translated to mean "trifling" and "flimsy" as well as "adroit." In the next six weeks, the franc fell more than 10 percent against the pound and the dollar. Lasteyrie's only recourse was brave words. On 18 August, in a formal statement from the Ministry of Finance, he attributed the decline to "speculative influences," not "economic causes," and declared that he would therefore watch the exchange rate "with the greatest sangfroid and the greatest calm." A month later, in a speech at Castres on 22 September, he offered reassurances that all was well and claimed that the franc would rebound upon recognition of French success in the Ruhr. The true state of his mind showed only before the Chamber, at the end of November, dur-

48. *Le Figaro,* 1 June 1923, for Vonoven; *Le Temps* and *Le Figaro,* 9 June 1923, for the Senate budget committee report; *Le Radical* and *L'Echo national,* 28 June 1923, for Herriot and Tardieu, respectively; J.O.S., Débats, 26, 30 June 1923; J.O.C., Débats, 30 June 1923.

ing a reply to complaints about the intrusiveness of tax collection, when he praised the votes in 1919 for the income tax and the turnover tax, "the two levies of salvation."[49]

By then, inflation was emerging as a critical issue in the forthcoming legislative elections. Demonstrations against high food prices were increasingly common in Paris, and the Sûreté générale was reporting political trouble for Poincaré and the Bloc national. To solidify traditional Radical support among fonctionnaires, who were among the most severely affected, Herriot proposed granting them all a cost-of-living indemnity of 1,800 francs, adding another 1.160 billion francs to the budget. Because there was general agreement that something had to be done, Lasteyrie rapidly prepared an alternative; apportioning the indemnity by local prices, that would cost only 263 million francs. But how could he prevail in the Chamber? Significant numbers from the Bloc national were ready to support Herriot's bill rather than risk being portrayed as uncompassionate with an election looming. To hold them, the issue would have to be made a vote of confidence, but that would be to admit the parlous state of the budget. When Poincaré resolved the dilemma in favor of economy, Lasteyrie bluntly told the deputies on 19 December that "to grant the fonctionnaires more would overwhelm the treasury. If I went ahead with such allurements, I could no longer consider myself a man of probity, for they would ruin the French economy. If the Chamber wishes to follow that policy, I declare in my name and in the name of the premier that it will do so with another cabinet." So confronted, the Bloc national held firm, easily adopting Lasteyrie's proposal by a vote of 392 to 169. Poincaré had finally backed his minister of finance—had it come too late?[50]

If Lasteyrie appeared unusually combative, even beside himself, before the Chamber in mid-December, he had the excuse of being harried over the François-Marsal convention, a technical and arcane issue but a vital indicator of France's fiscal condition. In 1920, Millerand's minister of fi-

49. Le Temps, 19 August 1923; Le Figaro, 23 September 1923; J.O.C., Débats, 28 November 1923.

50. A.N., F7 12952 2, "Notes Jean," F 9052, 14 December 1923, F 9056, 15, 21 December 1923; J.O.C., Débats, 19, 21, 22 December 1923; for commentary, see Le Figaro, 18–23 December 1923, Le Gaulois, L'Eclair, and La Victoire, 21 December 1923.

nance, Frédéric François-Marsal, devised a plan to reduce the amount of currency in circulation—and thus, in theory, inflation—by requiring the government to reimburse the Banque de France two billion francs each December, beginning in 1921. Briand's minister of finance, Doumer, had done so, but in December 1922, Lasteyrie, arguing against too rapid a deflation, had negotiated what he promised was an "exceptional" action, lowering the payment to one billion francs. On 9 December, Louis H. Aubert, writing as always in *Le Figaro,* asked what would be done at the end of 1923. While acknowledging that the François-Marsal convention was overshadowed in public opinion by the frenzy over the Ruhr, inflation, and the elections, he warned that "the consequences of failing to make reimbursement of the full two billion francs would be so grave for our credit, internationally and domestically, that one cannot imagine the minister of finance conceiving that eventuality." Instead of the anticipated pledge from the rue de Rivoli, Aubert's next column quoted Cachin, the leader of the Communists for whom *Le Figaro* never had a good word: Lasteyrie, he prophesied, would not be reimbursing the Banque de France but asking for advances; "we are where Germany was three years ago."[51]

This prediction was so dire that Aubert himself asked whether "at the moment when our foreign policy is bearing fruit all the effort will be compromised by financial blunders?" Finally, on 13 December, Lasteyrie issued an official communiqué explaining that the Ministry of Finance could not evade making the payment without the approval of the Banque de France—hardly a promise to do so. He was no more forthcoming before the Senate on 26 December, offering anodyne reassurances about an improving economy and criticizing "tendentious rumors" in the press about the reimbursement. In fact, Lasteyrie had already come to a secret—and unwritten—arrangement with the Banque de France that proved Cachin remarkably prescient. The Ministry of Finance agreed to reimburse 800 million francs as a concession to the François-Marsal convention, and the Banque de France promised to make certain unpublicized cur-

51. For Lasteyrie in 1922, see J.O.C., Débats, 28 December 1922; J.O.S., Débats, 30 December 1922; *Le Figaro,* 9 (Aubert), 11 (Cachin) December 1923; see also the articles by Tardieu, although somewhat less informed, *L'Echo national,* 9–12 December 1923.

rency advances, which over the first four months of 1924 would exceed 2.5 billion francs.[52]

By declaring the vote on the fonctionnaire indemnity an issue of confidence and through his equivocation on the François-Marsal convention, Lasteyrie had revealed the tenuous state of French finances. For that, *Le Figaro* denounced him as "un homme dangereux."[53] The blame belonged to Poincaré. He had gambled—on the Ruhr, on taxes, on a union sacrée—and lost. The only question remaining was how long before the magnitude of these disasters for the future of France would be generally recognized. Les jeux sont faits: the game is over.

52. *Le Figaro*, 13 (Aubert), 14 (report of communiqué) December 1923; J.O.S., Débats, 26 December 1923; Schuker, *End of French Predominance*, 42–54.

53. *Le Figaro*, 30 December 1923.

Georges Clemenceau
UPI/Corbis-Bettmann

Raymond Poincaré
Corbis-Bettmann

Aristide Briand
Corbis-Bettmann

André Tardieu
Corbis-Bettmann

Edouard Herriot
Corbis-Bettmann

6

■ ■ ■

Tragique roman d'amour

The figurative "high explosive love" of F. Scott Fitzgerald's *Tender Is the Night* could also be literal, the "tragique roman d'amour." On the evening of 11 March 1922, Captain Robinot-Marcy was found dead in his apartment on the rue Oudinot, in the fashionable seventh arrondissement of Paris, a single gunshot wound to the head. Police detectives assumed suicide, but there were troubling anomalies. They found a woman's glove beside the body. Another tenant in the building, a Mlle Smith, reported hearing the sound of a gun firing and then "feminine footsteps" on the stair. About an hour after the police were called, an elegant young woman confronted the building's concierge, demanding to see Robinot-Marcy and claiming he had telephoned asking that she come to his apartment immediately. When told that he was dead, she insisted on seeing for herself. Such obvious agitation attracted the attention of the detectives, who asked her name and address for later questioning. When this information proved false, the Paris prosecutorial office assigned examining magistrate Jean Lacomblez to pursue further inquiries.

The ranks of the *milieux mondains* close rapidly about their own, but after a month, detectives traced the mystery woman at the crime scene and, from her, the owner of the glove. They also thought they knew what happened that evening on 11 March: Mme Dhotel, the young wife of a prominent physician and involved in an affair with Robinot-Marcy, had met him to break off their relationship. Overcome with despair, he shot himself before her eyes. She fled, dropping a glove. Once home, she telephoned her closest confidante, Mme Reckling, another young society wife, who proved her friendship by going to Robinot-Marcy's apartment—surely to pick up the telltale glove, but too late. Her sudden appearance and unlikely story were enough by themselves to arouse suspicion. Her clumsy lies guaranteed it. But what the police thought they knew and what they could prove were, as often, entirely different. Dr. Dhotel claimed that he and his wife were invited to a masked ball for the evening of 11 March, but at the last moment "professional responsibilities" detained him. He had therefore suggested that she go escorted by their "mutual friend," Robinot-Marcy. Mme Dhotel explained that she met Robinot-Marcy at his apartment, and after they drank a glass of port, he decided to show off his pistol. Thinking that it was not loaded, he pressed it to his temple and pulled the trigger. In shock at the result, she had run from the room. Once at her own house, she called Mme Reckling. The next part of the story required the most careful retelling because for it there were witnesses. Mme Reckling recalled thinking that her friend was in no condition to investigate whether Robinot-Marcy had survived his mishap and had therefore volunteered to undertake the mission herself. The lie she told the concierge, the false name and address she gave to the police, were to avoid being further involved in this drama.

Lacomblez recognized that these affidavits meshed with each other too well. The Dhotels and Reckling had had time to coordinate their account and were clearly presenting a united front. Nevertheless, the testimony contained gaping holes: why had Mme Dhotel been at Robinot-Marcy's apartment, when propriety required his going to her house? Why, if he were a friend of the family, had she run away after the gunshot instead of seeking medical help? Why had Mme Reckling been so intent on avoiding identification? Was the reconstruction of the events by the police correct? If so, discreetly closing the case and overlooking the false depositions would save reputations while doing little harm to justice. This much hypocrisy did not disturb Lacomblez, but he worried that behind these facts might lurk a clever murder. To eliminate that possibility, he ordered the exhumation of Robinot-Marcy's body for examination by the coroner, Dr. Charles Paul, and by the forensic pathologist for the Paris Police, Dr. Victor Balthazard. When their findings were consistent with a verdict of suicide, Lacomblez returned Robinot-Marcy to his grave and the dossier of the case to the files. The Dhotel and Reckling marriages he left to their own moral calculus.[1]

How such reckoning could turn out was illustrated by the death of a wealthy businessman, Léonidas Basiliondis, who was discovered slumped across his office desk when his typist, Mlle Marie Bohant, arrived for work on 23 July 1923. It was a Monday, and from the state of the body, he had been dead at least twenty-four hours. Finding what appeared to be a single large bullet wound to his head and no signs of struggle, the police initially supposed that Basiliondis came to his office during the preceding weekend and for reasons unknown—because there was not a note—killed himself. They changed their conclusion to murder when the autopsy by Dr. Paul revealed two bullets in his brain. When that news was released, Mme Marie Dubot de Talhouet requested a meeting with Gustave Laroque, the examining magistrate for the case, and confessed to firing the shots. In 1898, when she was only seventeen, she had been seduced by Basiliondis and had borne him a son, Alfred Léonidis Dubot de Talhouet, the following year. They lived openly together for fifteen years, until 1913, when he decided that at thirty-four, she was older than he preferred for a mistress. Willing to abandon her and the adolescent boy but unwilling to leave them destitute, he promised to give her one hundred francs a month and had done so since. Ten years later, what had been barely sufficient was a pittance. Ten years later, the son had begun a career as a barrister, but his father refused to acknowledge him. Ten years later, Marie was a lonely woman of forty-four, but Léonidas sported a mistress in her twenties. It was, she told Laroque, too much: she would kill him. Although her knowledge of firearms was so rudimentary that Alfred had to load the pistol for her and demonstrate how to pull the trigger, the deed itself fazed her not at all. Firing the shots was easy. There was no option to charging mother and son with murder, but no one, least of all Laroque, thought they would be convicted. Their trial came seven months later, in February 1924, and after Marie repeated her story, the jury quickly voted their acquittal.[2]

1. *Le Figaro,* 16–23 April 1922.
2. *Le Matin,* 24, 27–29 July, 4 August 1923; *La Gazette des tribunaux,* 20–23 February 1924.

Alexandre Dumas fils had written, "Better to restore divorce to the law code than admit murder to the book of etiquette." Given exigencies and contingencies like those in the Basiliondis case, Georges Claretie, the long-time crime reporter for *Le Figaro,* was unfair in adding cynically: "But the Browning automatic is so much more convenient, economical, and speedy. Bang! Bang! And it's done. Before the jury, you weep and say that you killed only because you loved too much. The session of the Cour d'assises begins at noon, and by four o'clock you are free."[3]

Not always: consider the fate of Paul Boppe, whose case first came to sensational notice in 1921 because Suzanne, the wife he tried to kill, was the niece of Maurice Barrès. She had become "inconvenient": although willing to overlook his constant adultery, she would not consent to a divorce that would permit him to marry his latest mistress, a Mme Labouret, with whom he was besotted. In June 1920, griped by what he would describe as "madness and despair," he tried to murder Suzanne, first with poisoned tea and then with two bullets, one of them to the face. Somehow, she survived, but while the doctors worked over her, Barrès told him: "If my niece dies, you will be guillotined. If she recovers, the children must not be spattered by the shame of scandal." He meant that the family would dictate a private settlement: without the report of a crime and without a petition for divorce, no one outside need know. Suzanne would call the shooting an accident; Paul would agree to a separation and to financial support. In December 1921, he absconded with family money and yet another mistress, Mlle Thérèse Monier. To track him down, Barrès called in the police and, to limit the scandal, published his own version of events as an open letter in *Le Figaro.* No better at flight than killing, Boppe was quickly traced and, in October 1922, brought to trial for attempted murder and fraud. There, he mixed tears of repentance with bravado, encouraging Mlle Monier to describe him as "very sweet and very kind." He appeared to justify the prosecution's characterization of him as a "brute de luxe." In contrast to this pathetic performance, Barrès had the one great moment of the trial. After recounting how often Suzanne had forgiven her husband, he paused before crying out, "My niece may have pardoned, but I, as head of the family, demand justice!" The jury declared Boppe guilty, and the

---

3. *Le Figaro,* 13 March 1922.

judges sentenced him to five years' imprisonment at hard labor, the stiffest penalty available.[4]

For others, the roman d'amour was less sensational but equally "explosive" and "tragique." The prop master at the Ambassadeurs theater, Jacques Christophe, took up with Paule Delacourt, a dancer from the Folies Bergères. Finding them together, his wife, Eugénie, shot at Delacourt, but Christophe threw himself in front of his mistress to save her and was killed instead. A Mme Housseau also shot her husband, but he survived and refused to press charges, claiming that "the lesson he received was greatly merited." The separated but apparently well-matched Evezarts encountered one another on the boulevard du Temple, she firing a pistol at him, he at her—both missing. Jeanne Dedaumarde shot at her friend Louis William, Yves Peron at his mistress, Juliette Becfort Van Braet, and Georges Planchon at the woman he had lived with for five years, Suzanne Belloc, without inflicting serious harm—and then killed themselves out of shame or frustration. Although Yvon Brionne, serving with the 119th Infantry at St. Cloud, was presumably trained to use a bayonet, his wife, Annette, survived his slashing her four times during a jealous rage. Simone Barraud sought medical aid for a knife wound to her breast, insisting that she cut herself by accident, but her lover suddenly disappeared. A plumber named Dubos stabbed his mistress, a Mme Menigoz, and set their house on fire; both she and the house were saved. Perhaps the failure of aim—whether with gun or knife—was intentional.[5]

There was no doubting when it was not. Mme Tasillac threw vitriol in the eyes of her husband and then shot him twice in the arm. Maria Thalle threw vitriol on her lover and then killed herself. Augustine Trouillet attacked her husband with a razor and decapitated him. Maurice Bigot slit the throats of his mistress, Marthe Roland, and their daughter because she deserted him. Gaston Baudelot did the same to his mistress, Mathilde Rolland, and her daughter, after a quarrel. When Anna Dussard left her husband to live with Ben Omer Brahim, he traced them to Rosny-sous-Bois,

---

4. *Le Figaro,* 29 December 1921, for Barrès's letter; *La Gazette des tribunaux,* 25–28 October 1922, for the trial.

5. *Le Matin,* 7 March (Brionne), 8 March (Housseau), 14 April (Evezart), 26 April (Barraud), 12 May (Peron), 21 July (Dedaumarde), 30 December (Planchon) 1922; 12 June (Dubos), 29 June (Christophe) 1923.

shot her twice in the belly, and wounded her lover. Elie Pautel, a wine merchant, surprised his wife, Alice, betraying him with a cabinetmaker and gunned them both down. Five times Henry Postel forgave his wife, Félicie, for deserting him, but when she ran away a sixth, he tracked her to a bistro on the rue Simon-le-franc and threatened her with a pistol. Because she laughed in his face, he fired three times, to make certain that she was dead. Albert Brillmann, a businessman, found the girlfriend who jilted him, Suzanne Geiger, at a restaurant on the Champs-Elysées. He shot her, then himself. The plot was repeated on the boulevard Flandrin by Jérôme Grymonprez, a valet, and Marguerite Leblanc. André Desfondois proposed marriage to a young working girl, Denise Harry. Although she moved into his house, he kept putting off the ceremony until finally admitting his plans to wed another. She killed him with a single shot, afterward explaining to the police that as Desfondois prepared to leave, he insulted her obscenely. A goldsmith, Louis Lardier, married with children, fell under the spell of a divorcee, Juliette Charbotel, and began an affair with her. His wife demanded and obtained a divorce. Lardier then asked Charbotel to live with him, but she replied *by letter,* "I have changed my mind. I will stay where I am. Farewell." "Fou de douleur," he sought her out in a cafe and fired his pistol in her direction, hitting a glass. She begged at his feet to be spared, but he pulled the trigger twice more, carefully aiming at her head. A final shot at himself was more haphazard, and he recovered. At his trial, even the prosecution agreed that his having loved a woman like Charbotel required the granting of mitigating circumstances.[6]

Were more such summary judgments of the heart possible because relaxed regulations on the sale of firearms during the war had made "le Browning" too much at hand? One short-lived proposal called for each pistol to be declared, registered, and taxed—as if, *Le Figaro* jested, it were a child with "a birth certificate." Joseph Denais, the devoutly Catholic municipal councilman for Batignolles, instead blamed movie posters depict-

6. *Le Matin,* 2 April (Bigot), 23 May (Trouillet), 29 May (Tasillac), 17 June (Dussard), 22 July (Baudelot), 27 September (Lardier), 10 November (Grymonprez), 12 November (Thalle), 18, 29 December (Harry) 1922, 26 March (Postel), 4 June (Brillmann), 28 June (Pautel) 1923.

ing violent crimes and demanded to know why the Paris Police did not suppress them in the name of public morality. In 1922, the connection between religious upbringing and conduct was hazardous to advance because the most sensational murder of the year was by the product of a convent school. Marie-Zénobie Ollivier, who worked as a maid in the house of Dr. Armand Bernard, the celebrated chief surgeon at the Clinique Doyen, crushed the skull of his wife, Germaine, with a log of firewood. Afterward, she calmly wrote a letter to her mother confessing the crime, then took the train to Rouen, where she awaited her arrest in the company of the nuns who had taught her. Two months later, Bernard, who had been married for only three years, committed suicide in despair.[7]

The churchgoing *bien pensants* thought that the ideological table turned the following year, with the murder of Marius Plateau by Germaine Berton, the godless anarchist larcenist tubercular daughter of a laic schoolteacher. But that was before her trial the week before Christmas, when she appeared, dressed by her barrister, Henry Torrès, as "a kind of little smiling, made-up doll" in bobbed hair and a demure white blouse with a big bow. By late 1923, the violence of the Camelots du roi, Plateau's louts, had made them reprehensible to all but the extreme Right. The presiding justice for the court, Antoine Pressard, who would play an ambiguous role ten years later in the Stavisky scandal, permitted Torrès to exploit this animosity by portraying Berton as a heroine: "Plateau put himself outside the law by his transgressions. . . . What does the Action française want? To restore the king. What are its means? Violence!" The jury took less than half an hour to return a verdict of not guilty for an assassination Berton proudly claimed. *Le Libertaire,* the spokesman for anarchism, cheered, "Workers and great-hearted men rejoice, Germaine Berton is returned to us!" In *La République française,* Georges Bonnefous, as if training for his future career as a historian, pontificated: "A verdict such as yesterday's is the proof of the moral disarray that reigns among us. There are evidently too many in France who have not the slightest notion about the minimum of rules without which society cannot survive."[8]

7. *Le Figaro,* 5 March (Denais), 30 April (gun registration), 14, 15, 16 May (Ollivier), 22 July (Bernard) 1922.

8. *La Gazette des tribunaux,* 20–25 December 1923, Torrès quoted 25 December; *Le*

How silly! Societies survive much worse—as Bonnefous was personally to witness during the following two decades. For the moment, the public fascination with crime had supplements to murder. Larcenies on a grand scale had their usual allure: the theft of 875,000 francs by safecrackers from a post office on the rue Vauvenargues; an accountant embezzling 475,000 francs from the American Express office; audacious attacks on two jewelry stores, 300,000 francs from Léon Tcherkassky on the rue du Temple, 440,000 francs from R. Juelier et Cie. on the rue St. Honoré; the mugging of an American artist, Elysia Suddie, reckless enough to be carrying $4,000—when that was worth nearly 50,000 francs.[9] To applaud, there was the conspicuous success of the police in penetrating and arresting criminal gangs: the bande de la rue Beaubourg, the bande de la Bois de Boulogne, the bande de la Villette, all accused of multiple murders and robberies.[10] To deplore, there was the disturbing number of crimes—often with great violence—by soldiers, so recently national heroes: Louis Hervien from the 162nd Infantry strangled Marie Lenot; Emile Prévost, Henri Gillet, Jules Mercier, and Jean Pauligny from the aviation unit at Le Bourget stabbed Henri Huant; Edmond Godfry of the Fourth African Battalion murdered his sister, Elisa; and most shocking, Henri Baugaris, Clovis Valeron, and Léopold Maury of the Twenty-sixth Infantry attacked and robbed Lieutenant Léonce Lacarrière of the Ninety-eighth Artillery aboard the Paris-Nancy train, and then threw him, still alive, onto the tracks.[11]

Still better to deprecate, because of schadenfreude, were the cases touching *pudeur*—shame. On 22 March 1923, the Sûreté générale broke up a white slavery scheme preying on discontented young servant girls when agents arrested Judas Albon, Joseph Fontana, and Louise Dubois. Less than a week later, they traced other confederates to Dakar, Senegal, and caught men named Peuch, Aboucaza, and Girod red-handed preparing forged passports for the passage of the latest victims across the South

---

Figaro, 20 (Berton description), 25 December 1923; *Le Libertaire,* 25 December 1923; *La République française,* 25 December 1923.

    9. *Le Matin,* 13 February, 19 March (post office), 31 July (Tcherkassky), 12 September (Suddie), 13 December (R. Juelier et Cie.) 1922, 9 February (American Express) 1923.

    10. *Le Matin,* 16 June (Beaubourg and Bois de Boulogne), 21 June (Villette) 1922.

    11. *Le Matin,* 27 June (Hervien), 15 July (Prévost, Gillet, Mercier, Pauligny) 1922, 15 April (Baugaris, Valeron, Maury), 9 May (Godfry) 1923.

Atlantic and sale to procurers in Brazil.[12] By utter coincidence, on 27 March, the day of the arrests in Dakar, a modification of the criminal code went into effect, changing abortion from a *crime*—a felony—to a *délit*—a misdemeanor. The rationale was anything but to weaken enforcement. The minimum penalty for conviction of a crime was five years' imprisonment and for abortion, death or confinement for life. Juries, used in France only for felonies, were unwilling to impose such draconian justice and simply refused to convict either women or doctors. Prosecutors, in turn, declined to bring any but the most flagrant cases to trial—less than a hundred a year for the entire country. The need for more children to make up the losses of the war seemed to warrant ending this policy of the blind eye. Transforming abortion into a délit meant that it would henceforth be tried before three-judge panels, and though the maximum penalty could not exceed five years in prison, conviction became much more certain. Although newspapers rarely reported cases involving abortion, and then circumspectly, the perspicacious noted a change in tone accompanying the change in law. When a small-time actress and dancer, Paulette Duperrier (known on the stage as Ninette Peria), died in July 1922 after what appeared to be a botched abortion, when Marie Roussel, the unmarried daughter of the mayor in a Parisian suburb, was blackmailed by her abortionist in November 1922, *Le Figaro* observed a careful discretion. In April 1923, when the Paris prosecutorial office brought an abortion ring led by Denise Vigneron to trial before the judges of district court and won sentences ranging from six months' to four years' imprisonment, the report was much less chary.[13]

But at least for most of 1922, much the best of all the crime to follow was the descent upon Paris of the *vitrioleurs, coupeurs,* and *piqueurs,* their story a potent blend of resentment and sex and mystery that toyed with the anxieties of a society lacking equilibrium. At the end of January, all the major newspapers reported an outbreak of "vitrioleuses": women throwing vitriol on the furs and coats of well-to-do "ladies" in the Made-

12. *Le Figaro,* 28 March 1923.

13. *Le Figaro,* 24, 25, 26, 30 July (Duperrier), 1 November (Roussel) 1922; 20 April (Vigneron) 1923; Martin, *Crime and Criminal Justice,* 4–12; France, Ministère de la justice, *Compte générale* (Paris, 1922–23).

leine quarter, the motive ostensibly to ruin what they could not afford. By the beginning of February, the spelling changed to "vitrioleur" because the reports accused men as well as women, and the attacks spread to the grand boulevards and onto the Métro, where for the first time the acid burned through a coat to inflict burns. In mid-February came the first account of the *coupeur de manteaux,* a man surreptitiously using a razor to slash the coats of women whatever their social position. On 20 February, the Paris Police revealed that in barely more than three weeks, 323 women claimed to have been attacked by a vitrioleur. Most often, he was described as a tall man with a pince-nez wearing a raincoat. From his pocket, he would withdraw a syringe filled with the caustic, spray his target, and disappear into the crowd, all in seconds. Could one man acting alone account for so many attacks? Almost certainly, the initial incidents in the Madeleine were carried out by women. If this man—and perhaps others—had taken them as inspiration, the later victims were not prosperous dowagers parading fur but younger women working at white-collar jobs for whom damaged clothing had serious consequences. The coupeur appeared to have the same targets. Increasingly, women were attacked as they rode the Métro or the autobus to and from their jobs. Among them, there was a growing sense of panic. And rightly: for whether singled out as symbols of the "new woman" or simply easy prey numerous and crowded together on public transportation, they were under attack, the coats they needed for the penetrating Parisian winter burned and cut.[14]

Despite increased patrols and pleas for heightened vigilance, the police were baffled. The vitrioleur and the coupeur seemed to strike at will and then vanish, as if preternatural. The first break came on 8 March, as a woman waiting in line at the post office on the rue Glück, behind the Opéra, felt a tug at her clothing and screamed. The man behind her, Georges Sartor, twenty-nine years old and a commercial clerk, was immediately seized, in his hand an open pocket knife. A search of his room on the rue des Apennins turned up a razor and two pairs of scissors, but Sartor, who had previous arrests for eccentric behavior, was not the coupeur, only an imitator. The proof came when a Mme Leroy's coat was slashed

14. *Le Matin*: vitrioleur (29, 31 January, 2, 4, 7, 8, 9, 18, 22 February, 2, 9 March 1922), coupeur (14, 16, 22, 26 February, 5 March 1922), Paris Police (20 February 1922).

on the boulevard des Italiens five days later and, like previous victims, did not immediately notice. By then, nearly two months of sensationalism guaranteed political intervention, and René Lafargue proposed that the Chamber of Deputies enact a special law condemning to prison "anyone who purposely damages clothing belonging to another." A debate followed over whether such offenders should be considered criminal or insane. But before any action could be taken, the attacks by the vitrioleur and the coupeur ended nearly as abruptly as they had begun, with one exception. On 13 August, a Catholic schoolboy, Alfred Joly, seventeen, cut the dresses—no coats during the summer—of two salesgirls in a large department store. At his trial, he claimed to have been "offended by young women dressing in a flashy manner to attract attention to themselves. I wanted to make an example." Instead, the example was made of him, although he was clearly not the coupeur. Not one element in the mystery of the attacks during the winter and spring was resolved, but there was an arrest, a trial, and a conviction: a fatuous adolescent had sixty days in jail to consider his conduct. Bizarre behavior had been repressed, young women could rest easy, and that was that.[15]

But that was not that. On 5 December, a Mlle Servet, nineteen years old, was exiting the Métro at the Le Peletier station when she felt herself *piquée*—pricked—in the calf by a needle. The wound bled so freely that she had to stop at a pharmacy for a bandage. Over the next ten days, to be a young woman piquée became a grand vogue—the leg the preferred location, with the thigh slightly favored over the calf. The Paris coroner, Dr. Paul, proclaimed the women hysterics—there were hundreds of reports but not a single arrest. *Le Figaro* ridiculed, "Everyone is piquée, but as always, there are no piqueurs." That changed, briefly, on 14 December, when a Mme Herchkowicz accused Martial Fleury, the deputy administrator for the twentieth arrondissement in Paris, of jabbing her with a needle as they rode an autobus, but he was released when she was examined and found not to have a single wound. If she was imagining things, others that same day were as well. Five separate commuters walking through the

15. *Le Matin*: Sartor (9, 10 March 1922), coupeur (14, 17 March, 8, 18 May 1922), vitrioleur (28 April, 15 June 1922); *Le Figaro*, 23, 26 August 1922 (Joly); J.O.C., Débats, 25 March 1922.

tunnels of the Châtelet Métro station declared that they were struck from behind, but when they turned around, no one was there. At the end of the month, a sixteen-year-old typist was strolling on the rue Lepic in Montmartre when she felt a blow to the back of her neck and then saw a man running away, holding in his hand a hank of her long hair that he had just cut off. So much, it could be said, for the repression of bizarre behavior and for young women resting easy.[16]

For a much different set of crimes with a much different fascination, there was no shortage of repression but no resting easy: the "guerre à la cocaïne" declared in 1921 was clearly being lost by 1922. Speaking anonymously to *Le Figaro*'s Gilbert Charles, high officials of the Sûreté générale explained that cocaine had gained a foothold in France during the war, when opium from the Far East was unobtainable. Since 1918, more than eager to indulge this craving, laboratories in Germany—with Darmstadt the center—had been manufacturing a synthetic cocaine. So easy to conceal and so valuable in small quantities, its smuggling was as inevitable as impossible to prevent. In the first nine months of 1922, the Sûreté générale made nearly three hundred arrests for drug trafficking, and local police forces made at least that many more. Charles concluded that cocaine was nothing less than "un péril national."[17] Not just the sheer number but details of drug cases lent cogency to his alarm, portraying a France where, at least in Paris and along the frontiers and coastlines, cocaine was becoming banal. At Brest, it was sold "entre deux valses" in a dance hall, at tiny Saint-Vast-la-Hongue (Manche) on the English Channel by a sixty-year-old woman through her pharmacy, at Marseille by hotel clerks, at Avignon by cafe waiters, at Metz by soldiers.[18] Smugglers bringing in cocaine from the "German connection" were arrested at Thionville and Forbach (Moselle), Strasbourg, Montpellier, Metz, and, most often, Paris. Usually, the seizure was no more than a kilo—worth 1,250 francs when sold—but at the end of May 1922, the Sûreté générale tracked François-Marie Conquer

16. *Le Matin,* 6, 11, 13, 14, 15, 16, 17 December 1922 (piquées), 15, 16 December 1922 (Fleury); *Le Figaro,* 15 (Dr. Paul; Châtelet), 16 (ridicule), 30 (hair) December 1922.

17. *Le Figaro,* 19, 21 October 1922.

18. *Le Matin,* 6 April (Brest), 18 May (Metz), 9 June (Marseille), 14 July (Marseille), 23 July (Marseille and Avignon), 4 August (Saint-Vast-la-Hongue) 1922.

as he returned from Darmstadt with twenty-four kilos worth 30,000 francs.[19]

The Paris Police working undercover found it depressingly simple to make purchases, in the fashionable districts—from "l'Arabe" and "Joseph" at the place des Ternes near the shopping of the faubourg Saint Honoré, from a pharmacist on the rue Notre-Dame-des-Champs near the Luxembourg Gardens, from two Polish émigrés on the rue de Rivoli— and in the less fashionable—from a tourist on the rue d'Aboukir near the prostitutes of Saint Denis, from a Cuban émigré and his French girlfriend near the central railway stations, from two men selling openly at the place d'Italie, from waiters at cafes and from the down-and-out "mal vêtu."[20] Some drug dealers cultivated a certain notoriety: the dance instructor Henri Place, who sold to his students and whose supplier was known as "the aviator," the taxi driver called "le bel Henri," the kingpin of a Montmartre gang, Raoul Dianoux, feared as "Gros Raoul," and one of the gun molls, Anita Favergeon, "la belle Montmartoise." Others maintained a facade of propriety that collapsed only when they were arrested, like six physicians in Paris, practicing among the *milieux mondains* and prescribing—for a fee—morphine and cocaine.[21]

The varying combinations of self-indulgence and despair that drove the increasing use of drugs offered an interpretation for the many suicides of these years as well. Rachel Crakowski's tortured letter and death represented the end point—literally—of desperation. Marianne Le Marrec, nineteen years old and devoted to the reading of cheap novels, defined death as a vagary, stabbing herself repeatedly and using her own blood to write out the name of an imaginary lover because she dreamed of becom-

19. *Le Matin,* 19 May (Thionville and Metz), 30 May (Paris—Conquer), 9 June (Forbach), 11 July (Strasbourg), 16 September (Montpellier), 3 November (Paris), 21 November (Paris) 1922, 14 September (Paris), 21 December (Paris) 1923.

20. *Le Matin,* 28 May (Ternes), 26 July (*mal vêtu*), 11–12 August (Notre-Dame-des-Champs), 15 September (Aboukir), 9 October (Rivoli), 22 October (cafe) 1922, 6 March (cafe), 7 June (railway stations), 11 June (Italie) 1923.

21. *Le Matin,* 30–31 May (Place and the "aviator"), 13 August ("le bel Henri"), 19 September ("Gros Raoul" and "la belle Montmartoise"), 28–29 November (physicians) 1923.

ing the victim of passion.[22] Between them was every gradation, every excuse and every motive slightly different.

Some of the suicides had a minor prominence. The day after Marcel Sembat, one of Léon Blum's lieutenants in the Socialist party, died without warning from a cerebral hemorrhage, his wife turned a gun on herself. An attaché at the Polish embassy, a certain Bochencw, shot himself after writing letters to his friends and the ambassador describing his plan. Georges Aubry, editor of the *Correspondance parlementaire* and president of the Association des journalistes parlementaires, put a bullet through his temple in the Bois de Boulogne, a suicide note protruding from his coat pocket.[23] For the largely anonymous, there was sometimes—at least seemingly— hopeless love: Alice Rouillon asphyxiated herself for "chagrins intimes." André Bussa, a professor, and Sarah Bernart, his student, linked arms and jumped into the Seine, as did fifteen-year-old sweethearts Henri Cartier and Germaine Leboucher. Another student, Marcel Van Neenan, and his girlfriend blew out their brains after writing, "Disgusted with life, we do away with ourselves."[24] As with Mme Sembat, there was sometimes devastating personal loss: because Marcel Poirier's wife refused his pleas not to end their marriage, he told her, "You can have everything from me, even my life!" and shot himself before her eyes. Marie Lavieille and Julien Perrinet shot themselves, Jeanne Girard slashed her neck, and Marguerite Delarette took poison when abandoned by a lover. Jeanne Darcet shot herself at the tomb of her parents.[25] A few had been treated for nervous disorders: Emilie Karaviaz, who leaped from a fifth-story window, the lyric artist Poncet, who dived into the Seine, and Médéric Laquet, who hanged himself.[26] Occasionally, the excuse was penury—pulled from the Seine before she could drown herself, Louise Delaveine sobbed that she was "with-

22. *Le Figaro,* 24 January (Crakowski), 20 March (Le Marrec) 1922.

23. *Le Figaro,* 6–7 September 1922 (Sembat); *Le Matin,* 1 May 1922 (Bochencw); 1 March 1923 (Aubry).

24. *Le Matin,* 29 March (Bussa and Bernart), 11 April (Rouillon) 1922, 13 April (Van Neenan), 12 May (Cartier and Leboucher) 1923.

25. *Le Matin,* 16 March (Girard), 28 June (Poirier), 23 August (Delarette), 6 September (Lavieille) 1922, 19 May (Darcet), 9 August (Perrinet) 1923.

26. *Le Matin,* 21 March (Poncet), 3 April (Karaviaz), 26 April (Laquet) 1922.

out a job, without a home, and without a family to help her"—
occasionally, its opposite—Gilbert Lacombe aimed a bullet at his heart
because, as he had written his mother, he was "too bored."[27] And there
developed the curious custom of the final meal: Georges Legall paid for
his dinner at a cafe along the Seine, handed the waiter a twenty-franc tip,
complained that nothing had gone right for him in life, and threw himself
into the river. René Godard avoided paying the bill at a restaurant on the
boulevard Saint Denis by shooting himself in the heart as it was presented.
Georges Sibille did not even finish the dinner he ordered before firing a
gun at his head.[28]

For the rest, more often than not, only the means was known. Julia Gamant, Joseph Bridier, and a Mlle Guépal stepped in the path of a train.
Hérison Salomancanu, Louis Rousse, a Mlle Hermel, and Louis Legusguet took poison. Denise Mestas, Clothilde Roulier, Eugène Malassé,
Marie Raynaud, Suzanne Poyer, and Félicie Martin drowned themselves
in the Seine. Eugène Agasse, Henri Meunier, Narcisse Wattigny, Antonin
Barrazzi, Adrien Mancerot, Baptiste Guérin, and four unidentified men
hanged themselves.[29] Lucien Benoit, Pauline Thiébault, César Morin, Antoine Bochu, Marcelle Drouillon, Jeanne Wattier, Jeanne Maillard, Mar-
celle Charles, and Hélène Lartigue threw themselves from high windows;
Victor Schreider jumped from the Colonne de Juillet in the place de la
Bastille.[30] Edith Hirtz, Auguste Quiévreux, Commandant Cocillon, Paul
Dubar, Georgette Jeannot, Xavier Portarin, Juliette Desmarets, Ernest
Pringent, Victor Schenemberger, Edouard Fritsch, Emile Godard, Alexandre Devismes, Emile-Jean Dulong, Georgette Zuguier, Yvonne Aligue,

27. *Le Matin,* 2 February (Delaveine) 1922, 7 February (Lacombe) 1923.

28. *Le Matin,* 9 May (Legall), 9 June (Godard) 1922, 25 July (Sibille) 1923.

29. *Le Matin,* 5 April (Salomancanu), 11 April (three unidentified men), 16 April
(Rousse), 18 April (Mestas), 28 May (Roulier), 11 August (Gamant, Malassé, and Raynaud),
8 September (Agasse), 24 November (unidentified man) 1922, 10 February (Meunier, Wattigny, and Barrazzi), 28 March (Poyer), 20 May (Bridier), 15 August (Mancerot), 17 August
(Legusguet), 18 August (Guépal), 6 November (Hermel), 19 November (Guérin), 28 November (Martin) 1923.

30. *Le Matin,* 17 April (Benoit), 16 August (Thiébault), 18 August (Morin), 19 August
(Schreider), 13 November (Bochu) 1922, 19 January (Drouillon), 11 April (Wattier), 18
April (Maillard), 31 October (Charles), 28 November (Lartigue) 1923.

Georges Deschamps, and a certain elegantly dressed man without identification but his linen marked "H. H." shot themselves.[31] Pharmacist Georges Letourneau combined poison with the gun, drinking a glass of digitalis and then shooting himself five times to ensure the death he sought. His motive remained murky, but in a note left behind he captured something about the hopelessness of these years: "I am tired of living, tired of my business, tired of paying new taxes—I miss the good life of the countryside."[32]

Besides these ever-*retentissant faits divers,* the small change that jangled the loudest and overflowed pockets during the two Ruhr-crisis years was literally money—how topsy-turvy, the world had changed. *Le Petit parisienne* related how the nineteen-year-old daughter of a Russian aristocratic family once with uncounted riches now made her living as an actress for a minor theater. Caroline Otéro, "la Belle Otéro," a celebrated demimondaine during the Belle Epoque, suffered injuries to her eyes and one leg when her taxi crashed in May 1920. She asked 100,000 francs in damages, but the court, as *Le Figaro* reported, awarded her only 15,000 francs, ruling that a courtesan's beauty was a fugitive asset. "Intellectuals," facing eviction from Paris because their incomes—so many of them were rentiers—no longer matched their rents, found a champion in Maurice Barrès, who told the Chamber of Deputies that for such men and women, "their study is their very tool of work, so to speak. They need to have a library, solitude, and contemplation." This plight won a law limiting rent increases for them until 1926.[33] No one intervened to save rentiers trying—failing for the most part—to maintain large properties under the pressure of inflation. The real estate pages of the tonier newspapers like *Le Figaro* were filled with villas, châteaux, and estates for sale. They were described as "splendid," "important," "superb," or "magnificent," and

31. *Le Matin,* 11 April (Hirtz), 16 April (Quiévreux), 10 May ("H. H."), 11 May (Cocillon), 12 May (Dubar), 16 July (Jeannot), 30 July (Portarin), 13 August (Desmarets, Pringent, and Schenemberger), 8 September (Fritsch and Godard), 5 December (Devismes), 14 December (Dulong) 1922, 2 January (Zuguier), 20 August (Aligue), 6 September (Deschamps) 1923.

32. *Le Figaro,* 6 July 1922.

33. *Le Petit parisienne,* 7 February 1922 (Russian actress); *Le Figaro,* 16 March (Otéro), 20, 26 March, 14 July (intellectuals) 1922; J.O.C., Débats, 19 March 1922.

their prices were—in francs—225,000, 335,000, 650,000, 850,000. To expatriate Americans, that meant $18,000, $26,800, $52,000, $68,000—bargains indeed.[34]

The obverse for the still rich and the nouveaux riches was an abundance of full-page advertisements for automobiles such as the Delaunay Belleville, "the great French marque . . . if you desire the car of good form," the Irat, "the car of the elite," or the Amilcar, "the car of experts"—for women's fashions—like Premet, Paquin, Yionnet, or Parry, flaunting their international appeal by adopting English and Italian as well as French for the text, as in "Here are three ladies dressed by Joseph Paquin . . . there is not a country in the world where they would not be recognized immediately as 'Parisiennes' "—and for pricey products of all variety—such as Burberry, "synonym of perfection," or Vuitton, "trunks which impress through their convenience, their elegance, and their solidity."[35] For business there were new machines—imported: the Remington, "light, stylish, and portable," and the Underwood, "you do not risk an 'experience,' you profit from that by millions of users," or domestic: the M.A.P., "Is it reasonable to purchase a foreign machine when there is a French alternative better planned, better built, and less expensive?"—and for the home, new novelties such as movie projectors, the "Pathé-Baby," and even appliances for cleaning—sold at department stores expanding to keep pace.[36]

A somewhat larger denomination in historical currency was the playing out of the scandal involving the Banque industrielle de Chine. Its insolvency at the end of June 1921 placed in jeopardy not only depositors but France's prestige in the Far East. For Raymond Poincaré and his minister

34. For exceptional examples, see Le Figaro, 19, 20, 22 September, 1 October 1922, 10 April, 24 October 1923.

35. For examples, see Le Figaro, 16 February (Irat), 16 March (Delaunay Belleville), 20 March (Premet), 27 March (Parry), 18 May (Vuitton), 29 May (Paquin), 24 June (Amilcar), 3 September (Yionnet), 9 October (Burberry) 1923.

36. For examples, see Le Figaro, 5 November (Pathé-Baby) 1922, 6 January (Remington), 15 January (Underwood), 20 May (M.A.P.), 22 September (Au Bon Marché expansion), 30 September (Galeries Lafayette exposition) 1923; see also Robert L. Frost, "Machine Liberation: Inventing Housewives and Home Appliances in Interwar France," French Historical Studies 18 (Spring 1993): 109–30.

of finance, Charles de Lasteyrie, refloating the bank was imperative to national interests north of Indochina, but the means presented serious difficulties. Private investors were leery barring a contribution of treasury resources, and that was politically impossible because of the budget deficit and because of the revelations about Philippe Berthelot's role in the bank's collapse that forced his resignation as secretary-general of the Quai d'Orsay in December 1921. Eventually, Lasteyrie devised a complicated plan to use France's share of the indemnity pledged by the Chinese government for the damage done to foreign holdings during the 1900 Boxer Rebellion as the collateral for bonds to provide the initial capital. This sleight of hand was enough of a commitment for the investors but not too much for the senators and deputies.[37]

Much more interesting than these arrangements was the possibility of criminal culpability—rumored to include swindling and abuse of confidence, both felonies—involving the B.I.C., its officers, and principal shareholders. For Berthelot, subject to Poincaré's implacable rigor, the retribution was swift—suspension from government service for ten years. The rest had to await the investigation under Gustave Richaud, appointed as the examining magistrate for the case. And wait, for Richaud did not complete his work until April 1923, when he charged Alexis Pernotte, general manager of the B.I.C., André Berthelot, Philippe's brother, a senator, and chairman of the bank's board of directors, and six other directors, including Justin Perchot, also a senator, with relatively minor commercial violations. A jury might have treated them roughly, but juries did not hear misdemeanors. Before the three-judge panel of district court, Pernotte and Berthelot alone were convicted, with almost no significance because Pernotte received six months in prison and a 3,000-franc fine, Berthelot merely a 3,000-franc fine—an amount slightly more than the cost of two typewriters. Considering the outcome of previous financial scandals involving the political and the powerful in France, the result was predictable.[38]

37. J.O.C., Débats, 27 January, 15, 16 November, 31 December 1922; J.O.S., Débats, 3 March 1922, 12 January 1923.
38. *Le Figaro,* 24 February, 3, 4, 12, 14, 17, 26 March, 19 July 1922, 5 January, 24 April, 3 August 1923; *Gazette des tribunaux,* 3 August 1923; Philippe Berthelot's suspension was imposed on 16 March 1922; the French M.A.P. typewriter cost 1,250 francs.

Perhaps smaller in denomination than the B.I.C. intrigues, but more fascinating because of its nastiness, was the takeover of *Le Figaro* by perfume magnate François Coty. Agents for him had covertly bought up a majority of the shares in the holding company, and when his intention became public in early February 1922, Edouard Calmette, chief administrator of the newspaper and son of the "martyr-editor," Gaston Calmette, murdered by Henriette Caillaux in 1914, led some of the staff in crying foul. Titling his column "The Merchants in the Temple," Louis Latzarus, editor since 1920, approvingly quoted Charles Maurras's characterization of Coty as "the man whose sole qualification is wealth" and added his own: "Coty, rich but illiterate, buys a literary journal." But Coty, born François Spoturno and poor, then early orphaned, had not built an empire worth billions of francs without cleverness or brutality. To cut off the most damaging invective, he obtained a court order prohibiting further criticism in *Le Figaro* of himself or his allies until 28 February, the date of the annual shareholder meeting, when he would formally assume control and when his enemies would be shown the door. To counter sympathy for the son of the martyr-editor, he recruited his own Calmette, Gaston's brother Albert, a medical pioneer in Saigon and famous as the director of the Pasteur Institute of Lille. And to allay the broader disquiet that his presence might desecrate one of France's journalistic monuments or change its political tone, he lured back Alfred Capus, *Le Figaro*'s editor from 1914 to 1920 and one of Poincaré's few close friends. For Coty did not mean— yet—to run the newspaper, only to use its prestige in furthering his ambition of election to the Senate from his native Corsica. Following two failures, he won a close vote in 1923 that was quickly invalidated after revelations of corruption. Increasingly embittered, he turned toward extreme right political movements and in 1927 would push *Le Figaro* in that direction as well.[39]

The initial impact made by the smallest of the small change could never match that of the larger denominations, but sometimes the memory rang with curious reverberation. August, the month of heat and vacation in

39. *L'Action française,* 9 February 1922, for Maurras; *Le Figaro,* 10, 12, 14, 15, 27, 28 February, 1 March 1922; Latzarus joined the *Revue hebdomadaire*; Capus died on 1 November 1922 and was succeeded as editor by Henri Vonoven.

Paris, seemed to educe extravagant behavior. In 1922, the best example was Joseph Roche, who strode through the meat and vegetable stalls at Les Halles shouting, "The end of the world has come! I am the angel of destruction!" When a patrolman intervened, he raved on about the apocalypse and Napoleon. Exactly a year and a week later in 1923, a well-dressed man presented himself at the precinct station on the rue du Faubourg Saint Denis, just off the grand boulevards, and announced: "I am the Apostle Saint Paul. I come from God to inform President Millerand of danger threatening him." Police Captain Bénézech replied: "Wonderful! I will have you driven to the Elysée." Instead, the destination was a mental hospital: one more August lunatic, undoubtedly, but the prediction was prescient—doom was indeed stalking Millerand. He would prepare it himself that fall at Evreux and then flee from the consequences through the spring until they destroyed him in June. By then, whoever could recall that undelivered warning from the Apostle Saint Paul?[40]

40. *Le Figaro,* 9 August (Roche) 1922, 16 August (messenger for Millerand) 1923.

7

∎ ∎ ∎

Of Falling Francs, Shifting Blocs, and the
Uses of Resignation

By mid-January 1924, the steady decline of the franc became a precipitous collapse. From an average of 82.92 to the pound and 19.02 to the dollar in December 1923, the franc dropped to 90.46 and 21.19 by 12 January, losses of 9.09 and 11.41 percent, respectively, in less than two weeks. The next trading day, Monday, 14 January, the franc plunged to 96.11 and 22.80, down another 6.25 and 7.60 percent, respectively, in hours. At the Paris Bourse, the near free fall excited "la grande peur"—a sense of absolute panic that quickly spread to the front page of every newspaper. For the cabinet, especially for Raymond Poincaré as premier and foreign minister and for Charles de Lasteyrie as minister of finance, this calamity struck at a supremely inopportune moment. Legislative elections were only four months away in May, and the committee of experts under Charles G. Dawes was convening to consider the question of reparations. In the exchange rate of the franc could lie the fate of the Bloc national and France's occupation of the Ruhr.[1]

The voting for the Chamber of Deputies in 1919 had taken place under the system of répartition proportionnelle, but RP was not true proportional representation, for if a single list of candidates won an absolute ma-

---

1. Sauvy, *Histoire économique,* 1:445, for exchange rates; Schuker, *End of French Predominance,* 55–57.

jority of a department's vote, it received all the seats for the department, a provision known as the *prime à la majorité*. Since then, and without any sense of urgency, there had been recurrent debate over modifying the system for the elections to be held in 1924. Having won under the 1919 rules, most of the Bloc national deputies wanted to maintain RP—because it rewarded "blocs"—but divided over prime à la majorité. The fervent wish of the Radicals was for a return to the single-member districts (scrutin d'arrondissement) that had been their base of power for two decades after 1898, but with the creation of their own bloc, the Cartel des gauches, they began to find RP more palatable. Allied with the Radicals or not, the Socialists recognized that as a small party, true proportional representation would bring them more seats than they could possibly win any other way. Even smaller groups, like the clemencistes, the Far Right, and the Communists, came to the same conclusion.

When the discussion turned serious in late November 1923—after all, the elections were less than half a year away and no decision had been taken—the political atmosphere was heavily charged: President Alexandre Millerand's "Bombe d'Evreux," the proclamation of the Cartel des gauches, and the tergiversations of Aristide Briand, shrewd judge of the main chance. When Pierre Forgeot, one of the younger stalwarts in the Bloc national, warned that retention of RP with prime à la majorité might bring victory to the Cartel des gauches, he tried to goad Poincaré, who had thus far refused to take any position on the electoral law, by associating such abstention with Briand's "fine and candid cynicism" that "each should vote for 'the system most favorable to his party.'" And after Gaston Thomson, for the Radicals, demanded a return to single-member districts, after Marc Sangnier, for the liberal Catholics, and Bracke (the name taken by Alexandre Desrousseaux), for the Socialists, called for true proportional representation, Poincaré answered. He explained that while his personal preference was for RP without prime à la majorité, he was unwilling to make that an issue of confidence or even to recommend it to the Chamber at large. Disdaining the challenge—even the insolence—from Forgeot, he took the moral high ground: "You have a single question to answer: What is just? Which system guarantees the most genuine representation of the country?" The search for broad consensus had brought Poincaré to the position of implying that he cared more that the electoral law produce "the most genuine representation of the country" than that it produce a majority for the Bloc national.

This response left the field open to Briand. Although like Poincaré he favored true proportional representation, unlike him he was willing to make a recommendation—to retain the 1919 rules because at least they were a known quantity at a moment when so much was in upheaval. And as for the outcome:

> Forgeot cries "Beware! We are going to have very different results. The system that worked for us will now work against us." And Forgeot expresses the fear that our foreign policy may suffer as a consequence. I recall from before the war certain polemics, and the expectations to which they gave birth among our enemies. The war came. Men of the Left were in power. They were not unequal to their task. Let Forgeot be reassured. France senses profoundly her own vital interest and will not choose men likely to desert their duty. So let us set aside the issues of foreign policy and patriotism, which will not be placed in peril by the coming elections. For me, I see nothing wrong with France appearing in the eyes of the world always as the France of the Revolution.

These words cast the die: he would side with the Cartel des gauches. Poincaré might refuse to be "political"; Briand would not.[2]

The votes on the electoral law were anticlimactic: an effort by the Radicals to restore scrutin d'arrondissement failed overwhelmingly, 408 to 127, and with the cabinet "neutral" on prime à la majorité, the deputies split almost evenly, retaining it by the narrow margin of 290 to 275. All the debate had ended with the 1919 rules remaining in place for 1924. More important was the effect on the Bloc national, which interpreted Briand's decision as an indication that the Center was drifting dangerously left and recognized the acute danger of his discounting the effect on foreign policy of a victory by the Cartel des gauches. The Ruhr occupation was the greatest strength and the greatest weakness of the Bloc national, curbing Ger-

---

2. J.O.C., Débats, 27 (Forgeot), 29 (Thomson, Sangnier, Bracke, Poincaré, and Briand) November 1923.

man recalcitrance but at the cost of France's own financial destabilization. Sharing credit for the former but sole blame for the latter was a prescription for an election debacle. Friend to neither Poincaré nor Briand, André Tardieu had already echoed Alexandre Varenne's forecast, "If the majority of 1919 becomes the minority of 1924, it should recall that my friends and I warned them in time." No good could come from cornering Briand on the Ruhr—past master of foreign affairs and facile speaker, he had as well never wavered in supporting Poincaré's policy. The point of attack had to be at Edouard Herriot, the florid leader of the Radicals, and at the equivocal language that permitted agreement between them and the Socialists on the Ruhr—so making the Cartel des gauches possible. To mount it, the choice fell on Paul Reynaud, one of the bleu horizon elected in 1919, aggressive, and more poincariste than Poincaré. Only the timing was left to decide.[3]

The moment came on 28 December in the Chamber of Deputies, when Léon Blum, the leader of the Socialists, denounced Poincaré's Ruhr policy as "criminal" and merely an "electoral ploy" for the Bloc national. Reynaud responded by posing three questions to the Radical seats—aimed principally at Herriot, who would be premier if the Cartel des gauches won the elections: "Should you be offering your hand to those who declare the occupation of the Ruhr a crime? Will you combine your election funds with those of the Socialists [a reference to rumors of contributions from outside France]? And if you arrive at the Chamber in the majority, will you withdraw from the Ruhr?" As if in practice for answering interpellations, Herriot resisted precise answers to deadly questions. But his tone and his vocabulary were the reply Reynaud sought, unmistakably dividing the Cartel from the Bloc: "I criticized the operation of 10 January, because we were entering the Ruhr alone, but I say now that the business must be carried through to the finish. If the Ruhr was a disaster, it would not be a disaster for the cabinet but a disaster for France. And if tomorrow we were in power, we would not withdraw from the Ruhr—France plays there its last card—but our policy would be to substitute a more solid guarantee for this uncertain one." In his editorial the following day for *L'Oeuvre,* Herriot made the point even more clearly: "Reynaud does not

3. J.O.C., Débats, 4, 6 December 1923; *L'Echo national,* 3 December 1923.

want an accord between the French and German democracies . . . I see there a danger, not an element of security."[4] At the end of 1923, the lines were clearly drawn.

The beginning of 1924 blurred them again. Worrisome reports from the currency markets attracted attention less than a week into the new year. *Le Figaro*'s Henri Vonoven started his editorial bravely—"Anyone deserting the franc is an idiot"—but quickly revealed his anxiety—"one more time, we must hold firm." *L'Avenir* sounded the tocsin: "We all have a duty to perform, under penalty of treason, the banks, the cabinet, and the legislature." Stéphane Lauzanne in *Le Matin* suggested the means: "Let the government act! It can require exporters to repatriate all their foreign currency; it can guarantee the integrity of exchange rates; it can deny foreign riffraff access to the Bourse; it can close banking houses; it can lock up the French who bet against France; it can demand new laws in the name of national security." By comparison, the response from Lasteyrie, and therefore from the cabinet, lacked any sense of urgency. The franc's decline had no economic basis and was the result, he insisted, purely of speculation by foreigners, especially Germans hoping vainly to drive France from the Ruhr. If good French men and women worked hard, exported more, and imported less, all would be well. Meanwhile, he would seek the prosecution of anyone responsible for undermining confidence in the franc. When Robert de Jouvenel asked in *L'Oeuvre* whether that meant arresting the cabinet, Lasteyrie might well regard his credibility—questioned since the controversy over the François-Marsal convention in December—seriously damaged.[5]

The collapse of the franc on 14 January, France's "Black Monday," left the reputation in tatters, the man irrelevant. Poincaré called for the dossiers and applied his sedulous mind to the issues, reducing Lasteyrie almost to a factotum. Devising a set of austere economic and fiscal measures to restore international confidence required only his expertise; demanding their implementation required all his authority. And that Poincaré placed

---

4. J.O.C., Débats, 28 December 1923; *L'Oeuvre,* 29 December 1923.

5. *Le Figaro,* 5 January 1924, for Vonoven; *L'Avenir,* 4 January 1924; *Le Matin,* 8 January 1924, for Lauzanne; *L'Oeuvre,* 7 January 1924, for Jouvenel; *Le Temps,* 6, 9, 10 January 1924, for Lasteyrie.

at risk when he faced the Chamber of Deputies with his program three days after *la grande peur.* To defend the franc, speculation had to be repressed sternly. To defend the franc, revenues had to be increased significantly, through new measures to prevent evasion of current levies, through higher postal, telegraph, and telephone rates, through the sale of unprofitable state enterprises, and above all through a new imposition, the double décime, that 20 percent increase proposed a year earlier now revised to include all taxes. To defend the franc, expenditures had to be curtailed drastically, by a billion francs, through administrative reorganization so drastic and budget cuts so severe that the cabinet sought authorization to act by decree. His mien dour, Poincaré insisted that the deputies demonstrate their approval of these proposals, made "with sangfroid and great calm," through a resolution of confidence, after which "the cabinet will do its duty, and vindicate, before the country, the attitude of the Chamber. . . . The Chamber will once again have deserved well of the nation." As for the political risk of raising taxes and slashing spending four months before the elections, "The country will understand easily that the Chamber responds to the appeal of the cabinet, and will be grateful, come the elections in May, that the deputies present themselves with the treasury healthy, the franc stabilized, and the nightmare of inflation exorcised." He was right to be dour: the vote was 394 to 180, only the Bloc national willing to support him.[6]

The Left stood against Poincaré's economic program from the outset, with the division in the Chamber analogous to that of 15 June 1923, after the last previous major debate involving a domestic issue, the cabinet's margin on the vote of confidence then 193, now 214. Some of the opposition derived from a classical education that engendered among many French politicians of the Right but far more of the Left the sense that finances were utterly arcane and thus the temptation "to believe," as Denis Brogan put it with only slight exaggeration, "that the laws of economics, even of arithmetic, were inventions of reaction, to be safely ignored by the mandatories of universal suffrage, or to be refuted by eloquence." Instead

6. J.O.C., *Documents,* no. 6972–73, 1924, for the proposals; J.O.C., *Débats,* 17 January 1924, for Poincaré's presentation. On Poincaré during this period, see Miquel, *Poincaré,* 476–85, and Keiger, *Poincaré,* 305–11.

of the surtax, Radicals and Socialists would both call for a levy on capital, when such investment, not the wages of workers or the profits of shopkeepers, had been the great victim of the war and the Après Guerre. Paul Painlevé, despite (or because of) his mathematical training, even claimed that the double décime would provoke inflation.[7]

More important to the opposition was a calculation that imposing new taxes literally on the eve of the elections promised political disaster. On that basis, if not the first, the Cartel des gauches could expect defections from the Bloc national. Jules Lugol, seeking additional guarantees under the legislation he had sponsored for pensioners, sparred early with Poincaré, who replied brutally, "The cabinet will not vote a centime of expense without a centime of receipt." On 17 January, Pierre Taittinger on the Far Right had cried out to the Chamber that he preferred to be defeated for reelection rather than "risk through cowardice the ruin of France!" Only a week later, on 25 January, Léon Daudet accused the cabinet of "addressing its majority an invitation to suicide for nothing." And there was the uncertain effect of Tardieu's corrosive vituperation, supporting the Bloc national but not Poincaré and Lasteyrie: "I permit myself to recall that before attacking on the Marne, our Joffre began by dismissing the leaders already revealed to be incompetent. The majority will one day regret not having taken the same precaution."[8]

But most important was the recognition by the Radicals that the proposed economies would fall most heavily on their chief source of patronage, the *sous-préfectures*. By happy coincidence for the process of budget cutting, the committee formed in August 1922 under the direction of Louis Marin, a mainstay of the Bloc national and charged with proposing measures to simplify government operations, issued a report in early December 1923. The primary recommendation was that recent advances in transportation and communication would enable the state to centralize its various administrative functions at the level of the prefecture, at the departmental seat, and phase out the sous-préfecture, in each arrondissement, the districts making up a department. Substantial saving was pre-

---

7. Brogan, *Development of Modern France,* 156; *L'Oeuvre,* 20 January 1924, for Painlevé.
8. J.O.C., Débats, 17 (Lugol, Poincaré, and Taittinger), 25 (Daudet) January 1924; *L'Echo national,* 17 January 1924, for Tardieu.

dicted in the closing of many small offices, tribunals, even rural schools, and through the reduction of lower-level fonctionnaires. Exactly these men and women had gained what were essentially sinecures through their allegiance to the Radical party during its two decades of dominance after 1899. Because each deputy would surely fight furiously to defend his own, Poincaré asked the power to impose the cuts by decree, to be approved as a whole by the Chamber within six months. And no fool, he refused to reveal his targets: "I will not enter into detail before having the decrees in hand."[9]

The Radicals recognized that an undisguised fight for the preservation of patronage would be unseemly, especially with French troops in the Ruhr and the franc under siege. But there was another way, to attack as dictatorial the request for decree powers. Such a proposal was, Herriot exclaimed, "insupportable and terrible" and jeopardized the very essence of the Republic, almost a coup d'état. "I can only express my astonishment that a jurist of Poincaré's stature would present such a bill before the Chamber! . . . You invoke the public interest, but the citizens do not regard this moment as proper for dispossessing the legislature of its prerogatives." For the Socialists, Joseph Paul-Boncour asked similarly why Poincaré was abandoning his reputation for insisting on limited government. Both suggested an alternate source for economy, an audit of the expenses filed for reimbursement in reconstructing the devastated region. The great surprise of the attack was the desertion from the Bloc national of André Lefèvre, Millerand's minister of war in 1920 and Poincaré's close ally for more than a decade. After declaring that he could not countenance a "blanc-seing"—granting the cabinet a blank check—he also asked pointedly, "And what will the voters say if your plan does not save the franc?"[10]

One strident response to these arguments came from Gustave Hervé in *La Victoire*: "Let us be done with the stupidity that dictatorship is antirepublican, when it was the necessary condition for the very existence of the nation during the days of danger" (a reference to Georges Clemenceau's

9. For the Marin committee, see "Premier rapport de la Commission des réformes," *Journal Officiel*, Annexe, Documents administratifs, 10 December 1923; for Poincaré, J.O.C., Débats, 25 January 1924.

10. J.O.C., Débats, 25, 26 January (Herriot), 4 February (Paul-Boncour and Lefèvre) 1924.

methods); "Herriot and some good apostles of the Cartel des gauches experienced the need to assume the expression of horrified virgins when the word 'decree-law' was uttered"; "Without provision for difficult times, the constitution is scandalous in permitting babbling legislators to palaver interminably and so prevent the government from governing." Poincaré, his memory of défaitisme keener still than Hervé's, had an even more provocative response. He began innocuously: "It is not a question of granting to one man exorbitant power, but only of authorizing the cabinet to carry out reforms which in the end the legislature remains at liberty to reject. . . . Some orators have made reference to my republican convictions. No one has ever placed them in doubt." But that was not the case of all: after reading aloud a proposal to impose laws and constitutional change by decree, he thrust the knife: "No, it is not I who drew up this article, but I understand that the politician who did so dreamed once of using this text to cross the Rubicon."[11]

Poincaré did not have to name Joseph Caillaux because the allusion was sufficient for all. In 1916, bitter at the political isolation into which he had been cast by the aspersions of *Le Figaro* and then the revelations of his wife's trial, Caillaux had dreamed of returning to power and imposing a reckoning upon his enemies. Incautiously, he wrote down these plans under the title "Rubicon," and they were discovered a year later when he was charged with défaitisme. To continue the provocation begun by Poincaré, Fernand Engerand and Emmanuel Brousse of the Bloc national proposed substituting Caillaux's exact words for the original language in the decree-law proposal. An abashed Herriot tried to argue that Caillaux never meant what he wrote, but Edouard Ignace, Clemenceau's head of military justice, interrupted with a blistering attack. The much-despised Léon Daudet added his brand of calumny: "Down with Caillaux! Down with the traitor!" But the blocs in the Chamber were shifting, as the vote on the decree powers proved, and memories in past tense could not overcome fears in present. Although Poincaré won 333 to 205, his majority was down to 128, 86 fewer than only three weeks earlier.[12]

11. For Hervé, *La Victoire,* 19, 25, 30 January 1924; for Poincaré, J.O.C., Débats, 5 February 1924.
12. J.O.C., Débats, 7 February 1924.

Emboldened, the Cartel des gauches used every means to slow debate on the centerpiece of Poincaré's defense of the franc, imposing the double décime. The list of speakers and their speeches grew ever longer; amendments multiplied; interruptions became protracted. For more than a week, sessions lasted into the early morning, and deputies fell asleep at their desks. Paul-Boncour justified these tactics in *L'Oeuvre* as "the classic essence of all parliamentary opposition." But Raoul Péret, the moderate president of the Chamber, cautioned: "Think of France, of whom we are the representatives. She deserves our respect. We honor ourselves by acting worthy of her. For if France is watching, other countries are watching also." Poincaré was more pointed: "I ask what France can gain from such debates! In the name of the nation, I beg that you bring these discussions to an end." The Bloc national's Maurice Bokanowski, floor leader for the Chamber's budget committee, candidly addressed the Cartel: "We will take responsibility for this law. You can use it against us in the elections if you want. But let us vote it!" Vincent Auriol of the Socialists replied by proposing a tax on capital in place of the double décime. Not even the prospect of doing nothing could have frightened investors more, and four days later, on 18 February, the franc passed a psychological barrier, dropping to 100.50—triple digits—against the pound. That same day, Poincaré got his vote, the double décime passing the Chamber 305 to 219, but his support also passed a psychological barrier, falling to less than a hundred.[13]

Since 1919, Tardieu had been calling for a compact, disciplined majority: certainly, the 305 deputies remaining to Poincaré were the core of the Bloc national. Since 1919, Tardieu had been calling for a clear division in French politics between the Left and the Right: certainly, the Bloc national and the Cartel des gauches had all but eliminated the alternatives. Be careful what you wish for, so goes the admonition—because where was Tardieu now to stand? As the arch-clemenciste, he detested the Cartel but had to oppose Poincaré, even while belonging in the Bloc national. Above all, he feared that Poincaré's policies, especially these new economic and fiscal proposals, would lead to victory for the Cartel in May. His editorials had denounced the program from the outset: "That these hasty taxes are inad-

13. *L'Oeuvre,* 10 February 1924, for Paul-Boncour; J.O.C., Débats, 8 (Poincaré and Péret), 13 (Bokanowski), 14 (Auriol), 18 (vote) February 1924.

equate to their goal is grave. That they are the negation of justice while at the same time the ruin of the dreams nourished for the country by governmental eloquence is more grave still." He sided with Lefèvre on decree powers: "The majority has delegated to a worn-out cabinet the power which it holds from the voters, and which without their formal consent it does not have the right to give away." Before the Chamber, he explained to the Bloc national why he would vote against the double décime: "It is a question of your seats . . . and of the ideas you defend. For these dragnet unjust taxes, probably without effect upon the exchange rate, will profit only the Communists! The Communists are going to play the game of the Boulangists thirty-five years ago: attracting all the unhappy and the dissatisfied." Yet when a voice cried back, "But what would you do?" Tardieu had no response.[14]

And refusing to respond was the proper pose of any Cassandra having just uttered dire predictions. Tardieu had also hit upon a damaging description for the cabinet and perhaps Poincaré himself, "usé"—worn-out and used up. For despite the shock of Black Monday, the Chamber took a month to pass Poincaré's crisis legislation, and then by a much-diminished majority. More trouble was ahead in the Senate, which nine months earlier had stunned Poincaré by slapping down the prosecution of the "Communist Plot." Its budget committee was taking a hostile attitude toward his proposals. Its elections committee had already recommended that the voting in May for the Chamber revert to scrutin d'arrondissement, no matter that the deputies themselves wanted to maintain RP. When Poincaré forced a showdown on the elections law first, rumors flew that he was courting a defeat that would permit him to resign over an issue less critical than the Ruhr or the franc. To the senators on 21 February, he vehemently insisted, "I have not the slightest intention of deserting my post!" and then won a dangerously close vote, 150 to 134.[15]

Undaunted, the budget committee, dominated by Radicals, delayed two more weeks before formally opposing both the decree laws and the double décime on 8 March. The franc immediately dropped to record lows against the pound—113.05—and the dollar—26.22—on short sales by

14. *L'Echo national,* 27 January, 7 February 1924; J.O.C., Débats, 12 February 1924.
15. J.O.S., Débats, 20 (Poincaré), 21 (vote) February 1924.

speculators betting that Poincaré and his program were finished. They might have taken a lesson about him from the Germans. The fate of the elections law led Poincaré to believe that he had the votes in the Senate, and he shored up that support during the following week. On 13 March, he promised that "when you have voted these financial measures, the speculators who have warred against the franc will be forced to count their losses . . . but the battle will not be over until we have stripped from our adversaries the possibility of finding fault with our budget." When the following day the same thin majority approved the decree laws, 154 to 139, and then the double décime, 155 to 126, the franc rebounded spectacularly to 92.35 against the pound and 21.52 against the dollar, aided surreptitiously by credit to the French government from J. P. Morgan and Company, led by the Francophile John Pierpont Morgan. Ten days later, on 24 March, the franc was at 79.80 and 18.07. Poincaré had won a major economic and political victory. *Le Figaro's* editor, Henri Vonoven, celebrated "the end of the nightmare." Edouard Laskine in *La République française* predicted that the French knew who had saved the franc and would not forget. Like the speculators, Tardieu had been wrong: Poincaré was not yet usé.[16]

But Tardieu was right about the cabinet. On 26 March, Lasteyrie faced the Chamber of Deputies to defend the treatment of pensions under the new fiscal program. No domestic issue was more delicate because none more clearly recalled the sacrifices of the war, and thinking to protect himself against defections, Lasteyrie insisted on making the vote a question of confidence. He then watched in horror as the increasingly fissiparous Bloc national cracked apart entirely, defeating the cabinet 271 to 264. Poincaré was testifying before the Chamber's foreign affairs committee and knew nothing of this reverse until he left for the Quai d'Orsay and was told by an aide, "You are deposed!" Utterly astonished, he demanded an explanation, after which he proclaimed, "J'en ai assez! J'en ai assez!"—I have had enough! As he had the previous May after the Senate's Haute Cour vote,

16. J.O.S., Débats, 13 (Poincaré), 14 (votes) March 1924; *Le Figaro,* 19 March 1924, for Vonoven; *La République française,* 24 March 1924, for Laskine; see Schuker, *End of French Predominance,* for another assessment of the process in the Senate, 84–88, and of routing the speculators, 89–115.

he gathered his ministers together and headed for the Elysée to carry out the formalities of quitting office. Although Lasteyrie thought his own elimination would be sufficient, Poincaré insisted that the Chamber's vote was an act of defiance against the cabinet as a whole. When Millerand urged him to reconsider, he stormed out saying, "My departure is irrevocable!" The anger cooled overnight, and on the following morning, Poincaré bent to Millerand's entreaties by agreeing to reconstitute his cabinet.[17]

The new list of ministers combined the inevitable, the predictable, and one great surprise. Foreign policy Poincaré retained for his own, as before, and he kept on the principal executors of the Ruhr occupation, Yves Le Trocquer for public works and André Maginot for the army. The hapless Lasteyrie had to go, replaced by the symbol of deflation, Frédéric François-Marsal. For his labors on behalf of the double décime, Bokanowski gained the naval ministry. For not opposing the double décime, and as a sop to the moderate Radicals, Louis Loucheur, minister for reconstruction under Clemenceau, was made minister of commerce. The critical domestic post, the ministry of the interior, went to Justin de Selves, an even more moderate Radical and, since 1919, chairman of the Senate's foreign affairs committee. The choice of de Selves, as connoisseurs of political intrigue recognized immediately, was a shrewd gamble by Poincaré in the prelude to the elections: a turn slightly to the left, but not to Herriot's—meaning Caillaux's—Left. For through de Selves, minister of foreign affairs during the Agadir crisis in 1911, were revealed Caillaux's unofficial contacts with the German government throughout the diplomatic negotiations—by way of Oskar von der Lancken-Wackenitz, later sponsor of wartime défaitisme. Clemenceau's intense antagonism toward Caillaux and the willingness of Poincaré, Briand, and Louis Barthou to subsidize Gaston Calmette's editorial campaign against him in 1914 dated from that moment.

As *L'Homme libre* remarked, a certain cynicism lay behind the new cabinet: "If the skill of the leader lies in following the people he governs, Poincaré demonstrates that he possesses it as much as anyone." Vonoven in *Le Figaro* gamely hoped, "Other men, same policies." Perhaps so, but

---

17. J.O.C., Débats, 26 March 1924; *Le Temps* and *Le Figaro*, 27–28 March 1924, provided excellent coverage of the ministerial crisis; see also *Le Gaulois*, *L'Eclair*, and *L'Echo national*, 27 March 1924.

during a press conference for the new cabinet at the Quai d'Orsay, the comment from de Selves was that the ministers were "unanimously resolved to follow the foreign policy pursued thus far by Poincaré." After a pause, Maginot added, less than convincingly, "And the domestic policy, likewise." The franc had been saved; the Dawes committees had yet to report; the elections were only six weeks away: the time had well and truly come for politics.[18]

Like a plunger certain of his choice, Briand had laid down his bet more than a month earlier by addressing a banquet of Radical party leaders on 24 February, in Carcassonne, notably far from his seat in Brittany. So often since January 1922, he had couched his opposition to the Bloc national in rhetorical ambiguity. Now, he declared war. Now, in the divide between Left and Right, his words placed him unmistakably on the side of the Cartel des gauches: "France will have a foreign policy conforming to her true interest only when she stands as the France of the Revolution and of liberty. She will take up her place in the world, she will play the role which has fallen to her, she will appear entirely worthy of her victory only when she will be the 'republican' France that overcame the enemy." And that would be "tomorrow, after the elections, France showing her true face, faithful to her past and to her traditions" because of the victory by "Radicals and Socialists. . . . They belong to the same family, and if liberty were threatened, they would all be ready to unite in its defense. . . . It is not enough to say that the Bloc national should disappear; it must disappear. The triumph of the Bloc national's policies would compromise our external position and place our security in jeopardy. Because the country is convinced of that, because wherever the gravity of the hour is felt, accords are arranged, and our union is realized in the desire to be free from the Bloc national."[19]

Two provocative responses quickly followed. The first was from Millerand, who multiplied by an infinite factor the political risk to himself and the presidency of the Republic undertaken at Evreux. In a speech on 26 February to representatives from local chambers of commerce, he left be-

18. *L'Homme libre,* 28 March 1924; *Le Figaro,* 29 (Vonoven), 30 (press conference) March 1924.
19. *Le Temps* and *Le Figaro,* 25 February 1924.

hind any hint of nonpartisanship by praising Poincaré's occupation of the Ruhr and defense of the franc. When he asked these business leaders to help in "repulsing the attack of which we are the object," the specific context was exchange rates, but many understood the "attack" to be from the Cartel des gauches and the "we" to be the Bloc national. A second response came from Georges Mandel, speaking three days later before the Chamber of Deputies because he had so isolated himself in vindictive solitude that no banquet or rally was open to him. Vonoven at *Le Figaro* normally reserved his invective for caillautistes, but this "evil spirit" of the clemencistes, even though almost always a supporter of the Bloc national, had been, he claimed, "taught by Beelzebub all the sordid stories of political intrigue" and how to use them for extortion. Like his mentor, Clemenceau, Mandel scornfully dismissed Briand as a duplicitous lightweight who at Carcassonne betrayed the "majority that faithfully supported him for a year." The real danger, he insisted, was that Herriot and the Cartel were merely a front for Caillaux. With characteristic malice, he wondered whether a majority for the Cartel would mean a pardon of the Haute Cour sentence. Herriot had to interrupt, but with his answer an equivocation, he could only offer an insult, "We would show that the methods of the vice squad applied to politics when Mandel reigned are not ours!" That accusation spurred Daudet and Painlevé to exchange ugly words, some Far Right deputies to shout "canaille!" at the Left, and one Socialist deputy foolish in raising his fists to wind up with a bloody nose. Throughout, Mandel waited in icy calm at the tribune to deliver the point of the entire exercise: "You must choose between two majorities, one which includes Herriot, Painlevé, and Paul-Boncour, the other which goes from Reynaud to General [Edouard de] Castelnau. You must say to which you grant your sympathies. Know that there are those who, although not making pact with the Cartel des gauches, acquiesce in the supreme disgrace, to lose without having fought!"[20]

Briand, Millerand, Mandel, Herriot—all were drawing distinct lines for the election. That was continued on 6 March, when the three Radicals

20. *Le Temps* and *Le Figaro,* 27 February 1924, for Millerand; J.O.C., Débats, 29 February 1924, for Mandel, Herriot, Painlevé, and Daudet; *Le Figaro,* 1 March 1924, for Vonoven's comment.

serving in Poincaré's cabinet—and under attack for that since the previous June—Albert Sarraut, Paul Strauss, and Paul Laffont, were formally read out of the party by its executive committee. The great question remained what Poincaré would now say, whether Radical and Socialist obstruction of the double décime and the decree powers had changed his mind about seeking a broad and centrist majority. The answer Poincaré gave the very next day before the Chamber was that he had not: others might have changed, but not him. He was speaking about political matters in the midst of the struggle to save the franc only, he insisted, because recent incidents required a reply. Mandel might divide the political world between light and darkness, but Poincaré declared his willingness to rest upon a majority he defined as "republican and national . . . seeking neither monarchy nor Bolshevism, neither reaction nor revolution . . . prepared to sustain the ministry in its policy of integral enforcement for the treaty." Herriot interrupted by exclaiming, "And the decree powers?" To which Poincaré retorted with telling irony, "Is that why you voted against me on 15 June?"—seven months before decree powers were proposed. He reminded the Radicals that he had sought a union sacrée by including three of their own in his ministry, for which they had just been hounded from the party. And for Briand, Poincaré professed astonishment that the speech at Carcassonne could so indict the Bloc national, when Briand had sided with it to sustain the ministry on every vote involving foreign policy.[21]

Poincaré was defining out no one, at least by name, and defining in everyone who wanted to be. With these rules, he had already lasted twenty-six months as premier, one of the longest-lived cabinets of the Third Republic, and had done so facing nearly constant crisis. But what had worked thus far foundered on the rock of election fears. Slipping seriously since January, his majority in the Chamber simply disappeared three weeks later, on 26 March, when Lasteyrie mishandled the debate over pensions. A few days afterward, when the revamped cabinet came before the deputies, four sessions of remarkable posturing ensued. Everyone recognized that making de Selves minister of the interior meant a side step

21. *L'Oeuvre* and *Le Radical,* 7 March 1924, for Sarraut, Strauss, and Laffont; J.O.C., Débats, 7 March 1924, for Poincaré and Herriot.

to the left, but Poincaré insisted, "Nothing will be altered in either our foreign or our domestic policy." That was what the Bloc national wanted to hear. Herriot then echoed Poincaré by claiming that new men did not new ideas make. That was what the Cartel des gauches wanted to hear. Varenne of the Socialists announced, "If Germany supposes that a victory by the Left will mean having its quittance handed over on a platter, Germany is mistaken!" That was what Radical voters wanted to hear of their Cartel partners. The firebrand Forgeot delivered a bitter valedictory declaring his disgust with politics and refusal to stand again as a candidate. He had already turned on Poincaré over the election law, and now he lectured the man he had believed would "do better" than Briand: "I have taken your measure! You are decidedly too little for me!" That was what the disillusioned wanted to hear. And then, by a vote of 408 to 151, the Chamber voted its confidence in Poincaré and his new ministers, the largest margin since the end of 1923.[22]

The easy explanation lay in the reluctance of anyone to create a cabinet crisis with the elections only six weeks away. But underlying that motive was the realization that the government could not be crippled or placed in caretaker hands with the announcement looming of what the Dawes committees had decided. On 9 April came the word, as the experts presented their report to the Reparations Commission. The United States would formally return to European affairs and thereby make possible, through the confidence that its presence would generate, the mobilization of private foreign capital to restore Germany's fiscal stability, an amount estimated to be 800 million gold marks. The so-called London Schedule of reparations payments, agreed upon in May 1921 but never once met in full, would be abandoned. Instead, German payments would be set at 1 billion gold marks for 1924 and 1925 and rise to 2.5 billion by 1928 and 1929, assuming that all went well. Half of the annual payments was to be generated from taxes, the other half by interest on first mortgage bonds issued against the assets of industry and railroads. In addition to granting Germany a four-year partial moratorium, this "Dawes Plan" also meant

22. J.O.C., Débats, 31 March, 1 (Forgeot), 2 (Poincaré), 3 (Herriot, Varenne, and the vote) April 1924.

an end to the Régie because Franco-Belgian exploitation of the Rhineland and Ruhr rail lines would make issuing the mortgage bonds impossible. To reassure investors, all other "material guarantees" would have to be returned to German control, thereby ending the means by which Poincaré was paying for the seizure of the Ruhr. Although a strictly "military" occupation was not ruled out, its expense and the likelihood of its exciting extreme criticism as economically disruptive would make the continuation difficult and a renewal all but impossible.[23]

When presenting his new cabinet, Poincaré had spoken briefly of France's position in advance of the report: "Even if we are asked to modify the use of our material guarantees, there is no reason for us to withdraw before complete payment. . . . But it is possible that we will be asked to exploit them differently or to comprehend them within more general pledges. Of course, in all cases we will conserve our means of pressure." Almost every word he had uttered was now in jeopardy. On 11 April, he conferred with Louis Barthou, France's representative, and president, of the Reparations Commission. They agreed that the Dawes Plan had little appeal. The accomplishments of the Ruhr occupation—assurance of payment and German capitulation—would be undone. Although the total sum owed by Germany was not reduced, reparation income would be drastically lowered over the next four years. If Germany returned to recalcitrance after the limited moratorium, what intervention other than bankruptcy court could be mounted? The Reparations Commission had to approve the Dawes Plan, but France had no hope of blocking it there. And in making the effort, the French would risk emphasizing their isolation: the British, whose argument about reparations the experts most closely adopted, now had the support of the Italians, anxious to be on the winning side, while the Belgians, exhausted from the occupation and fearful of the future, wavered. With the franc still under duress and no solution to the question of war debts even under discussion, the French could also not afford to offend the Americans, who were sponsoring the plan. Did Barthou recall his striking analogy from January 1923, when with France and Great Britain divided over the Ruhr occupation he called them travelers

23. Schuker, *End of French Predominance*, 174–86.

who having journeyed long together take separate paths through a woods but join up on the other side? If so, he altered the ending to make the reunion considerably less friendly.[24]

The international context played havoc with the strategy of the Bloc national in the election campaign. If Poincaré had to admit that the Dawes Plan was a diplomatic debacle, for what did France sacrifice in occupying the Ruhr? To the charge of the Cartel des gauches that government by the Bloc national meant staggering new taxes and the loss of liberty through decree laws would be added utter failure in foreign policy. Some immediate limitation of the damage had to be attempted, and Poincaré did so in the first of his three major speeches during the campaign, this one on 15 April at Luna Park in Paris. There, he selectively embraced the work of the experts by claiming that their proposals were the "most brilliant justification" of the Ruhr occupation because before France acted, Germany had refused to pay. The very basis of the Dawes Plan was the assumption that Germany could and would pay, and with this fact now demonstrated, France could welcome its broad conception. That left the details, which he called critical to "safeguarding our interests" and therefore subject to negotiation, above all the "exchange of France's material guarantees for pledges more ample and productive" and "retaining the means to reestablish our occupation rapidly if needed." Usually so punctilious, Poincaré was practicing extraordinary casuistry in taking credit for the conclusion of the experts and was wishing on a star about these details.

The rest of his speech was predictable praise of the outgoing majority and his familiar call for a union sacrée—in his words, "union républicaine et concorde nationale"—because "rarely will a Chamber of Deputies have a more glorious mission: to consummate the recovery of the treasury so courageously undertaken by this legislature, to finish the restoration of our devastated regions, to ratify the administrative reforms which the cabinet will soon decree, to stimulate industrial and agricultural production, to enhance our magnificent colonial possessions, to consider new social reforms, to improve the lot of the unfortunate or poor, especially families with many children—great tasks which will demand as much compassion and

24. J.O.C., Débats, 2 April 1924, for Poincaré; Schuker, *End of French Predominance,* 187–206.

benevolence as intellect and diligence." Election rhetoric is election rhetoric, but these stirring challenges were carefully calculated. Although pronounced before a banquet of Bloc national leaders, they were more centrist than conservative and had appeal to moderate Radicals of the de Selves stripe, men uneasy about the coalition with the Socialists that was the basis of the Cartel des gauches.[25]

In Poincaré's second speech, on 23 April before another Bloc national rally in Paris, the appeal became a denunciation of "these heterogeneous alliances where, here and there, men whose convictions differ on the gravest issues of politics, become reconciled momentarily. The Socialists want to abolish private property; they decry capital as responsible for inequalities and human misery. Republicans believe that inequality is a fact of nature and not of civilization; they want capital to work and labor to possess; they do not dream of suppressing property but of making it more widely expanded and general throughout society. . . . How can any republicans, if they find revolutionary means repugnant, found the hope of a new majority on such contradictions? . . . Socialists and Radicals are thus separated by a chasm. No engineer however clever can throw across this pit a lasting footbridge." Even the moderate Radicals had been uncomfortable with the Ruhr occupation, and to reassure them, he pointed to France's joining with the other members of the Reparations Commission to make the adoption of the Dawes Plan unanimous on 17 April. Yet they could rely on his not falling prey to illusions about Germany and peace—he was Poincaré, not Herriot or Blum: "We must persevere in our spirit of conciliation without sacrificing prudence. That will be not only the task of tomorrow but the long, patient, and thankless work of further vigilant years."[26]

Proof that the strategy of trying to peel off the centrist Radicals from the Cartel des gauches had possibilities came in Briand's speech at Nantes the same day. The plunger early, now he hedged his bet—slightly. The Bloc national was the enemy, he clarified, not Poincaré. The Ruhr occupation deserved the support of all French citizens, and indeed, besides always backing the decision, he had himself seized the three river ports when pre-

25. Extensive report in *Le Figaro,* 16 April 1924.
26. Extensive report in *Le Figaro,* 25 April 1924.

mier. He would have voted for the decree laws if the proposed economies had been specified, but he could not countenance granting a blank check. How different this language was from his speech at Carcassonne two months earlier in February. Then, he was clearly within the Cartel. Now, he was not. The weather-wise Briand noticed that Poincaré was campaigning less for the Bloc national than against the Cartel. One interpretation was that he expected losses among the Bloc and hoped to make them up among dissident Radicals, thereby moving the cabinet's majority into the Center. In that case, he would need, eventually at least, the supreme centrist Briand. And so Briand adjusted his position accordingly.[27]

A better interpretation was that Poincaré simply did not know what to do in this campaign in which the Bloc national controlled none of the issues. Within France, inflation, the double décime, and the decree laws were easy targets for the Cartel des gauches. Without, the Dawes Plan seemed little return for the enormous risks of the Ruhr occupation. One last time Poincaré replied, on 6 May, again at Luna Park, his cabinet ministers arrayed beside him. The impression was of an embattled martial government justifying sacrifices present and future, with Poincaré concluding thunderously, "We seek only our due from the peace, but of that we will not be despoiled!" In marked contrast, the Socialists promised international peace through brotherhood with Great Britain's first Labour government, which took power in January under Ramsay MacDonald, and with the Weimar Republic in Germany. If that strained credulity, Herriot was sincerity personified, pudgy and rumpled, his ever-present pipe a reassuring domesticity. Of course, victory for the Left would mean a certain satisfaction for Caillaux after all the indignities he had faced since 1918 and would encourage the future ambitions of the Communists, who far outdid the Camelots in disrupting electoral rallies and once managed to rough up Tardieu. But Caillaux was still exiled to Mamers, and the Communists were persona non grata with the Cartel. The victory of the Right-Center in 1919 had been exceptional for the Third Republic and was based on promises that four and a half years later were largely unfulfilled—and in all likelihood impossible to fulfill. The Third Republican tradition was government by the moderate Left: voting for the Cartel was

27. See reports in *Le Temps* and *Le Figaro,* 25 April 1924.

voting for the only "retour comme avant" realizable. When the result went against him, Poincaré was saying as much when he sighed, "Clearly, the French are too tired to follow me."[28]

Although both the electoral coalitions demonstrated much less than perfect cohesion, in approximately two-thirds of France there was a head-to-head contest between the list of the Bloc national and the list of the Cartel des gauches. This stark divide and so many dramatic issues drew the largest number of voters since 1871, 8.9 million, a 12 percent increase over 1919. Although the Bloc national did not lose popular votes, the Cartel gained nearly all the new ones. The result was a political massacre. In 1919, there were 616 seats, of which the Bloc won 380 (62 percent) and its Far Right allies another 57. In 1924, with the number of seats reduced to 584, the Bloc won only 205 (35 percent), the Far Right 28. The Cartel won 286 seats (49 percent)—just short of a majority—and could count on at least some of the 37 centrist Radicals to provide a working cushion. Like the Far Right, the Communists won 28 seats. Despite the rancor over prime à la majorité, true proportional representation would have changed the results only slightly, mostly in favor of the Communists and against the Cartel. To this general disaster for the Bloc national was added the defeat of prominent—if always difficult—conservative figures, Tardieu, Mandel, Daudet, and Castelnau. In his editorial for *L'Echo national,* a bitter Tardieu wrote, "Tant pis pour la France!"—Too bad for France! Hervé added in *La Victoire,* "We must be ready for anything, now that we have seen what was unimaginable a mere five years ago, the revenge of Joseph Caillaux."[29]

The election won, the Cartel des gauches manifested its broad humanitarianism in seeking spoils and shooting the wounded. Socialist veteran Pierre Renaudel defined the terms for patronage: "Toutes les places et tout

28. *Le Figaro,* 28 April (Tardieu assaulted), 7 May (Poincaré and cabinet at Luna Park) 1924; Jacques Chastenet, *Raymond Poincaré* (Paris, 1948), 260, for the quotation; Keiger, *Poincaré,* 308–9, concludes differently; Brogan, *Development of Modern France,* 583–84; Schuker, *End of French Predominance,* 229–313.

29. For election analysis, see Jean-Marie Mayeur, *La Vie politique sous la troisième république* (Paris, 1984), 271–77, which improves on Georges Lachapelle, *Elections législatives du 11 mai 1924* (Paris, 1924), 26–27; see also the Paris press, notably *Le Temps,* 12–14 May 1924; *L'Echo national,* 13 May 1924, for Tardieu; *La Victoire,* 13 May 1924, for Hervé.

de suite"—All the jobs, right now. The wounded targets were Poincaré and Millerand. Poincaré immediately proved that he knew where the better part of valor lay. Acknowledging the will of popular suffrage, he announced that his cabinet would formally resign on 1 June, the day before the new Chamber of Deputies convened. Barring emergencies, during this two-week interim the ministers would undertake no initiatives. To set the example, Poincaré canceled discussions with MacDonald scheduled for 19 May, leaving them for the next premier, presumably Herriot. Back home in Bar-le-Duc, where he had delivered so many of his important speeches, he called on the Bloc national to grant the new majority a sense of "fair play." Departing in this fashion removed Poincaré from the sights of Cartel snipers, enhancing or refurbishing—depending on the individual view—his reputation as a "good republican." Of course, the decision was made easier by his having a Senate seat to which he could return.[30]

Millerand's situation was vastly different. Elected for a seven-year term by the deputies and senators, the president of the Republic was in theory immune to the vagaries of shifting legislative majorities. The price of that protection was a careful and official political neutrality. Millerand was exactly halfway through his term and from the beginning had asserted executive power in a manner distinctly troubling to the traditional defenders of legislative dominance, above all the Radicals. His idea of strengthening the office of the president accorded too closely with the predilections of the Bloc national. But then, he was the founder of the Bloc national. The speech at Evreux in October 1923 implied strongly that even in the Elysée palace he remained its leader, and his words during the election campaign sealed the proof, shedding his immunity. Controversy about the so-called electoral franc generated further animosity, some Radicals accusing Millerand of using the Banque de France to manipulate the value of the currency for political purpose: driving it up in advance of the elections to indicate the success of the Bloc's economic program, then letting it fall back abruptly afterward to imply lack of confidence in the Cartel. Rumors

---

30. Renaudel is quoted by both Brogan, *Development of Modern France,* 584, and Schuker, *End of French Predominance,* 130; for Poincaré's official actions, see *Le Temps,* 14 May–2 June 1924; for a full report of Poincaré's speech at Bar-le-Duc, see *Le Figaro,* 27 May 1924.

about how seriously he was in jeopardy flew during the last two weeks of May. On 1 June, most of the Radical deputies met at the Hotel Terminus for a banquet to celebrate their victory and adopted a resolution declaring that "Millerand's continued presence at the Elysée would wound the republican conscience, create incessant conflicts between the cabinet and the chief of state, and represent a constant danger to the regime itself." Herriot himself had yet to speak, but his decision was now effectively forced.[31]

Not that Herriot lacked other besetting complications: the rickety character of the Cartel des gauches was apparent as he sought to assemble a cabinet. Maintaining their prewar policy, the Socialists declared that while they would pledge their votes to Herriot, Marxist doctrine precluded actually serving in a "bourgeois" government. That eliminated as ministers Blum, Paul-Boncour, and Auriol—all energetic and innovative. Briand had also removed himself from consideration, although not by choice. His adjustment of position at Nantes during the finale of the campaign had seemed an equivocation, and especially to the Radicals, for whom anticlericalism was in the blood, he was already suspect for having reestablished diplomatic relations with the Vatican. Herriot was therefore short on talent to carry out the program of the Cartel and most critically so where the gravest danger to French interests lay, in finance and diplomacy. Since the turn of the century, the great spokesman for the Radical party on economic matters had been Caillaux, but he was a manifestly impossible choice for the Ministry of Finance, barred not least by the sentence of the Haute Cour stripping his political rights. As a pale substitute, Herriot chose Etienne Clémentel, who had gained some respect in business circles while minister of commerce and industry from 1915 to 1919 and adviser to Clemenceau at the peace negotiations. For foreign affairs, the Radicals had no one of stature—making their spite toward Briand all the more gratuitous. With utterly misplaced self-confidence, Herriot awarded the Quai d'Orsay to himself. Although filled out with more of the inexperienced and politically lightweight, this cabinet-in-waiting proposed an agenda nothing short of annulling the four and a half years of rule by the Bloc national: "the suppression of the decree laws . . . the elimination of the

---

31. For the "electoral franc," see Schuker, *End of French Predominance,* 128–31; for the Radical banquet, see *Le Radical, L'Oeuvre, Le Temps,* and *Le Figaro,* 2 June 1924.

Vatican embassy . . . the mitigation of burdens created by levies on consumption, especially the turnover tax . . . the engendering of peace through understandings among peoples . . . the restoration of normal relations with Russia . . . the acceptance without conditions of the report by the experts . . . the resolution of security problems through treaties of guarantee placed under the authority of the League of Nations." To accomplish this program, Herriot needed to bind his majority to him as if on crusade, and nothing could stoke crusading ardor better than political advantage cloaked as principle. The Radicals were demanding Millerand's head, and Herriot had no choice but to be the executioner. The guillotine would be a ministerial strike: the refusal to form a cabinet as long as Millerand remained at the Elysée.[32]

To defend the constitutional basis of the presidency, to save his own political career, and to attenuate the Cartel program, Millerand resisted. He had on his side the opinion of Henry Barthélemy, dean of the Paris Law Faculty: "I do not contest that in actual fact the legislature can force the president out, but to do so would violate the constitution." And if the conservative newspapers reacted predictably—"When you want to shoot your dog, you say he's rabid" was Hervé's ridicule of the charges—even moderate ones like *La République française* did not shy from writing "un coup d'état." But the Cartel had the votes, as it proved on 4 June, in electing Painlevé as president of the Chamber over Maginot by 296 to 209. The next day during a tense, brief meeting at the Elysée palace, Herriot declined the offer to form a cabinet and asked instead to discuss Millerand's resignation. Afterward, Millerand issued a terse communiqué that revealed the state of his nerves: "The constitution has fixed at seven years the duration of the presidential mandate. Called for seven years to the Elysée, President Millerand believes that his duty to the Republic and to France lies in remaining there until the expiration of his mandate. He is resolved to do whatever he must in order that respect for the constitution be assured and that a precedent of incalculable peril be averted." By contrast, a relaxed Herriot, certain of the eventual outcome, told reporters simply that the Cartel was unwilling to govern with Millerand.[33]

32. *Le Temps*, 3 June 1924.

33. *Le Figaro*, 8 June 1924, for Barthélemy; *La Victoire*, 1 June 1924, for Hervé; *La République française*, 1 June 1924; J.O.C., *Débats*, 4 June 1924, for the election of Painlevé; *Le*

Over the next five days, Millerand cast desperately for salvation. He called in the debts owed him by men among the moderate Left, hoping that one of them would dare to present a cabinet and perhaps splinter the Cartel. Théodore Steeg, a traditional Radical stalwart, whom Millerand had made minister of the interior in 1920 and then governor-general of Algeria in 1921, considered the proposition seriously enough to travel from Algiers to Paris before recognizing its futility. Millerand turned finally to François-Marsal, who agreed out of longtime friendship to run the gauntlet of certain defeat in the Chamber for the slender chance that the Senate might vote differently because leery of the constitutional implications. Slender chance indeed: if the Senate did oppose the Chamber, an equally serious constitutional crisis would loom; Millerand could exercise the presidential prerogative—last used, and disastrously so, in 1877—to ask the consent of the Senate in dissolving the Chamber and calling for new elections. Even Millerand's defenders regarded that possibility as "un grand risque."[34]

But not a risk that would be run: the implacable consequences of May reached their conclusion on 10 June. Before the Chamber of Deputies, François-Marsal read an exculpatory message from Millerand. Although the Bloc national mounted a defense, not a single member of the Cartel even bothered to speak. The few Communist deputies, detested by the Bloc and rejected by the Cartel, demonstrated their contempt for both in shouting gross insults, slamming their desks, and singing the "Internationale." All was merely a prelude to the inevitable vote, 329 to 214, against the cabinet. In the Senate, without any Communists, there was utter decorum and the same result, the vote 154 to 144. Early the following day, Millerand submitted a one-sentence letter of resignation. The assessment of Jacques Bainville in *L'Action française* was prescient but yet to be proved: "After the fall of Poincaré, that of Millerand tolls the knell for the Treaty of Versailles. The era of integral execution is finished." The comment from *La Victoire* had just been confirmed: "It is the end not only of a presidency but of a man."[35]

Temps, 6 June 1924, for the meeting at the Elysée, the presidential communiqué, and Herriot's remarks.

34. Farrar, *Principled Pragmatist,* 360–76; see Vonoven in *Le Figaro,* 10 June 1924, as an example of the attitude toward new elections.

35. J.O.C., Débats, 10 June 1924; J.O.S., Débats, 10 June 1924; *Le Temps,* 12 June 1924,

The election for Millerand's successor was set for two days later, 13 January, at Versailles, as was the custom under the Third Republic. Also as was the custom, "republican" legislators gathered the evening before to take a preliminary ballot, Painlevé, president of the Chamber, defeating Gaston Doumergue, president of the Senate, 306 to 149. But the definition of "republicans" had never been so exclusive, defined this time as partisans of the Cartel, and therefore eliminated nearly half of the deputies and senators, including all of the Bloc national. At Versailles, the excluded had enough votes to determine the result, although the choice could have little appeal: Painlevé was an architect of the Cartel, Doumergue a symbol of the Senate's refusal to hear the "Communist Plot." The deciding factor was that Painlevé could be clearly counted an enemy, Doumergue not necessarily so. And there was the satisfaction of flouting the result of the "republican" caucus by electing Doumergue over Painlevé on a vote of 515 to 309.[36]

Herriot preferred Painlevé, but Doumergue was a Radical of excellent standing, a minister under the arch-anticlerical Emile Combes and the last premier to include Caillaux in a cabinet. Immediately accepting the new president's invitation to present the Cartel's cabinet-in-waiting, he proclaimed its agenda before the Chamber of Deputies. The majority that had destroyed Millerand then made him premier on 19 June, the vote of confidence 313 to 234. Herriot had won a grand political victory. All that remained was to govern. At this critical moment in French history, the destiny of the nation rested with a man who when consulted about economic matters literally held his head in his hands, who could not even grasp how calves developed teeth. Ten months before, a madman calling himself the Apostle Saint Paul had tried to warn Millerand of coming disaster. France needed such a madman.[37]

---

for the resignation letters; *L'Action française,* 11 June 1924, for Bainville; *La Victoire,* 11 June 1924.

36. See the accounts and commentary in *Le Temps* and *Le Figaro,* 13–16 June 1924.

37. J.O.C., Débats, 18–19 June 1924; *Le Temps,* 18–20 June 1924; Peter J. Larmour, *The French Radical Party in the 1930's* (Stanford, 1964), 71, for Herriot's reaction to economic details.

Conclusion: Illusions

Born in 1900, Antoine de Saint-Exupéry was too young—barely—for the war. He learned the sangfroid and stoicism that characterized his life and writing during long hours as a pilot, flying the most difficult routes when aviation was new and inherently perilous. In *Terre des hommes,* he defined existential courage through this marker experience: "Once again, I skirted a truth that I did not understand. I believed myself done for. I reached the depth of despair, and then having embraced renunciation, I knew peace. It seems to me now that at these hours a man discovers who he is and becomes his own friend."[1] The Après Guerre was such a moment, but for France, it bore not truth but illusion.

On 21 June 1924, less than thirty-six hours after his investment as premier and having accepted only the most cursory briefing from the permanent officials at the Quai d'Orsay, Edouard Herriot hied himself to Chequers for the conference with Ramsay MacDonald that Raymond Poincaré had deferred. Over two days of talks, the British displayed none of the international brotherhood so blissfully extolled by the Cartel des gauches during the elections but much of the cleverly disingenuous and hard-headed proposals from the pre-Ruhr diplomacy of David Lloyd George. Armed as always with every detail, Poincaré would have shouldered

---

1. Antoine de Saint-Exupéry, *Oeuvres* (Paris, 1959), 244; *Terre des hommes* was originally published in 1939.

through them. Utterly unprepared, Herriot dazedly acquiesced. Here was the warning of much worse to come when Herriot crossed the Channel again three weeks later for the London conference, where the United States joined Great Britain, France, Belgium, and Italy to discuss the Dawes Plan. After a month of negotiations, 16 July to 16 August, the original provisions were accepted essentially without modification. The sole concession to French pride was a year's delay in completing the *military* withdrawal from the Ruhr—a minor sop indeed because the *economic* occupation and the Régie for the railroad had to be dismantled immediately.[2]

During the next six years, Germany paid approximately 8 billion gold marks in reparations (10 billion gold francs or 2 billion gold dollars) under the terms of the Dawes Plan. Had the London Schedule remained in effect, and if Germany could have been made to meet its requirements, the total would have been 12 billion gold marks, 50 percent more. To ask whether Poincaré or any other French leader could have done better is to play history in the subjunctive. And useless, for there could be no turning back: the "era of reconciliation" supplanted the "era of confrontation," for all practical purposes eliminating alternative policies no matter who was premier. How profoundly the terrain had changed was proved during the rest of the 1920s. Herriot lasted not quite ten months, to April 1925, destroyed by his own economic incompetence and the fears it generated among bondholders. Paul Painlevé continued Cartel rule for eight more months, characterized by two returns, the impossible, Joseph Caillaux at the rue de Rivoli, and the inevitable, Aristide Briand at the Quai d'Orsay. After that, from November 1925 until November 1929, France would be governed by the men of confrontation, Briand and Poincaré, now become the men of reconciliation.

The new reality had several facets. If Caillaux could be rehabilitated, Louis Malvy, the other *défaitiste* in chief, deserved no less, and Briand restored him to the ministry of the interior in March 1926. After their relatively brief, relatively mild, antagonism from 1922 to 1924, Poincaré and

2. Schuker, *End of French Predominance*, 236–382; McDougall, *France's Rhineland Diplomacy*, 360–79; Bettina Mercedes Söhnigen, "French Interwar Security Policy Reconsidered," M.A. thesis, Louisiana State University, 1993.

Briand quickly patched up their long friendship. Once Poincaré returned as premier, he hesitated not at all in choosing Briand as his foreign minister, the partnership lasting three years. And both of them excused the many past asperities from André Tardieu, whom Poincaré added to his cabinet first as minister of public works and then the interior. Georges Clemenceau never forgave Tardieu for choosing office over personal allegiance. Georges Mandel alone kept the faith of clemencisme, meaning that like his mentor he would remain in self-imposed political exile. The Communists and the Far Right were left in outer darkness: reconciliation went only so far.

As foreign minister during all these years—and beyond to 1932— Briand presided over another facet, the "quest for peace," which was actually the undoing of France's victory in 1918. On 25 August 1925, the last French soldiers left the Ruhr, appropriately departing from Düsseldorf, Duisburg, and Ruhrort, the river ports occupied first, since March 1921, when Briand himself gave the order. Six weeks later, in October, Great Britain, France, Belgium, Italy, and Germany agreed to the Locarno treaties, each guaranteeing to uphold the existing boundaries in western Europe; for eastern Europe, meaningless arbitration treaties were substituted. Germany was thereby giving willing acceptance to the result of the war at least in the west, and Briand finally had the commitment, however undefined, of British support in case of German aggression against France. A certain warm glow of hope and security, the "spirit of Locarno," encouraged an end to all the trammels from Versailles. On 8 September 1926, Germany was admitted to the League of Nations, the international good-citizenship certification, and not five months later, on 31 January 1927, the League took over enforcing—meaning ignoring—the disarmament strictures that the Germans had already contrived to evade. Regular payment of reparations encouraged this sense of good feelings. To simplify the transfer of marks into other currencies, the Dawes provisions were modified in June 1929 by the Young Plan, which also slightly reduced German payments while extending the final installment to 1988. As the seal of reconciliation, the Rhineland occupation was ended by June 1930, four years ahead of schedule. Perhaps the ultimate expression of the period had come some months earlier, on 27 August 1928, when twenty-three nations gathered in Paris to sign the Pact of Peace drawn up by Briand and Frank B. Kellogg, the American secretary of state, renouncing offensive war as an instrument of national policy.

If Poincaré, who was premier from July 1926 until July 1929 and thus throughout this quest for peace, had thought any other diplomacy possible, he would surely have jettisoned Briand and taken over the Quai d'Orsay himself. Instead, he was engaged in economic reconciliation. By the Mellon-Bérenger agreement of April 1926, France finally reached a settlement with the United States over war debts, further French resistance to repayment made impossible by the weakness of the franc and by the argument that even Germany was voluntarily meeting its obligations. This new imposition, the effect of the war and the Après Guerre, and the experience of Cartel economics sent the franc into another tailspin. The Radicals swallowed hard and accepted Poincaré's return as premier, taking solace that he constructed a union sacrée cabinet. His austere and rigorous fiscal policies, but more his presence, restored confidence. Ultimately, he was able to stabilize the currency at 20 percent of its 1914 value, and for that was called the "savior of the franc." Poincaré knew better. Here was no retour comme avant but the limits of the possible. So too with the quest for peace: Briand and Poincaré both recognized that the Dawes and Young plans were not much more than international pyramid schemes, which would generate impressive returns early but ultimately collapse. Both also recognized that the "spirit of Locarno" might well be evanescent. The quest for peace thus depended on Germany, but in the context of the late 1920s, betting on the good intentions of the Germans was the only wager left. Each, before he died, recognized that the bet was a loser. This admission and this attitude were not far from proof that France had ceased to be a great power. The implication was that a second general European war in the twentieth century had become inevitable.[3]

The large bills in the currency of French history during the Après Guerre turned out to be counterfeit: the Armistice itself, the Treaty of Versailles, the election of the Bloc national and then of the Cartel des gauches—all promises broken. France's leaders, Clemenceau, Alexandre

---

3. Schuker, *End of French Predominance*, 383–93, argues the point with cogency and eloquence.

Millerand, Briand, Poincaré, Herriot, failed, none of them and no one else rising, in Briand's notable line, "to do better." Certainly, France was betrayed by her wartime allies, but French politics of the Après Guerre were betrayal personified. What was left but the small change of personal grief, ruined lives and ruined fortunes, the passions, crimes, suicides, and drugs of tragiques romans d'amour, the definition of la vie est bête. Who could blame the French in 1924 from shying away from further sacrifice? Who could blame them for embracing the illusions that followed? Illusions last as long as they can compel belief. Their shattering came soon enough.

Around the walls of the study at Bélébat, his retreat on the Vendée coast, Clemenceau hung the stuffed heads of animals he had shot on safari. "Believe me," he explained, "they provide encouragement. I get up at the stroke of two in the morning for my writing, and if I feel drowsy, I stare at these brutes and say, 'You idiots, I'm still doing better than you!' Then, I get down to work quickly."[4] Perhaps in addition to madman Apostle Saint Paul, France needed more tiger heads.

4. René Benjamin, *Clemenceau dans la retraite* (Paris, 1930), 69–70.

BIBLIOGRAPHY

Unpublished Government Documents
Archives Nationales, Series AJ, Fonds divers
4 43   Photographies de villes et villages endommagés pour faits de guerre
4 49–52   Mélanges: photographies, documents, coupures de presses, rapports sur la conduite des Allemands
5 86–102   Dommages de guerre en France et évaluations
5 227–30   Evaluations des dommages: principes, études générales
5 231–41   Evaluations des dommages de la France: correspondances, rapports, observations des ministères
Archives Nationales, Series AP, Archives personnelles et familiales
151   Papiers Deschanel
Archives Nationales, Series BB 6 II, Dossiers personnels de magistrats
961   Jousselin, Louis
Archives Nationales, Series F7, Police général
12821   Elections des présidents Poincaré, Deschanel, Millerand et Doumergue (1912–24)
12951   Notes confidentielles dites "notes Jean": on political parties, politicians, domestic and foreign affairs, 1918–22
12952   1 Notes confidentielles dites "notes Jean": on political parties, politicians, domestic and foreign affairs, 1923
12952   2 Notes confidentielles dites "notes Jean": on political parties, politicians, domestic and foreign affairs, 1923–24
12952   3 Notes confidentielles dites "notes Jean": on political parties, politicians, domestic and foreign affairs, 1924

12967	Synthèse mensuelle sur la situation politique, 1920–24
13191	Radicals-Socialistes
13970	Dossier Malvy
13971	Dossier Caillaux
13978	Journalisme, politique, et spéculation, 1920–30
13980	Action française (Philippe Daudet)
14608	Grèves en 1920

Parliamentary Papers

Journal Officiel, Chambre des Députés, Débats parlementaires, 1917–24.

Journal Official, Chambre des Députés, Documents parlementaires, 1917–24.

Journal Officiel, Sénat, Débats parlementaires, 1917–24.

Journal Officiel, Sénat, Documents parlementaires, 1917–24.

Journal Officiel, Annexe, Documents administratifs, 1923.

Newspapers

L'Action française, 1918–24

L'Avenir, 1918–24

L'Echo de Paris, 1918–24

L'Echo national, 1922–24

L'Eclair, 1918–24

Le Figaro, 1918–24

Le Gaulois, 1918–24

La Gazette des tribunaux, 1918–24

L'Homme libre, 1919–24

L'Humanité, 1918–24

L'Intransigeant, 1918–24

Le Journal des débats, 1918–24

La Lanterne, 1918–24

La Liberté, 1918–24

La Libre parole, 1918–24

Le Matin, 1918–24

L'Oeuvre, 1918–24

Le Petit journal, 1918–24

Le Petit parisien, 1918–24

Le Radical, 1918–24

La République française, 1918–24

Le Temps, 1918–24

La Victoire, 1918–24

Books, Articles, and Dissertations

Abensour, Léon. *Clemenceau intime: Souvenir de son ancien secrétaire.* Paris, 1928.

Adamthwaite, Anthony P. *Grandeur and Misery: France's Bid for Power in Europe, 1914–1940.* London, 1965.

———. *The Lost Peace: International Relations in Europe, 1918–1939.* London, 1980.

Agulhon, Maurice. *La République.* Rev. ed. 2 vols. Paris, 1992.

Allain, Jean-Claude. *Joseph Caillaux.* 2 vols. Paris, 1978–81.

Aubert, Louis, et al. *André Tardieu.* Paris, 1957.

Audoin-Rouzeau, Stéphane. *14–18: Les Combattants des tranchées.* Paris, 1986.

Auffray, Bernard. *Pierre de Margerie et la vie diplomatique de son temps.* Paris, 1976.

Bainville, Jacques. *Les Conséquences politiques de la paix.* Paris, 1920.

———. *Journal, 1919–1926.* Paris, 1949.

Barbier, Jean Baptiste. *Un frac de Nessus.* Rome, 1951.

Bardel, Pierre, ed. *Eugène Dabit et Roger Martin du Gard: Correspondance.* 2 vols. Paris, 1986.

Bardoux, Jacques. *De Paris à Spa, la bataille diplomatique pour la paix française.* Paris, 1921.

———. *Journal d'un témoin de la Troisième.* Paris, 1957.

———. *Lloyd George et la France.* Paris, 1923.

Bariéty, Jacques. *Les Relations franco-allemandes après la première guerre mondiale.* Paris, 1977.

Barré, Jean-Luc. *Le Seigneur-chat: Philippe Berthelot, 1866–1934.* Paris, 1988.

Barthou, Louis. *Le Traité de paix.* Paris, 1919.

Baumont, Maurice. *Les Questions européennes en 1919.* Paris, 1956.

Beau de Loménie, Emmanuel. *Le Débat de ratification du Traité de Versailles.* Paris, 1945.

Becker, Jean-Jacques. *Les Français dans la grande guerre.* Paris, 1973. Translated by Arnold Pomerans as *The Great War and the French People.* New York, 1986.

Becker, Jean-Jacques, and Serge Bernstein. *Victoire et frustrations, 1914–1929.* Paris, 1990.

Benjamin, René. *Clemenceau dans la retraite.* Paris, 1930.

Benoist, Charles. *Les Nouvelles frontières de l'Allemagne et la nouvelle carte d'Europe.* Paris, 1920.

———. *Souvenirs.* 3 vols. Paris, 1932–34.

Berenson, Edward. *The Trial of Madame Caillaux.* Berkeley, 1992.

Berger, Marcel. *Les Dessous du Traité de Versailles.* Paris, 1933.

Berger, Marcel, and Paul Allard. *Les Secrets de la censure pendant la guerre.* Paris, 1932.

Bernard, Philippe, and Henri Dubief. *The Decline of the Third Republic, 1914–1938.* Cambridge, Eng., 1985.

Binion, Rudolph. *Defeated Leaders: The Political Fate of Caillaux, Jouvenel, and Tardieu.* New York, 1960.

Blum, Antoinette, ed. *Correspondance entre Charles Andler et Lucien Herr, 1891–1926.* Paris, 1992.

Blumenthal, Henry. *Illusion and Reality in Franco-American Diplomacy, 1914–1945.* Baton Rouge, 1986.

Bonnefous, Georges, and Edouard Bonnefous. *Histoire politique de la IIIe République.* 7 vols. Paris, 1956–67.

Bonnet, Georges. *La Quai d'Orsay sous trois républiques, 1870–1961.* Paris, 1961.

Bourgeois, Léon. *Le Traité de paix de Versailles.* Paris, 1919.

Bournazel, Renata. *Rapallo, naissance d'un mythe: La Politique de la peur dans la France du Bloc national.* Paris, 1974.

Bréal, Auguste. *Philippe Berthelot.* Paris, 1937.

Brogan, Denis W. *The Development of Modern France, 1870–1939.* London, 1940.

Bruun, Geoffrey. *Clemenceau.* Cambridge, Mass., 1944.

Bury, J. P. T. *France: The Insecure Peace, from Versailles to the Great Depression.* London, 1972.

Caillaux, Joseph. *Mes mémoires.* 3 vols. Paris, 1942–47.

———. *Mes prisons.* Paris, 1920.

Cairns, John C. "A Nation of Shopkeepers in Search of a Suitable France, 1919–40." *American Historical Review* 79 (June 1974): 710–43.

Cambon, Paul. *Correspondance, 1870–1924.* 3 vols. Paris, 1940–46.

Carls, Stephen D. *Louis Loucheur and the Shaping of Modern France, 1916–1931.* Baton Rouge, 1993.

Carly, Michael Jobara. "The Origins of the French Intervention in the Russian Civil War, January–May 1918: A Reappraisal." *Journal of Modern History* 48 (September 1976): 413–39.

———. "The Shoe on the Other Foot: A Letter from Raymond Poincaré to Alexandre Millerand, December 1922." *Canadian Journal of History* 26 (December 1991): 581–87.

Chastenet, Jacques. *Histoire de la Troisième République.* 7 vols. Paris, 1952–63.

———. *Raymond Poincaré.* Paris, 1948.

Clemenceau, Georges. *Au soir de la pensée.* 2 vols. Paris, 1930.

―――. *Grandeurs et misères d'une victoire.* Paris, 1930. Translated by F. M. Atkinson as *Grandeur and Misery of Victory.* New York, 1930.

Clémentel, Etienne. *La France et la politique économique interalliée.* Paris, 1931.

Cobb, Richard. *French and Germans, Germans and French: A Personal Interpretation of France Under Two Occupations, 1914–1918/1940–1944.* Hanover, N.H., 1983.

Collet, Georges-Paul, ed. *Correspondance (1916–1942): François Mauriac et Jacques-Emile Blanche.* Paris, 1976.

Corday, Michel. *L'Envers de la guerre: Journal inédit, 1914–1918.* 2 vols. Paris, 1932.

Cornilleau, Robert. *Du Bloc national au Front populaire.* Paris, 1939.

Coston, Henry. *Dans les coulisses de la République: Ministres, préfets, et policiers, agents d'exécution de la dictature maçonnique.* Paris, 1944.

Craig, Gordon A., and Felix Gilbert, eds. *The Diplomats, 1919–1939.* Princeton, 1953.

Crémieux, Benjamin. *Inquiétude et reconstruction: Essai sur la littérature d'après guerre.* Paris, 1931.

Cruikshank, C. G. *Variations on a Catastrophe: Some French Responses to the Great War.* New York, 1982.

Dallas, Gregor. *At the Heart of a Tiger: Clemenceau and His World, 1841–1929.* London, 1993.

Daniélou, Charles. *Le Vrai visage d'Aristide Briand.* Paris, 1935.

Dansette, Adrien. *Histoire des présidents de la République: De Louis Napoleon à Vincent Auriol.* Paris, 1953.

Daudet, Léon. *L'Agonie du régime.* Paris, 1925.

―――. *La Chambre nationale du 16 novembre.* Paris, 1923.

―――. *Député de Paris, 1919–1924.* Paris, 1933.

―――. *Moloch et Minerve ou l'après-guerre.* Paris, 1924.

―――. *Paris vécu: Rive gauche.* Paris, 1930.

―――. *Souvenirs des milieux littéraires, politiques, artistiques et médicaux.* 2 vols. Paris, 1926.

Derfler, Leslie. *President and Parliament: A Short History of the French Presidency.* Boca Raton, Fla., 1983.

Doughty, R. A. *The Seeds of Disaster: The Development of French Army Doctrine, 1919–1939.* Hamden, Conn., 1985.

Ducatel, Paul. *Histoire de la IIIe République, vue à travers l'imagerie populaire de la presse satirique.* Paris, 1973.

Duhamel, Georges. *Entretiens dans le tumulte: Chronique contemporaine, 1914-1918.* Paris, 1949.

Dulles, Eleanor Lansing. *The French Franc, 1914–1928: The Facts and Their Interpretation.* New York, 1929.

Duroselle, Jean-Baptiste. *Clemenceau.* Paris, 1988.

———. *Les Relations franco-allemandes de 1914 à 1945.* Paris, 1965.

Engelmann, Larry. *The Goddess and the American Girl: The Story of Suzanne Lenglen and Helen Wills.* New York, 1988.

Farrar, Marjorie Millbank. *Principled Pragmatist: The Political Career of Alexandre Millerand.* Oxford, 1991.

Ferro, Marc. *The Great War, 1914–1918.* Boston, 1973.

Ferry, Abel. *Les Carnets secrets d'Abel Ferry (1914–1918).* Paris, 1957.

Field, Frank. *British and French Writers of the First World War: Comparative Studies in Cultural History.* New York, 1991.

———. *Three French Writers and the Great War: Barbusse, Drieu la Rochelle, Bernanos.* Cambridge, Eng., 1975.

Fink, Carole. *The Genoa Conference: European Diplomacy, 1921–1922.* Chapel Hill, 1984.

Fitzgerald, F. Scott. "The Crack-Up: Pasting It Together." *Esquire* 7 (March 1936): 35–39.

———. *Tender Is the Night.* New York, 1933.

Flanner, Janet [Genêt]. *Paris Was Yesterday, 1925–1939.* Edited by Irving Drutman, from *The New Yorker Magazine,* 1925–39, originally published in book form in 1972. New York, 1979.

Fleury, Maurice de. *Manuel pour l'étude des maladies du système nerveux.* Paris, 1904.

Foch, Marshal Ferdinand. *Mémoires pour servir à l'histoire de la guerre.* Paris, 1931.

France, Ministère de la justice. *Compte générale de l'administration de la justice criminelle.* Paris, 1913, 1920–24.

François-Marsal, Frédéric. *Les Dettes interalliées.* Paris, 1927.

François-Poncet, André. *De Versailles à Potsdam, la France et le problème allemand contemporain.* Paris, 1948.

———. *Souvenirs d'une ambassade à Berlin.* Paris, 1946.

Frost, Robert L. "Machine Liberation: Inventing Housewives and Home Appliances in Interwar France." *French Historical Studies* 18 (Spring 1993): 109–30.

Gatineau-Clemenceau, Georges. *Des pattes du Tigre au griffes du destin.* Paris, 1961.

Gombin, Richard. *Les Socialistes et la guerre: La S.F.I.O. et la politique étrangère entre les deux guerres mondiales.* The Hague, 1967.

Greer, Guy. *The Ruhr-Lorraine Industrial Problem: A Study in the Economic Interdependence of the Two Regions and Their Relation to the Reparation Question.* New York, 1923.

Guilleminault, Gilbert, ed. *La France de la Madelon, 1914–1918: Le Roman vrai de l'arrière.* Paris, 1965.

Haig, Robert Murray. *The Public Finances of Post-War France.* New York, 1929.

Hanotaux, Gabriel. *Le Traité de Versailles du 28 juin 1919: L'Allemagne et l'Europe.* Paris, 1919.

Hayne, M. B. *The French Foreign Office and the Origins of the First World War, 1898–1914.* Oxford, 1993.

Herriot, Edouard. *Jadis: D'une guerre à l'autre, 1914–1936.* 2 vols. Paris, 1952.

―――. *Notes et maximes inédits.* Paris, 1961.

Horn, Pierre L., ed. *Handbook of French Popular Culture.* Westport, Conn., 1991.

Huber, Michel. *La Population de la France pendant la guerre.* Paris, 1931.

Huddleston, Sisley. *Poincaré: A Biographical Portrait.* Boston, 1924.

Hughes, Judith M. *To the Maginot Line: The Politics of French Military Preparation in the 1920s.* Cambridge, Mass., 1971.

Hunt, Persis Charles. "Revolutionary Syndicalism and Feminism Among Teachers in France, 1900–1921." Ph.D. dissertation, Tufts University, 1975.

Jackson, John L. *Clemenceau and the Third Republic.* London, 1946.

Jacobson, Jon. *Locarno Diplomacy: Germany and the West, 1925–1929.* Princeton, 1972.

―――. "Strategies of French Foreign Policy After World War I." *Journal of Modern History* 55 (March 1983): 78–95.

Joffre, Joseph. *Mémoires du maréchal Joffre.* 2 vols. Paris, 1938.

Joffroy, A. *La Vie réinvitée: L'Explosion des années 20 à Paris.* Paris, 1982.

Jones, Adrian. "The French Railway Strikes of January–May 1920: New Syndicalist Ideas and Emergent Communism." *French Historical Studies* 12 (Fall 1982): 508–40.

Jouvenel, Bertrand de. *D'une guerre à l'autre.* 2 vols. Paris, 1941.

Kaplan, Jay L. "France's Road to Genoa: Strategic, Economic, and Ideological Factors in French Foreign Policy, 1921–1922." Ph.D. dissertation, Columbia University, 1974.

Keiger, John F. V. *Raymond Poincaré.* Cambridge, Eng., 1997.

Kemp, Tom. *The French Economy, 1913–1939.* London, 1972.

Kent, Bruce. *The Spoils of War: The Politics, Economics, and Diplomacy of Reparations, 1918–1932*. Oxford, 1989.

Keynes, John Maynard. *The Economic Consequences of the Peace*. London, 1920.

Klotz, Louis-Lucien. *De la guerre à la paix: Souvenirs et documents*. Paris, 1924.

Kriegel, Annie. *Aux origines du communisme français, 1914–1920*. 2 vols. Paris, 1964.

Krüger, Peter. *Deutschland und die Reparationen, 1918–1919*. Stuttgart, 1973.

Lachapelle, Georges. *Elections législatives du 11 mai 1924*. Paris, 1924.

Larmour, Peter J. *The French Radical Party in the 1930's*. Stanford, 1964.

Laroche, Jules. *Au Quai d'Orsay avec Briand et Poincaré, 1913–1926*. Paris, 1926.

———. *La Pologne de Pilsudski: Souvenirs d'une ambassade, 1926–1933*. Paris, 1953.

Leffler, Melvyn P. *The Elusive Quest: America's Pursuit of European Stability and French Security, 1919–1933*. Chapel Hill, 1979.

Lévy-Leboyer, Maurice, ed. *La Position internationale de la France: Aspects économiques et financières*. Paris, 1977.

Loucheur, Louis. *Carnets secrets, 1908–1932*. Edited by Jacques de Launay. Brussels, 1962.

McDougall, Walter A. *France's Rhineland Diplomacy, 1914–1924: The Last Bid for a Balance of Power in Europe*. Princeton, 1978.

Maier, Charles S. *Recasting Bourgeois Europe: Stabilization in France, Germany, and Italy in the Decade After World War I*. Princeton, 1975.

Mantoux, Etienne. *The Carthaginian Peace, or the Economic Consequences of Mr. Keynes*. New York, 1946.

Margueritte, V. *Aristide Briand*. Paris, 1932.

Marin, Louis. *Le Traité de paix*. Paris, 1920.

Marks, Sally. *The Illusion of Peace: International Relations in Europe, 1918–1933*. New York, 1976.

Martet, Jean. *Le Tigre*. Paris, 1929.

Martin, Benjamin F. *"Briand à la barre:* Aristide Briand and the Politics of Betrayal." *French Politics and Society* 15 (Summer 1997): 57–64.

———. *Count Albert de Mun: Paladin of the Third Republic*. Chapel Hill, 1978.

———. *Crime and Criminal Justice Under the Third Republic: The Shame of Marianne*. Baton Rouge, 1990.

———. *The Hypocrisy of Justice in the Belle Epoque*. Baton Rouge, 1984.

———. "Political Justice in France: The Dreyfus Affair and After." *The European Legacy: Toward New Paradigms* 2 (August 1997): 809–26.

Martin du Gard, Roger. *Les Thibault.* 8 vols. Paris, 1922–40. Translated by Stuart Gilbert as *The Thibaults* (Parts I-VI) and *Summer 1914* (Parts VII-VIII). New York, 1939–41.

Mayer, Arno J. *Political Origins of the New Diplomacy, 1917–1918.* New Haven, 1959.

———. *Politics and Diplomacy of Peacemaking: Containment and Counterrevolution at Versailles, 1918–1919.* New York, 1967.

Mayeur, Jean-Marie. *La Vie politique sous la troisième république, 1870–1940.* Paris, 1984.

Meunier, Raymond. *Les Ames en peine, les désemparés.* Paris, 1913.

———. *Les Ames en peine, les fous.* Paris, 1913.

———. *Les Ames en peine, les rêveurs.* Paris, 1913.

Meyer, Jacques. *La Vie quotidienne des soldats pendant la grande guerre.* Paris, 1966.

Michel, Edmond. *Les Dommages de guerre de la France et leur réparation.* Paris, 1932.

Minart, Jacques. *Le Drame du désarmement français, 1918–1938.* Paris, 1959.

Miquel, Pierre. *La Paix de Versailles et l'opinion publique française.* Paris, 1972.

———. *Poincaré.* Paris, 1961.

Mordacq, General Jean J. H. *Clemenceau.* Paris, 1939.

———. *Clemenceau au soir de sa vie, 1920–1929.* 2 vols. Paris, 1933.

———. *Les Légendes de la Grande Guerre.* Paris, 1935.

———. *Le Ministère Clemenceau: Journal d'un témoin.* 4 vols. Paris, 1930–31.

Nadeau, Maurice. *Histoire du surréalisme.* Paris, 1964.

Nelson, Keith L. *Victors Divided: America and the Allies in Germany, 1918–1923.* Berkeley, 1975.

Néré, Jacques. *The Foreign Policy of France from 1914 to 1945.* London, 1975.

Newhall, David S. *Clemenceau: A Life at War.* Lewiston, N.Y., 1991.

Noiriel, Gérard. "Les Grèves de 1919 en France: Révolution manquée ou mouvement d'humeur?" *French Politics and Society* 8 (Winter 1990): 48–55.

———. *Workers in French Society in the 19th and 20th Centuries.* Translated by Helen McPhail. Oxford, 1990.

Noulens, Joseph. *Mon ambassade en Russie soviétique, 1917–1919.* Paris, 1923.

Nye, Robert A. *Masculinity and Male Codes of Honor in Modern France.* New York, 1993.

Oudin, Bernard. *Aristide Briand, biographie.* Paris, 1987.

Paléologue, Maurice. *La Russie des tsars pendant la Grande Guerre.* 3 vols. Paris, 1921–22.

Paoli, François André. *L'Armée française de 1919 à 1939*. Paris, 1969.

Paul-Boncour, Joseph. *Entre deux guerres: Souvenirs sur la Troisième République*. 3 vols. Paris, 1945–46.

Payen, Fernand. *Raymond Poincaré: L'Homme, le parlementaire, l'avocat*. Paris, 1936.

Pedroncini, Guy. *Les Négotiations secrètes pendant la Grande Guerre*. Paris, 1969.

Perreux, Gabriel. *La Vie quotidienne des civils en France pendant la grande guerre*. Paris, 1966.

Persil, Raoul. *Alexandre Millerand, 1859–1943*. Paris, 1949.

Pierrefeux, Guy de. *Le Revenant: Propos et anecdotes autour de Caillaux*. Strasbourg, 1925.

Poincaré, Raymond. *Au service de la France*. 11 vols. Paris, 1926–74.

Porch, Douglas. "A Reappraisal of French Strategy in the First World War." *Journal of Military History* 53 (October 1989): 363–86.

Prévost, Jean. *Histoire de France depuis la guerre*. Paris, 1932.

Prost, Antoine. *Les Anciens combattants et la société française, 1914–1939*. 3 vols. Paris, 1977.

Recouly, Raymond. *Le Mémorial de Foch, mes entretiens avec le maréchal*. Paris, 1929.

Renouvin, René. *Le Traité de Versailles*. Paris, 1969.

Ribot, Alexandre. *Journal d'Alexandre Ribot et correspondances inédits, 1914–1922*. Paris, 1936.

Richter, Hans. *Dada Art and Anti-Art*. New York, 1965.

Roberts, Mary Louise. *Civilization Without Sexes: Reconstructing Gender in Postwar France, 1917–1927*. Chicago, 1994.

———. "Samson and Delilah Revisited: The Politics of Women's Fashions in 1920s France." *American Historical Review* 98 (June 1993): 657–84.

Roche, Emile. *Caillaux que j'ai connu*. Paris, 1949.

Rogers, James Harvey. *The Process of Inflation in France, 1914–1927*. New York, 1929.

Saint Aulaire, Auguste Félix Charles de Beaupoil, Comte de. *Confession d'un vieux diplomate*. Paris, 1953.

———. *La Mythologie de la paix*. Paris, 1929.

Saint-Exupéry, Antoine de. *Oeuvres*. Paris, 1959.

Sanouillet, Michel. *Dada à Paris*. Paris, 1965.

Sauvy, Alfred. *Histoire économique de la France entre les deux guerres*. 3 vols. Paris, 1965–75.

Schrecker, Ellen. *The Hired Money: The French Debt to the United States, 1917–1929*. New York, 1978.

Schuker, Stephen A. *The End of French Predominance in Europe: The Financial Crisis of 1924 and the Adoption of the Dawes Plan*. Chapel Hill, 1976.

Schmitt, Bernadotte E., and Harold C. Vedeler. *The World in Crucible, 1914–1919*. New York, 1984.

Selsam, J. Paul. *The Attempts to Form an Anglo-French Alliance, 1919–1924*. Philadelphia, 1936.

Seydoux, Jacques. *De Versailles au Plan Young: Réparations, dettes interalliées, reconstruction européenne*. Paris, 1932.

Shattuck, Roger. *The Banquet Years: The Origins of the Avant-Garde in France, 1885 to World War I*. Rev. ed. New York, 1968.

Sherwood, John M. *Georges Mandel and the Third Republic*. Stanford, 1970.

Sicot, Marcel. *Servitude et grandeur policière: Quarante ans à la Sûreté*. Paris, 1959.

Siebert, Ferdinand. *Aristide Briand, 1862–1932: Ein Staatsman zwischen Frankreich und Europe*. Zurich, 1973.

Silverman, Dan P. *Reconstructing Europe After the Great War*. Cambridge, Mass., 1982.

Slater, Catherine. *Defeatists and Their Enemies: Political Invective in France, 1914–1918*. New York, 1981.

Smith, Leonard V. *Between Mutiny and Obedience: The Case of the French Fifth Infantry Division During World War I*. Princeton, 1994.

Söhnigen, Bettina Mercedes. "French Interwar Security Policy Reconsidered." M.A. thesis, Louisiana State University, 1993.

Soulié, Michel. *Le Bloc national républicain*. Paris, 1924.

———. *La Vie politique d'Edouard Herriot*. Paris, 1962.

Soutou, Georges-Henri. *L'Or et le sang: Les Buts de guerre économiques de la Première Guerre mondiale*. Paris, 1989.

Suarez, Georges. *Briand: Sa vie, son oeuvre, avec son journal et de nombreux documents inédits*. 6 vols. Paris, 1938–52.

Tabouis, Geneviève. *Jules Cambon par l'un des siens*. Paris, 1938.

Tardieu, André. *La Paix*. Paris, 1921. Translated as *The Truth About the Treaty*. Indianapolis, 1921.

Tirard, Paul. *La France sur le Rhin: Douze années d'occupation rhénane*. Paris, 1930.

Tournoux, General Paul-Emile. *Haut commandement, gouvernement et défense des frontières du Nord et de l'Est, 1919–1939*. Paris, 1960.

Trachtenberg, Marc. *Reparation in World Politics: France and European Economic Diplomacy, 1916–1923*. New York, 1980.

Wandycz, Piotr S. *France and Her Eastern Allies, 1919–1925: French-Czechoslovak-Polish Relations from the Paris Peace Conference to Locarno*. Minneapolis, 1962.

———. *The Twilight of French Eastern Alliances, 1926–1936: French-Czechoslovak-Polish Relations from Locarno to the Remilitarization of the Rhineland*. Princeton, 1988.

Watson, David Robin. *Clemenceau: A Political Biography*. London, 1974.

Weber, Eugen. *Action Française: Royalism and Reaction in Twentieth-Century France*. Stanford, 1962.

———. *France: Fin de Siècle*. Cambridge, Mass., 1986.

———. *My France: Politics, Culture, Myth*. Cambridge, Mass., 1991.

Weill-Raynal, Etienne. *Les Réparations allemandes et la France*. 3 vols. Paris, 1947–49.

Weiss, John, ed. *The Origins of Modern Consciousness*. Detroit, 1965.

White, Stephen. *The Origins of Detente: The Genoa Conference and Soviet-Western Relations, 1921–1922*. New York, 1985.

Wileman, Donald G. "What the Market Will Bear: The French Cartel Elections of 1924." *Journal of Contemporary History* 29 (Fall, 1994): 483–500.

Wishnia, Judith. *The Proletarianizing of the Fonctionnaires: Civil Service Workers and the Labor Movement Under the Third Republic*. Baton Rouge, 1990.

Wohl, Robert. *French Communism in the Making, 1914–1924*. Stanford, 1966.

Wolfe, Martin. *The French Franc Between the Wars, 1919–1939*. New York, 1951.

Wormser, Georges. *La République de Clemenceau*. Paris, 1961.

Wright, Gordon. *Raymond Poincaré and the French Presidency*. Stanford, 1942.

Wurzburg, Frederick. "The Politics of the Bloc National." Ph.D. dissertation, Columbia University, 1961.

Young, Robert J. *Power and Pleasure: Louis Barthou and the Third Republic*. Montreal, 1991.

INDEX